Welcome to the *EVERYTHING*® se

These handy, accessible books give you all you need to tackle a difficult project, gain a new hobby, comprehend a fascinating topic, prepare for an exam, or even brush up on something you learned back in school but have since forgotten.

You can read an *EVERYTHING*® book from cover to cover or just pick out the information you want from our four useful boxes: e-facts, e-ssentials, e-alerts, and e-questions. We literally give you everything you need to know on the subject, but throw in a lot of fun stuff along the way, too.

We now have well over 100 *EVERYTHING*® books in print, spanning such wide-ranging topics as weddings, pregnancy, wine, learning guitar, one-pot cooking, managing people, and so much more. When you're done reading them all, you can finally say you know *EVERYTHING*®!

E FACTS
Important sound bytes of information

Essentials
Quick handy tips

ALERT
Urgent warnings

QUESTIONS?
Solutions to common problems

EVERYTHING®
Series

Dear Reader,

My first encounter with hypnosis was twenty years ago, when I was hired to play piano for a stage show. As the hypnotist and I discussed the evening, I began to feel some kind of strange pull—the room started to swirl around me, and I focused hard, trying to resist. I had to learn what this hidden magic was! That quest has consumed my life ever since.

Shortly after the stage show, I began to read every book on hypnosis that I could find. I began to practice self-hypnosis for stress control, establishing a daily routine. I used to be a very intense person, described as having different shades of anger—from very mad to moderately mad, but never happy. After practicing self-hypnosis, my mental attitude began to change.

In 1989 I was hit by a car. As I lay injured, I automatically entered a calming hypnotic trance. Since then I have used hypnosis on myself for better health, weight loss, stress reduction, and even eye surgery. Hypnosis is still magic to me.

It is my hope that in this book you will discover some of the magic of hypnosis.

Michael R. Hathaway

THE

EVERYTHING

HYPNOSIS
BOOK

Safe, effective ways to lose weight,
improve your health, overcome bad
habits, and boost creativity

Dr. Michael R. Hathaway, D.C.H.

SA PL

Adams Media Corporation
Avon, Massachusetts

EDITORIAL
Publishing Director: Gary M. Krebs
Managing Editor: Kate McBride
Copy Chief: Laura MacLaughlin
Acquisitions Editor: Bethany Brown
Development Editor: Julie Gutin
Production Editor: Khrysti Nazzaro

PRODUCTION
Production Director: Susan Beale
Production Manager: Michelle Roy Kelly
Series Designer: Daria Perreault
Cover Design: Paul Beatrice and Frank Rivera
Layout and Graphics: Colleen Cunningham,
Rachael Eiben, Michelle Roy Kelly,
Daria Perreault, Erin Ring

An Everything® Series Book.
Everything® and everything.com® are registered trademarks of Adams Media Corporation.

Published by Adams Media Corporation
57 Littlefield Street, Avon, MA 02322 U.S.A.
www.adamsmedia.com

ISBN: 1-58062-737-4
Printed in the United States of America.

J I H G F E D C B

Library of Congress Cataloging-in-Publication Data
Hathaway, Michael R.
The everything hypnosis book / Michael R. Hathaway.
p.   cm.   —(An Everything series book)
ISBN 1-58062-737-4
1. Mental suggestion. I. Title. II. Everything series.
BF1156.S8 H38 2003
154.7—dc21
2002009818

This publication is designed to provide accurate and authoritative information with regard to the subject matter covered. It is sold with the understanding that the publisher is not engaged in rendering legal, accounting, or other professional advice. If legal advice or other expert assistance is required, the services of a competent professional person should be sought.
—From a *Declaration of Principles* jointly adopted by a Committee of the American Bar Association and a Committee of Publishers and Associations

Illustrations by Barry Littmann.

*This book is available at quantity discounts for bulk purchases.
For information, call 1-800-872-5627.*

Visit the entire Everything® series at everything.com

To Carter, Brenda, Marc, Brian,
and my soul mate, Penny.

Contents

Introduction

Self-hypnosis is fascinating and fun to use. You can practice it occasionally, or it can become a daily routine in your life. Instant self-hypnotic techniques allow you to enter a trance for a brief moment of relaxation that no one else will notice. Self-hypnosis can help you communicate with others and with yourself, it can enhance your focus at work and at school, and it has the potential to give you a whole new view of life.

This book is written as a complete guide to self-hypnosis. You will learn a self-hypnotic technique in the first chapter, and then as you progress, you will have the opportunity to learn how your mind works, how it is unique and different from all other minds in the world. You will understand what hypnosis is, and that it is already a natural part of your life. You will receive step-by-step instructions on how to create and use self-hypnotic trances.

You do not need any previous training in hypnosis to use *The Everything® Hypnosis Book*. However, this book does offer fresh concepts for professionals, who are always seeking new ideas to help their clients. You can experience this book alone or use it with others. It is intended to provide fun and easy ways to make positive changes in your life.

Hypnosis is an important tool for curbing bad habits such as overeating or smoking, and for improving or enhancing sports performance. It can help resolve stress—you can create powerful hypnotic anchors that help you feel calm and relaxed as you go about your daily routines.

Hypnotherapists are now associated with many hospitals, where they assist patients in areas such as pain control, hypno-anesthesia during operations, and hypno-birthing. Several organizations for the promotion and safe practice of hypnosis offer extensive hypnosis training.

Hypnosis is used in law enforcement to help witnesses with recall. Its principles are widely practiced in sales and marketing, and its concepts are taught in communication classes. We are constantly subjected to hypnotic imagery in all forms of advertising.

We often read media reports on the widespread benefits of hypnosis, and we hear sensational stories of hypnosis used in the metaphysical field and in popular stage shows. Many books have been written about using hypnosis to recover lost memories of alien abductions and to learn of past lives.

Edgar Cayce used self-hypnotic trances when he gave readings for his subjects; more than 12,000 of his readings were written down and are still being used. More than half a century after his death, Cayce's predictions for the future and his readings on the lost continent of Atlantis receive constant attention in the tabloids. And who knows, perhaps you too have a psychic ability that can be enhanced by self-hypnosis.

After reading this book, you will have the chance to try simple exercises that show you how your mind images. It is fun to do them with friends or family members, and they are also easy to do alone. As you learn, you will begin to have a great advantage in understanding how other people think. You will actually be able to anticipate someone else's actions and reactions.

Hypnosis is a natural state. When experiencing hypnosis, you are always in control. There are many levels of hypnotic trances, from light daydreams to deep, sleeping states, in which you may have no waking memory of what took place during the trance. If you are ready, by the end of the first chapter you will be counting backward, from five to zero . . .

CHAPTER 1

You Are Getting Sleepy

The popularity of hypnosis has increased steadily over the past several decades. Hypnotherapy is now recognized as a valuable tool to bring about positive changes in people's lives. You may not yet realize it, but hypnosis is a part of your daily existence. Learning how to use self-hypnosis can enrich your life in many ways, from habit change and better health to creative development and higher psychic levels.

Mystique of Hypnosis

The mystique that surrounds hypnosis is as old as history. Primitive people throughout the world used trance states for religious and healing ceremonies. The Australian Aborigines entered trance states during Dreamtime. Native American medicine men used trance states, and sweat lodges provided a venue for mystical experience.

In Africa, traditional rituals included chanting and dancing, accompanied by the beat of drums. And in America, African slaves would congregate in places such as Congo Square in New Orleans, where they would dance their way into trance states. Slaves also sang and chanted in cotton fields as a way to find some relief from their deplorable environment.

Early Pioneers in Hypnosis

Franz Anton Mesmer (1734–1815) is credited with being the founder of modern hypnosis. Using a magnet, and later just his hand, Mesmer believed he was able to unblock an invisible fluid in his patient's body. Once this invisible fluid returned to a normal flow, the patient's circulation improved, and he would be cured. Unfortunately for Mesmer, his theory of animal magnetism was proved unfounded, and he was pronounced a fraud by the French government.

FACTS

In 1842, James Braid renamed Mesmer's technique *hypnotism* (from the Greek for "sleep"). Later, Braid concluded that the hypnotized patient wasn't actually going to sleep but into a trance, a heightened state of awareness. Nevertheless, the term *hypnosis* had become too well known to change.

His technique, however, actually produced a hypnotic trance in his patients. It turned out to be the comments he made during the séance that effected the cure. His method of "mesmerizing" became the model of inducing a trance for those who followed, including his student, the Marquis de Puysegur (1751–1825), who concluded that changes in a patient's condition were brought about by suggestion, not animal magnetism.

Hypnosis in Medicine

Medical doctors continued to experiment with hypnotism, refining its use during the 1800s. In England, Dr. Elliotson successfully treated patients for epilepsy, hysteria, asthma, headaches, and rheumatism. He used hypnosis to perform over 200 painless operations during the 1840s and 1850s.

Through the late 1800s, alternative healing gained popularity in America. One alternative practitioner was Oscoe Whitman, a Doctor of Healing who had a successful practice in Lewiston, Maine. Whitman would go into a trance and a feel power coming into his body through his shoulders. It would continue down his arms and out his hands, bringing about miraculous healing in those he touched.

The development of chemoanesthesia at the end of the nineteenth century nearly brought the use of hypnosis in medicine to a standstill. Doctors began to rely on drugs such as chloroform, ether, and nitrous oxide, which were easier to use and effective with a wide range of patients. It was not until the 1950s, with the growing interest in holistic medicine, that hypnosis made its comeback.

Development of Hypnosis in the Twentieth Century

One man who played an important role in the development of hypnosis was Edgar Cayce, the "Father of New Age Health." When he was young, Cayce was a very poor student, often unable to concentrate on his lessons. One night he fell asleep on his books, and when he awoke, he knew all the material inside. At fifteen he was hit in the spine with a ball. That night he went into a coma, and when he came to, he told his parents that an old monk had appeared to him and told him how to cure his injury. His parents followed the monk's instructions, and Edgar was cured.

In his early twenties Cayce lost his voice, but he discovered that he could speak when he was under hypnosis. When he induced his own trance to find the cure, his throat turned bright red, he spat some blood, and when he awoke he could talk again.

The medical community rejected Cayce's work, but when he gave trance readings there were a high percentage of cures. He also gave readings on past lives and the lost continent of Atlantis, and made predictions of the future.

ESSENTIALS

When Edgar Cayce was young, an angel told him that he would help many people during his lifetime. His trance readings helped thousands of people and continue to do so today, through the Association for Research and Enlightenment located in Virginia Beach, Virginia.

To give a reading, Edgar Cayce would loosen his tie, lie down on a couch, and put himself into a hypnotic trance. When he reached his deepest trance state, he would answer questions regarding the condition of his subject. If the person were not at the same location, he would project himself to the address. As soon as he "had the body" in view, he would scan it and provide a complete health analysis.

Milton Erickson

The model for modern hypnosis was developed by Milton Erickson, a psychiatrist. Erickson had a natural ability to bring about dramatic changes in his patients. He would tell boring stories about his relatives or acquaintances, which seemed to have nothing to do with the patient's therapeutic visit, but these stories served to create a hypnotic trance that brought the patient face to face with the very reason she was there.

Erickson was color-blind, dyslexic, tone-deaf, and arrhythmic. He almost died of polio at seventeen, and the disease left him bedridden. Every day he would imagine getting out of bed and walking to the window. His muscles began to respond, and eventually he was able to walk again. At age fifty-one, he was stricken with another form of polio that confined him to a wheelchair for the rest of his life.

FACTS

In the 1970s, therapist Richard Bandler and linguist John Grinder observed Erickson's work in Phoenix, Arizona. Influenced by Erickson, they developed Neuro-Linguistic Programming (NLP), a technique that helps create thinking models of the mind. NLP has become a valuable tool for hypnotherapists, psychologists, and businessmen alike.

Trance States

Hypnosis is not easily defined—it is a state of mind, not a tangible substance. Many people fear that hypnosis requires you to give up control of your mind. However, you need to understand that you will not do anything in a hypnotic trance that you would not do while in a normal waking state. When in hypnosis, you have a heightened state of suggestibility.

There are many levels of hypnotic trance. You may have experienced driving down a highway, when all of a sudden you become aware that you've missed your turn. You were driving just fine, and yet your mind was focused on something else. You were in a hypnotic trance.

A daydream is a light trance. So is reading a good book, watching a television program, or having a conversation with friends. Even words are hypnotic; they stimulate your imagination, creating a suggestible state in your mind.

Meditation and prayer are forms of trance as well. During meditation, the practitioner strives to quiet the mind, finding peace as thoughts drift away into space. Prayer sends the thoughts to a specific source, with the expectation of a positive response. Either of these techniques is a good way to enter a hypnotic trance. If you already have a habit of meditating or praying, it may be useful to you when doing the exercises in this book. If you have your own way of entering a trance, you can rely on it as well.

The deepest level of trance experience is somnambulism. In it, the subject has no conscious awareness of his actions. He can experience negative hallucinations, where things disappear before his very eyes.

Hypnosis in Advertising

Companies spend millions of dollars annually researching how to sell you their products. They study packaging, age groups, colors, tastes, smells, feelings, and marketing areas. Their goal is to create an image that you cannot resist. They want you to follow their suggestions, to enter their hypnotic trance, to purchase their products.

Most marketing companies research their potential customer base. Then they write a presentation program and train their salespeople to follow it to the letter. Salespeople are often supplied with motivational tapes for inspiration and success. The potential customer also receives literature written around the sales profile. This whole process uses hypnosis concepts, with both the salespeople and the customers.

Like the stage show hypnotist, the salesperson takes full control of his presentation. Ernie, who had a very successful career in sales, learned early on to use this method. Regardless of what he was trying to sell or the level of his customer's intelligence, Ernie would assume control by taking away the customer's ability to think critically, until he landed the sale.

There are now several television networks devoted entirely to sales. They have succeeded in creating a consistent viewer base of people who actually feel obligated to purchase items that they may never use. These watchers often relate more to the show's host than to the product; they make the purchase because their "good friend" the salesperson recommends it.

Hypnosis Concerns

Is hypnosis mind control? Cult leaders often employ hypnosis concepts to bring potential members under their control. Their objective is to systematically take away the individual's critical decision-making ability. Hitler may have been the greatest hypnotist who ever lived.

Major problems can result when someone who is not properly trained in hypnosis tries to use it on another individual. It is easy to induce a suggestible state in someone; however, the hypnotist must be very careful of his words and constantly aware of the subject's mental and physical state. If something unexpected happens, an untrained operator could make the situation worse. On the other hand, self-hypnosis is safe and effective.

FACTS

Autohypnosis or autosuggestion is achieved when a posthypnotic suggestion is given during a trance. The subject will continue to experience the suggestion after the trance has ended. The use of posthypnotic suggestion is the difference between hypnosis and meditation.

Suggestibility Tests

A suggestibility test measures your potential to enter a hypnotic trance. The more you are able to experience the suggestions, the deeper you may go into trance. Even if you don't have much success, it doesn't mean that you cannot reach a good trance level. In a light trance you are aware of everything that happens, and yet you experience some of the suggestions.

To see how suggestible you are, try the following five tests. You can read each test first and repeat it from memory, or you can record it and play it back. Or ask someone to read it to you, while you give it a try. It's fun to do the exercises with others and compare the results. (You should all be a little different.)

Eyelid Closure Test

Don't try this test if you have an eye condition. The first experience is quite simple. Look straight forward with your eyes open. Now try to look up while pulling your eyelids down over your eyes.

Can you do this? Do your eyelids flutter? Did you resist the exercise? This test is a good indicator of your ability to enter a hypnotic trance.

If for any reason you feel uncomfortable while participating in an exercise, discontinue the exercise, open your eyes, and relax. Don't force yourself to do anything that makes you uncomfortable.

Arms Rising and Falling Test

Stand up, put your feet together, and hold both arms straight out in front of you. Turn your left hand over so the palm is facing up, and with your right hand, make a fist with the thumb upward. Now close your eyes and imagine that you are holding a bucket filled with heavy cement in your left hand, while your right hand is holding on to a rope that is gently tugging your hand and arm upward. It is almost impossible to hold them down.

Up and up your right arm and hand are pulled—up and up and up. You are feeling the heavy weight on your left arm and hand from the bucket of cement—heavier and heavier, pulling your hand and arm down and down, heavier and heavier. It is so hard to hold the left arm up. At the same time, your right hand and arm are being pulled up and up, rising and rising, up and up and up.

Your left arm and hand are going down and down, heavier and heavier, heavier and heavier. Your right hand is doing the best it can to hang on to the rope. Up and up it is pulled. Now stop. Hold that position and open your eyes.

Did your arms move? Did you feel the heavy weight in the bucket and the upward pull of the rope? There was, of course, no difference in actual weight on either arm or hand. If you felt a difference, it was because your mind followed the suggestions. You just experienced hypnosis.

Balancing Test

Stand with your feet together and your hands and arms down at your side. Close your eyes and imagine you are standing on the deck of a boat.

If you have never been on one, imagine standing on a big round beach ball, or perhaps on a train or subway car. Let yourself feel it rocking back and forth, back and forth. You feel yourself swaying back and forth, back and forth, and you have to move your body to keep your balance.

Now imagine you've arrived back on shore. Before you can get comfortable, however, you find yourself standing on a wide wooden plank one foot above the ground. It holds your weight easily, and you stand on it comfortably, gently bouncing up and down, up and down. Now you're on firm ground again.

Now you are back on the deck of the boat, rocking back and forth, back and forth, adjusting your body to keep your balance, back and forth, back and forth. Now you're back on firm ground. Oh dear, now you are standing on the plank again, but it is fifty feet up in the air! You can feel it bounce up and down, up and down, as the wind blows against your body. You look around; you are way up in the air, bouncing and bouncing and bouncing.

Finally you are back on firm ground! Take a deep breath and open your eyes. What were your experiences like? Did you work to keep your balance on the moving boat or react to the height of the plank as it was raised into the air? If you did, you entered into a hypnotic trance.

Warm and Cold Test

Let's try something easier. You can stay seated for this one. Take a deep breath of air and slowly exhale. Close your eyes. Let your body relax.

Imagine that beside your right hand there is a large pail of ice. You can feel the cold as you place your hand on the ice. Now push your hand into the ice. You can feel the cold, colder and colder.

As you continue to keep your hand in the ice, it becomes so cold that you can feel it turning numb. Your hand is getting colder and colder, so numb it does not even feel a light pinch by your left hand. Take it out of the ice. It is still numb.

Now imagine you are placing that hand in a pan of slightly warm water. Your hand begins to feel the warmth, warmer and warmer. It is returning to its normal temperature. You feel comfortable again.

The deeper into hypnosis you go, the more vividly you'll experience this.

Pendulum Test

Now you can try a focus experiment. You will need some kind of pendulum: it can be a necklace with a pendent, a string with a washer, a pocket watch on a chain, a set of keys on a ring—anything with a small weight that you can dangle from your hand.

Hold the chain or string between your thumb and forefinger so the heavy part (the pendulum) is able to swing freely. Place your hand about eighteen inches in front of your eyes and focus on the pendulum. Try to keep your hand and arm as still as possible. Take a deep breath and relax.

Mentally ask the object to turn in a circular motion. Watch the pendulum turn, and ask the circle to get bigger and bigger. Now tell it to change directions, and watch it begin to swing in the opposite direction. Focus on it, and ask it to stop swinging. Concentrate on it coming to a stop.

Set the object down, take another deep breath, and notice how relaxed and calm this exercise has made you feel. Focusing on a pendulum can produce positive, relaxing results. This technique can be used for many things.

FACTS

Many dowsers use a pendulum to get answers from the unconscious mind. The first step, as you hold it, is to ask it to show which way it swings for *yes*. Then ask it to show you *no*. Next ask if it is appropriate to ask questions. If the answer is *yes*, you may begin. Remember to ask short yes-or-no questions.

Stage Hypnosis

The stage hypnotist uses a form of depth testing to see if the subject will follow his commands in an entertainment setting. He will check for muscle resistance when he lifts an arm, moves a head, or shakes a hand. He watches eye movements, how relaxed the body becomes, and the ability to follow his suggestions. If a subject resists, he sends her back into the audience. Sometimes he uses only a few of the tested subjects in his performance.

The stage hypnotist will stand before his subject, lower his voice, and say, "You are getting sleepier and sleepier." The audience watches in amazement as the subject lowers his head, relaxes his body, and slips into a sleeplike state. He will command the subject to return to this position many times during the show.

QUESTIONS?

Who are the best hypnosis subjects for a stage show?
The best hypnosis subjects have fantasy-prone personalities. They have great imaginations. Teenagers and young adults are at the best age for hypnosis. People in repetitive occupations and those who are used to following orders are also good subjects.

Mr. Re was a successful stage hypnotist in the 1960s and 1970s who worked on major cruise lines. His first encounter with hypnosis was accidental. One day in grade school he had to stay late for some extra help. The soft-spoken youngster was talking quietly with his teacher, when she suddenly slumped over and he could not waken her.

Panic-stricken, he ran for help, and the local doctor was summoned. The doctor recognized that the teacher was in a hypnotic trance; he told her to wake up and she did. Mr. Re had hypnotized his first subject without even knowing what he had done.

Hypnosis Inductions

There are two basic types of hypnosis inductions, authoritative and permissive. The difference is in the language used. Authoritative induction makes use of direct orders such as "you will" and "you are." The stage hypnotist is authoritative when she guides her subject into a trance. She wants to retain control. This induction method is still used by many traditional, old-school hypnotherapists.

Permissive hypnosis phrases include "you may" and "if you would." NLP technique generally follows the permissive style. This technique is innovative, progressive, and on the cutting edge of twenty-first-century hypnosis.

A Relaxation Exercise

The first step in establishing a hypnotic trance is to use a basic relaxation exercise. You should now be ready to try it. This is a good way to get yourself focused and ready to go deeper into hypnosis.

The choice of words and the manner and speed in which they are said is very important. You will notice that key words are used over and over in an induction. "Relax" is one of them; repeat it slowly, and feel relaxed while you are saying it. When you say the word "heavy," feel the heaviness. The same goes for "lighter" and "deeper." When you come back to normal consciousness, feel refreshed in your mind and body.

Get Comfortable and Relax

Make yourself as comfortable as possible. You may sit or lie down, and loosen your clothing. Take a breath of air, fill your lungs to a comfortable level, and focus on an object in front of you. (Or you may prefer to look up with your eyes, as if you were peeking under your eyelids.) Slowly exhale your breath, and then fill your lungs again. Slowly let your eyes go out of focus, as you continue breathing in this slow manner.

Now start relaxing the muscles throughout your entire body. You can work either from the feet upward or from the head down. Locate individual muscles that are tense, and relax each one. Every time you relax a muscle, you will relax a little more. Breathe in and out, in and out, relaxing and relaxing.

Count Down

In a moment you may begin counting slowly down from five to zero. As you count, you may continue to breathe slowly and relax your body, as you feel yourself going deeper and deeper. It is very relaxing, and you know that you may come back to full consciousness anytime you want. Nothing is keeping you in this relaxed state except your wish to be there.

When you start to count back from five to zero, you may want to close your eyes. You can open them anytime you want. If you are ready, you may begin to count slowly:

- **FIVE,** relax, breathe deeply
- **FOUR,** relax, breathe in and out
- **THREE,** relax, breathe deeply
- **TWO,** relax, breathe deeply
- **ONE,** relax, breathe in and out, in and out
- **ZERO,** so peaceful, so calm, so relaxing

Count Up

Remain in this state for a brief moment, or for a little longer if you like. It is so peaceful, so calm, so relaxing. When you are ready, slowly count yourself back up to five. At five, you will open your eyes and feel calm and relaxed, refreshed and positive:

- **ZERO,** slowly
- **ONE,** breathe
- **TWO,** coming back up to the surface
- **THREE,** coming back, slowly and positively
- **FOUR,** almost there
- **FIVE,** deep breath in and exhale, back at the surface, fully awake, positive and relaxed, feeling very refreshed

Take a moment to reaccustom yourself to your environment. Even with this short exercise, it is possible to feel relaxed and refreshed.

The more you practice this induction, the easier it will be to do, and the easier it will be to relax yourself.

The next time you try this relaxation induction, when you have counted down to zero, you may want add the following suggestion: "You will now remain relaxed for five minutes. You are comfortable and relaxed. At the end of five minutes you will count yourself back up to five."

ESSENTIALS

There are many mechanical aids to help induce a trance. You can use a "hypnosis wheel," a strobe light, a candle, soft music, a metronome, a clock, the sound of water, a smell, or even the sound of traffic.

Hypnosis Wheel

When you are doing a self-hypnosis induction, you may want to use the word *I* instead of *you*. The goal of self-hypnosis is to establish positive and productive communication with yourself. You have already started that process. Hypnosis is like practicing a musical instrument or playing a sport. The more you practice, the more you improve.

CHAPTER 2

Your Mental Makeup

It's time to develop an understanding of your mental makeup. You will examine how you use images in each of the five senses, and how your senses already impact your life. Then you can begin to use this sense model to help deepen your self-hypnotic relaxation trance.

The Mind Is Like a Computer

The workings of the mind still remain, to a large extent, a great mystery. The mind can be compared to a very complex computer in that it processes and stores information. It is influenced by many things, including your physical environment, mental state, and genetic makeup. And just as your physical DNA is different from anyone else's, the makeup of your senses is also unique.

FACTS

DNA is short for deoxyribonucleic acid, which is present in almost every cell in your body. DNA produces a genetic blueprint, unique in each individual except identical twins, which determines physical makeup. You inherit your genetic code from your parents.

You process, store, and recall information through five senses: sight, hearing, feeling, taste, and smell. It is possible that you may produce excellent images in all five senses, but it is more likely that you have a different level of response in each of them. The following exercises will help you build a sensory model of your imagery, which is your natural ability to imagine in the five senses.

Take your time, and give yourself a moment after each question to evaluate your experience—you might never have considered questions like these before, and it is perfectly okay not to have answers for all of them. Also, try to determine how clear each of your images is. There could be no image at all, a fuzzy image, a moderate image, or a very clear image.

The Sense of Sight

You can do this exercise with your eyes open or closed, whichever works the best for you. As you read or hear each question, answer yes or no.

First take a deep breath and exhale slowly. Do this a couple more times. Now imagine a place that's special to you. It can be indoors or outdoors, real or imaginary.

Can you see this special place in your mind? If you can see it, is it clear? Very clear? Fuzzy? Do you see it in brilliant color, normal color, faded color, or black and white? Can you see it as a moving picture, like watching a video? Can you rewind it and play it over again, or freeze one frame? Can you change the picture's colors, seasons, or contents; can you dim or brighten it?

Now try to change your perspective. Can you look at your special place from a different location, zoom in for a close-up, step back for a broad view, look over it or under it? Can you see yourself in the picture? Can you change the picture and see yourself at a different age? Can you see the picture without your presence?

You may have been successful in answering yes to these visual questions, or you may not have been able to see any images in your mind at all. If this is the case, you may be nonvisual. Remember that the sense of sight is only one of five.

Effects of Color

Have you noticed how color affects your life? You may find that you are attracted to a certain color of clothing. See if there is a relationship between what you wear and your moods. It's possible that certain colors may affect your moods positively or negatively.

Here is a list of how certain colors affect some people. How does it compare with your experience? It's possible that you do not respond the same way.

- **Blue:** Calming, lowers blood pressure, decreases respiration
- **Green:** Mentally and physically relaxing, relieves anxiety and nervousness
- **Red:** Increases heart rate, blood pressure, respiration, and brain waves
- **Yellow:** Energizes, improves memory, stimulates appetite
- **Violet:** Peaceful, relieves migraines
- **Pink:** Relaxes muscles, relieves tension
- **Orange:** Energizes, stimulates appetite and digestive system
- **Black:** Enhances self-confidence, power, and strength

Can You See Auras?

Can you see colors or energy lines around people? If so, you are actually seeing an energy field, called an aura, that each person projects. Some individuals project their auras a good distance from their bodies, while others only expand a small distance.

A few people do have the ability to see this energy. You may see colors, or you may see wavy lines instead. If you have the ability to see auras, you may be able to determine another person's mood or health by the colors or lines you see.

ESSENTIALS

Here's how to see your aura. Spread two fingers apart in a V position. Hold them up to the light and look through the V without focusing on either finger. You should see a wavy line similar to what you would see in an old pane of glass. That's your aura.

The Sense of Hearing

Next you will measure your sense of hearing. Again, get comfortable, take a deep breath and exhale slowly. Can you imagine any sounds in your special place? Are there sounds of nature, such as birds singing, water running, wind blowing, or is there just the sound of silence? Can you hear sounds coming from different directions in your special place—from the left or the right, from above or below? Can you hear the sounds fading or getting stronger?

Relaxing or Emotional Sounds

Can you imagine a sound that relaxes you? Does listening to it help you feel calmer? Can you imagine a sound that gives you energy? Can you imagine happy or sad sounds?

Can you replay conversations or sounds from the past? Can you change them or turn the volume up or down? Do you hear your own voice in your head? Do you hear other voices in your head?

Music or Noise

Think of how sound influences your life. Do you seek out places with loud, energetic music, or do you search for peace and quiet? Can you imagine music in your head? Can you turn the volume up or down, slow the music or speed it up? Can you pick out different instruments or voices?

Do you have trouble holding a focus when you are surrounded by a lot of sound? Do loud sounds bother you? Can you "zone out" so nothing bothers you?

Throughout history sound has been used to help induce trances. The powerful performance of Stravinsky's "Rite of Spring," which debuted in Paris in the early 1900s, caused concertgoers to riot in the streets. In the 1950s, it was feared that rock-and-roll music would corrupt the minds of teens.

Scottish bagpipers piped armies into battle, Aborigines played didgeridoos, and Tibetan monks used gongs and cymbals. In America, Revolutionary War soldiers marched to the fife and drum, Native Americans used war chants, and even today, football teams leave locker rooms yelling and chanting to psyche themselves up for a game.

Mood Music

Many stores play music that has a light, airy tempo to get you in the mood to shop. Restaurants combine music with lighting to produce a comfortable, intimate atmosphere for their patrons. In the same way, you may find yourself listening to certain radio stations, tapes, or CDs to create a specific mood while driving.

If you drive to work, try listening to upbeat music like rock-and-roll. When you arrive, you will be full of energy, psyched up for the workday. When you drive home, find softer and gentler music to listen to—you will arrive relaxed and ready for a quiet evening.

The Sense of Touch

The kinesthetic, or feeling, sense is experienced in two different ways. Your tactile sense represents physical feelings, which you may experience both internally and externally. Your kinesthetic sense also has an emotional component. Emotional images are often linked strongly to all the senses. To continue the exercise, answer the following questions and explore your sense of touch.

Can you imagine feeling the temperature in your special place? Is it hot, warm, cool, or cold? Is it dry or damp, windy or calm? Can you raise or lower the temperature? Can you feel the texture of things close to you: the ground, your clothes, or other objects? Can you hold or touch an object and feel its history? Can you picture its past?

Do you feel emotions in your special place? Can you relax there, get energized, let your worries go, or feel the creative flow of the universe?

Emotions

Do you hold emotional encounters inside long after the event has occurred? Do you pick up and hold on to others' feelings? Do you have a sense of space around you, and do others intrude on it? Can you change your emotions?

Another type of feeling is intuition. It is the gut emotion that tells you something is wrong, or that something is right. Often people do not acknowledge their intuition; they try to cover it up. Have you ever said to yourself, "I knew I should have . . ." but you didn't.

The Sense of Taste

By now you may have discovered a connection between the senses: emotions may be experienced in colors, sounds, or sensations. There are still two more senses to evaluate. The next one is taste. Sit back, take a deep breath, exhale slowly, and experience the questions one at a time.

Do you have a favorite food? Can you imagine its taste? Can you change the taste, add a different seasoning, or cook it a different way? Can you blend the tastes of different foods on your plate?

Do you like to cook? Can you read a recipe and know what the result will taste like? Do you use recipes, or do you cook by feel?

Are there foods that comfort you? Are there foods that bring back memories, good or bad? Are there foods that you do not like? Do you dislike a food because of the taste, smell, feel, or appearance? Can you imagine a little bit of an unpleasant taste? If so, now remember a pleasant taste.

FACTS

In 1954, researchers at the National Institute of Mental Health developed a deep relaxation environment called a sensory deprivation tank. It was a floatation tank filled with a solution of Epsom salts that was five times denser than seawater, and it was completely soundproof. When floating inside, a person had a complete experience of her sense modalities, without interference from outside.

Many people love the comfort that certain foods provide. Chocolate is smooth and soothing. Tea provides a warm, comfortable feeling, both when you hold the cup and when you sip it. A crunchy food can help burn off stress. The emotions that accompany certain foods often cause a diet to fail; when you diet, you give up much more than calories.

The Sense of Smell

Last but not least of the five senses is the sense of smell. You can do the next exercise just like the others. Take a deep breath, exhale slowly, let your body relax, and contemplate the questions one at a time.

Can you imagine any smells in your special place? Is there more than one? Can you experience one smell and then another, or can you inhale a combination of smells at the same time? Can you imagine moving about in your special place, experiencing smells as you go?

Can you imagine a smell that relaxes you? Is there more than one? Do certain smells bring back memories? Do these smells help you remember sights, sounds, emotions, or tastes?

Emotional Smells

Are there smells that create feelings within you? Do they make you sad or happy, give you energy or make you tired? Are there smells that remind you of feeling ill or being healthy? If so, remember a healthy smell.

Fragrances impact our lives in many ways. Think about the smells you experience on a daily basis. You may visit a restaurant or bakery, pass by freshly cut grass, or get a whiff from a bouquet of flowers. You may wear a favorite perfume or cologne. You may have endured smells coming from a city dumpster or exhaust fumes on a busy street.

You might burn candles and incense or put fragrant oils in your bath. You may enjoy the aroma of fresh-brewed coffee, a wood fire, or spices and herbs. Do you have a favorite street, where each step you take brings different and enchanting smells to your nose?

Evaluation of the Senses

This exploration of the senses may have helped you create a hypnotic trance. Specific words will often trigger a memory, which for a brief moment replays itself in your mind. Words can evoke several of the senses.

Colors can be linked to feelings by using phrases such as "hot pink," "cool blue," "pure white," "spicy yellow," or "peaceful green." Foods are often experienced by all five senses. Taste may not be the only reason that you dislike a certain food: it might be the color, the feel, or the smell. Perhaps it reminds you of an unhappy memory, a place, or a person from that time.

The Importance of Sensory Imagery

It is very important to understand how your sense modalities function. In the upcoming chapters of this book, your sensory imagery will play a key role in hypnotic suggestion. It will be helpful for you to know both what you like and what you do not like: your positive and negative responses in each sense. This is a major component of Neuro-Linguistic Programming.

The skilled hypnotherapist can detect your slightest reaction to her words. She will watch the movements of your mouth for indications of your sense of taste. She will watch your eye movements to read your visual, auditory, and kinesthetic senses. Your breathing patterns will show her your sense of smell. Soon you will be able to read the same signals.

A nonvisual person is more likely to tilt his head downward than a visual person. The eyes of a nonvisual person may sit back in the skull, giving the impression of blindness. The nonvisual person may develop a strong kinesthetic sense.

Range of Vision

There are interesting links between your DNA and your senses. The most noticeable is the shape of your head. The position of your eye sockets in the skull has a strong impact on your visual and kinesthetic senses. Eyes that are far apart have a wider range of vision.

When basketball legend Bob Cousy first played for the Boston Celtics, his teammates had trouble with his play making. He had such good side vision that he would pass the ball before they were prepared to make the catch. They had to learn to be prepared to make a play anytime Cousy had the ball.

ALERT

If you are a visual person, you may be sensitive to light. You may have a heightened need to shade your eyes in bright light, and even the flickering of fluorescent lighting might produce headaches. Also, lack of daylight during the winter can cause feelings of lethargy, irritability, sadness, and increased desire for sleep. This condition is known as seasonal affective disorder, or SAD.

How far to the side can you see? To find out, hold your arms straight out at your side, elbows bent and hands pointed upward, fingers spread apart. With your eyes looking straight ahead, move your hands foreword until you can see them. Now move your hands away from your head, and you will be able to determine your side vision range.

Life Changes

Your mental makeup is based on your physical makeup, but unlike your genetic code, the strength of your imagery perception can change. Any traumatic event, such as abuse, an intense change in your life, or a situation where your mind is called upon to deal with survival, will heighten the senses.

The near-death experience is a prime example. Once a person has been through such an experience, she is not the same. The person herself often does not know she has changed, but everyone else is aware of the difference.

Without the understanding of friends and family, people who have had near-death experiences often feel out of place. Many times their relationships fall apart. Their emotional sense may become so strong that they are consumed with mental pain and may turn to drugs or alcohol to deaden their feelings.

A near-death experience does not have to be a tragedy. When properly understood, it can be a great opportunity to use your increased sensory ability for positive improvements. The greatest challenge is to give yourself permission to try. Enhanced senses can be especially beneficial when they are experienced through hypnotic trance.

ESSENTIALS

Increasing your ability to experience sensory images will be a great help in deepening your self-hypnotic trance. This awareness will help you create your own relaxation "capsule" in your mind, giving access to the inner peace that is deep within you.

Develop Your Sense Model

Now it's time to evaluate the results of your sense modality exercises. Rate each of your senses as none, weak, moderate, or strong.

- Can you image with your visual sense? Can you detach from it and view it with no emotional feelings? Can you step into the image and experience it?
- Can you image sound? Can you raise and lower the volume, and slow it down or speed it up?
- How did you experience the kinesthetic, feeling sense, internally and externally? Can you image texture and emotion?
- How strong is your taste imagery?
- How do you rate your sense of smell imagery?
- Could you image each sense by itself, or was it tied to other senses?

Relaxation Exercise

You may now begin to integrate your sensory imagery into the basic relaxation induction. This exercise is written to give you an opportunity to experience all your senses. If you do not image in one or more sense, just focus on the senses that are the strongest for you.

Find a comfortable position, take a deep breath, and slowly let it out. If you can imagine a favorite smell, you may do so now and all during the exercise. Remember that you can stop the induction anytime you wish and continue on with your regular activities.

Take another deep breath, inhaling your favorite smell, and pick a spot for your eyes to focus on. You may feel your body begin to relax with each breath you take. You may let your eyes go out of focus as you smell your favorite relaxing smell. Perhaps you can imagine some music or other relaxing sound. You will always be aware if your phone rings or if someone speaks to you.

As you hear the sounds and smell the air, you may allow yourself to relax more and more, going deeper and deeper into hypnosis. In a few moments you may begin to count backward from five to zero. You may look forward to being in your favorite relaxing place in your imagination when you reach zero. This may be a place you remember or one you create. When you reach this place, you may have a positive experience through all your senses: seeing, hearing, feeling, tasting, and smelling.

Count Down

You may now count down at a comfortable speed.

- **FIVE,** relax, breathe slowly
- **FOUR,** going deeper and deeper into hypnosis
- **THREE,** relax, feel how comfortable you are—you may look forward to the next number and going to your special place
- **TWO,** going deeper and deeper, relaxing and relaxing
- **ONE,** you're almost there—you're looking forward to the next number, to being in your special place that is so comfortable, so relaxing
- **ZERO,** it is so good to be here

Take a few moments and enjoy where you are. Look around and see how relaxing it is here. You may hear the sounds and smell the smells. Imagine a favorite taste. You may stay for a few moments and feel comfortable and relaxed.

Count Up

It is now time to come back to the surface of your mind. You may count up from zero to five at a comfortable pace. ONE, coming upward. TWO, THREE, FOUR, coming back to the surface. At the next number you may open your eyes, fresh and relaxed, taking a deep breath of your favorite smell. FIVE.

ESSENTIALS

You have just experienced an induction designed to take you deeper into hypnosis than the previous relaxation exercise did. This is an excellent method to practice before going to sleep. If you give yourself the suggestion that you will drift off peacefully into a restful sleep when you reach zero, you may fall asleep even before you get there.

You may now have a much better understanding of how your five senses work for you. This knowledge about your sensory imagery model of your unique mental makeup can help you develop confidence in your natural abilities.

CHAPTER 3

Your Conscious and Unconscious

As you explore your conscious and unconscious minds, you'll learn the difference between the two, how they function, how they can communicate with each other, and how they get out of sync. The exercises in this chapter are designed to help you understand your own message system, what it is trying to tell you, and how to begin making productive and positive responses.

Conscious and Unconscious

Perhaps the best way to illustrate the relationship between the conscious and unconscious minds is the story of Jason's spring. When he was a boy, Jason used to visit his grandfather's camp, deep in the woods. It was located down in a valley, with the nearest neighbor over a mile away. The camp had no telephone, electricity, or indoor plumbing.

When Jason visited, one of his chores was to fetch water from the spring behind the camp. The spring was very shallow, and when he scooped up water, he was only able to fill his pail half full. The pail always scraped along the bottom of the spring and roiled up the debris that had settled there. Then he would have to wait until the water cleared.

When Jason tried to fill his pail again, he lost the water he had already scooped up and was only able to fill it to the same level as before. Try as hard as he might, he was only able to fill half the pail. He finally returned to the camp, disappointed at his failure to complete his chore.

When Jason's grandfather saw his dejected face, he asked Jason what was the matter. Jason showed him the pail, only half full of water. Grandfather laughed. He took a dipper from a hook near the old iron sink and led Jason back to the spring.

Grandfather bent down, carefully filled the dipper, and emptied it into the pail. Soon water spilled over the top. Jason took the dipper and filled another pail. He could have filled pails all day long. Under the surface of the shallow spring was a source of water that flowed upward from deep in the earth.

Like Jason's childhood spring, your mind has two levels. Your conscious mind is the surface and your unconscious mind is the deep reservoir underneath. The conscious mind makes up only about 10 percent of your total mind. When you try to get too much information from your mind at one time, you can roil up your critical thinking. As you develop skills in self-hypnosis, you will find it easier to get information from your reservoir at a comfortable pace.

Communication and Storage

Your conscious mind is the communication center where you process thoughts and ideas. Here you think, calculate, plan, feel emotions, and direct the outcome of your conscious actions. It is in your conscious mind that you set long- and short-term goals. The conscious mind deals with all the information that enters it, both through the unconscious mind and through your external image sensors: your senses of sight, hearing, touch, taste, and smell. It can be a very busy place.

Your unconscious mind is your storage center; it contains all the experiences you've had since birth. Some believe that it may even retain information from before birth, recognizing the idea of a universal mind that is accessed through the unconscious mind. Your memory of experiences takes place through your sensory images.

FACTS

"In self-hypnosis, we focus the conscious mind and use it as a tool to instruct and to guide the unconscious in the direction that we consciously want our lives to go. Self-hypnosis can be symbolized by a microscope focusing on a specific goal or objective."
—Henry Leo Bolduc, *Your Creative Voice*

The unconscious mind hosts your belief system. It sends you subtle messages regarding actions you are contemplating in the conscious mind. Should I? Shouldn't I? The unconscious mind is responsible for your intuitive or gut feelings.

Time Zones of the Mind

Your mind processes information from three different time zones: the past, the future, and the present. Mentally, you constantly move between these zones as you deal with information from both the conscious and the unconscious. The more you are aware of this, the easier it will be to understand how you recall information from the past, which is retrieved from your unconscious mind.

To imagine an event or action in the future, your two minds have to work together. The unconscious mind provides memory images of past events, and the conscious mind critiques, changes, and projects the image into the future. The future may or may not manifest as you imagine. As time passes, conditions may change, affecting your image of the future.

Recalling the Past

If you are visually strong, you will recall your memories as visual images. If you are kinesthetic, you will remember what you felt. Chances are your image recall is connected to more than one sense. Using the model of your sensory images that you developed in the last chapter, allow yourself to experience the following questions in terms of your strongest senses.

Visual Recall

Get comfortable, take a deep breath, exhale, close your eyes if you wish, and begin. If you recall visual memories, also ask yourself what the image feels like, emotionally and physically. See if you can hear any sound images with your picture: natural, mechanical, musical, or conversational. How strong is your ability to experience visual replay?

Sound Recall

If you recall sound memories, how are they linked to your other senses? Do you also feel emotions or energy, do you see pictures, or do you associate sounds with tastes or smells? Can you immerse yourself in a pleasant sound as if you were wearing a pair of headphones? If the sound is music, do you listen for the words, the beat, the melody, or the harmony?

Kinesthetic Recall

If you recall tactile memories including touch and temperature, or emotional memories including happiness and sadness, can you also generate pictures, sounds, smells, or tastes? Can you image a memory and increase or decrease its emotional content? Can you experience, and amplify or diminish, heat or cold?

Taste Recall

If you recall taste memories, do you link them to pictures, sounds, feelings, or smells? Can you see the food that you remember tasting? Can you see the location of the taste experience; can you see the people you were with, hear the conversation, feel the mood, and remember the smells?

Smell Recall

If you recall smell memories, do you see pictures, hear sounds, feel emotions, or experience tastes at the same time? Can you inhale your favorite aroma in your mind and relive a related memory from the past?

Your subconscious is more powerful than your conscious mind. It can influence you to take impulsive actions that override the critical mind. Afterward, an argument can take place between your two minds. You may have experienced this when you tried to break an unwanted habit.

Projecting into the Future

We project our minds into the future by using memory data from the past. As you do these exercises, rate yourself according to how clearly you experience the images. Are they clear and bright, fuzzy or hazy, dark and weak, or nonexistent? Contemplate the questions one at a time. Get comfortable, relax, take a deep breath, exhale, and begin.

Visual Projection

If you are visual, imagine a pleasant outdoor memory. Can you change this picture in your imagination to a different season? Can you change the hour from morning to noon, to sunset, or to night? Can you change the weather conditions from sunny to cloudy? Can you pick out an object in the picture, such as a house, and change its color?

Can you remove or add objects or people to the picture? Do you see yourself in the picture as though you are watching a video, or do you experience yourself actually being there? Can you do both? Can you move this picture ahead in time? Can you see it in a week, a month, a year, or in five or ten years from now?

Can you imagine a picture of an indoor scene? Can you rearrange items or people? Can you change the color scheme? Can you move yourself and others forward in time? Can you see the scene from different angles?

Can you imagine abstracts, such as colors or energy lines? Can you change colors or swirl them together like a kaleidoscope? Can you do the same with energy patterns? Can you speed up these images or slow them down? Can you brighten or dull them?

Today's world is very different from the world of only a hundred years ago. Your senses are constantly bombarded with outside interference. Pollution is everywhere—noise pollution, odor pollution, visual pollution, and taste pollution, and these all have an impact on your emotional sense.

Hearing Projection

Can you imagine sounds in your mind? Can you relate sounds to a picture image that is projected into the future? If so, can you change the sounds as the picture changes? Can you imagine a future conversation with one or more people? Can you change the conversation, running through several different scenarios?

Can you raise or lower the volume of sounds in an image of the future? Can you slow the sounds down or speed them up? Can you change the pitch? Can you change the intensity? Can you run one sound over another?

Can you set music or other sounds to color or energy images? Can these sounds move in sync with images that are dancing or pulsating? Can you slow or speed up the picture and the sound? Can you change your selection of sounds or music? Can you imagine sounds with no pictures?

Kinesthetic Projection

Can you take a tactile memory from the past and project it into the future? Can you relate the sensation of touch to a picture? Can you feel the temperature in an outdoor or indoor location? Can you change the temperature from cold to warm, to hot, to very hot? Can you imagine the warm sun, and feel the change in temperature as a cloud covers it? Can you feel your bare feet walking in sand or wearing a comfortable pair of shoes?

Can you imagine holding an object in your hand and feel its texture, temperature, size, and weight? Can you change it in your mind and feel the difference? Can you imagine your muscles moving? Can you imagine playing a musical instrument, dancing to music, playing a sport, or doing some other activity? Can you feel yourself slow down or speed up while doing an activity?

Can you imagine someone else touching you? Can you imagine the feel of your own touch, or the texture and weight of different clothing? Can you feel a warm blanket covering you from head to foot? Can you feel the texture of a color or energy?

Can you feel emotion when imagining music? Can you change the music and get another emotion, or does it stay the same? Can you imagine feeling the emotion of a future conversation with others? Can you change that emotion? Can you imagine how you would feel participating in a future activity, such as playing a sport, acting a character in a play, or being with family or friends? Can you project emotions into images of the future?

Taste Projection

Can you imagine going to a favorite restaurant sometime in the future and dining on your favorite food? Can you taste a combination of different foods? Can you change the seasoning or spices, or taste the different ways it might be prepared? Can you change the menu? Can you imagine eating a five-course dinner and drinking the beverages that accompany it?

Can you read a recipe and imagine how it will taste when prepared? Can you imagine the taste of the individual ingredients in the recipe? Can you imagine what the dish would taste like if you changed the ingredients? Can you picture yourself eating and tasting the finished recipe?

If you hear the crunch of certain foods, do you anticipate the taste in your mouth? Can you imagine eating a sour food and feeling your mouth pucker up? Can you imagine a taste when you picture a color? Can you imagine tasting a spoonful of sugar, salt, or fat?

Do you relate an emotion to the taste of certain foods? Can you imagine the taste of a happy food, a sad food, a calming or relaxing food, or an energy food? Do you identify the taste of certain foods with an anticipated event? Can you imagine the taste of a future meal with friends?

Smell Projection

Can you imagine any smells in the outdoor picture you created? Can you sense different smells as you move about in the picture? Can you diminish or intensify the smells? Can you imagine smells in your indoor picture? Can you move about and smell different smells?

Can you imagine a smell that would calm you down? Can you imagine one that would wake you up? Can you think of a place that has a relaxing smell? Can you imagine a sound and relate a smell to it? Can you change your mood by imagining a smell?

Can you imagine smelling the different ingredients that make up a recipe, such as spices, herbs, meats, or other items? Can you smell it cooking? Can you smell the difference between frying, baking, grilling, barbecuing, boiling, and steaming?

Can you imagine a bouquet of fresh flowers? Can you take individual flowers out of the arrangement and smell each one, noting the different fragrances? Can you imagine the smell of burning candles or incense? Can you feel the warmth of a bath and smell the soaps or oils?

Living in the Present

Your mind is constantly reaching into its memory banks and projecting thoughts into the future. As it does this, your mind passes through the present moment. The present is where action takes place. Athletes call awareness of the present moment "being in the Zone." Peak performances are often achieved in this state.

ESSENTIALS

Unfortunately, it is impossible to stay in the present for long periods of time. Both your internal and external senses are constantly being bombarded, which brings you back to normal awareness. In the next chapter you will learn to use self-hypnotic anchors that can help you stay in the Zone.

When you are able to stay in the present Zone, your mind may be able to alter time, distance, speed, strength, tastes, smells, pictures, artistic performances, emotions, and even pain. Perhaps you can remember a time when you were called upon to react quickly to a serious situation. Looking back, you might describe the experience as "being in slow motion." Actually, your mind had sped up, and you entered the Zone. The Zone often produces an adrenaline rush, a high that keeps athletes coming back for more and causes thrill seekers to push themselves to the edge.

Physical Characteristics That Affect Your Experience

Your mental and physical makeup affects how you experience and react to the present. You may have physical conditions that have been with you since birth: sense-altering conditions such as blindness, deafness, or little ability to smell or taste, or birth defects, or other physical or mental conditions. You may have been born with overdeveloped sensitivity in one or more of the senses, making it difficult for you to filter out what others experience as normal.

You may have experienced physical or mental changes during your lifetime. You may have lost your ability to taste, smell, hear, or see. You may not be able to use parts of your body that you once relied on. An emotional trauma may have changed your sense of focus. All of these conditions, and others not mentioned here, may affect how you react in the moment.

FACTS

Temporary situations affect the way your senses take in information. A common cold can hamper your ability to hear, smell, taste, or see. Drugs or alcohol can impair your senses, providing inaccurate information. In these conditions, your experience can affect your memory or distort the way you perceive the future.

You Are Unique

You may be able to have a total sensory experience with all five senses, roaming freely through time. You may be able to dissociate and observe yourself in the past, the present, and in the imagined future. You may be confined by your experiences, or you may be detached from them. Your sensory images may work in only one or just a few of the five senses. However you process with the senses, this is central to your uniqueness.

When you become comfortable with your own mental makeup, it can become a great ally as you journey through life. The secret is to give your two minds the opportunity to communicate. You want to give them permission to use all your internal resources to determine positive and productive decisions. The secret is to listen to what you're telling yourself.

Imagine that you live in a three-room house that looks like a motel. The rooms are side by side and are connected by doorways. Each of the rooms also has a door to the outside. The rooms represent your past, present, and future.

You may be able to roam freely through this house, entering all three rooms whenever you want to, and you may also be able to look at the house from the outside. Or it may be that you can't go outside, or you can't come in. You may be confined to one or two rooms.

If you have felt confined because you don't understand how you are different, you need not feel so any more. If you seem to live in only one of the rooms, it may mean that you have developed extraordinary abilities there. That orientation can make up for what you may be lacking in the others.

Flooding Technique

Flooding is a hypnosis induction technique designed for people who have trouble focusing on a single thing because something always interrupts their attention. If you are this type of individual, you probably have at least one especially heightened sense.

Self-Hypnosis Flooding Exercise

Before you do this exercise, you may want to turn on the television, the radio, a tape player, and/or a CD player. The object is to have several sensory stimulants going on at the same time, the more the better, as long as they do not bother anyone else and they are comfortable for you. Think of something you have been trying to make a decision about, and ask your minds to work together on an answer while you're in your sensory flooding trance. You may allow yourself to find a comfortable position, loosen your clothes, take a deep breath, exhale, and begin.

As you slowly breathe in and out, you may be aware that there are many different sounds around you. Every time you focus on one of these sounds, you may hear another sound. You may also be aware that some of your muscles are stiff and some are relaxed, and your muscles may be in constant motion as you breathe in and out, listening to all the sounds around you.

There may be other sounds that you hear: talking, traffic, the telephone, or perhaps even an airplane. You may be aware of smells that are near you or the temperature where you are. You may think of anything you want to.

You may think pleasant thoughts from the past or positive thoughts about the future. You may also be aware of all the sounds, feelings, and smells that you are experiencing at the same time. You may breathe in and out slowly, and look forward to being aware of all that is happening around you.

As you experience all of this sensory stimulation, you may slowly count down from five to zero. Allow plenty of time in between numbers to experience all your senses. You may count at a speed that is comfortable for you. Five, four, three, two, one, zero.

Now that you are at zero, you may experience all the sounds, smells, and feelings that are around you, and you may feel your muscles relax and flex as you breathe in and out. You may think a pleasant thought from the past, or think about a positive event in the future. You may be aware of as much or as little as you want.

When you are ready, you may count slowly from zero back up to five. Zero, one, two . . . you may feel yourself coming back to the surface of your mind. Three, four . . . you are almost there, feeling relaxed and refreshed as you come back to the surface. You may open your eyes now and have an answer about your decision. Five.

QUESTIONS?

Will the flooding technique work for me?
The flooding technique can be very effective if you have an active mind. However if you seek peace and quiet, this approach may not be for you.

Difficulty Focusing

Mitch studied self-hypnosis, and although he enjoyed practicing it, he was able to put himself only into a light trance. He could relax, but his mind never stopped thinking. The more he tried to focus, the harder it was to quiet his conscious mind. Then he tried the flooding induction.

Mitch could never remember weather reports; every time one came on the television or radio, he would automatically think of something else. He exercised on a treadmill twenty minutes a day, and he decided to put on a pair of headphones and play a weather station while he walked. He asked his minds to work on solving a problem while he exercised.

He started the weather report and began to walk, giving his mind permission to think of whatever it wanted, from the past to the future to the present. As he concentrated on exercising, he did not hear the weather report playing through his headphones. After twenty minutes, an idea suddenly lit up in his conscious mind, like a light bulb switching on. From then on Mitch practiced self-hypnosis on his treadmill.

Sleep on It

Many people have learned that if they ask themselves a question in the evening, they often wake up with the answer the next morning. Your dreams are similar to the flooding induction in self-hypnosis. While the conscious mind sleeps, the unconscious mind weighs the pros and cons, calculates all the probabilities, and relays the answer when you awake. The conscious mind then makes a decision.

To take advantage of this technique, try the self-hypnosis induction at the end of Chapter 2 with the following additions: Before you begin, give yourself a suggestion; ask your unconscious mind to address a decision you have been pondering. Then ask your conscious mind to carefully consider the answer that you receive at the end of your self-hypnosis session.

Proceed with your induction at a pace that is comfortable for you. Once you reach zero, spend some time enjoying your sensory images. Let your mind wander positively wherever it takes you. When you're ready, count yourself back to the surface, returning relaxed and refreshed and open to the enlightenment you may receive from the unconscious mind.

If you use this self-hypnosis induction before going to sleep, suggest to yourself that you will fall asleep by the time you reach zero, and that you will let your unconscious mind work on the answer overnight.

Universal Consciousness

Many people believe in the existence of a third form of consciousness: universal consciousness. Universal consciousness is a continuation of the unconscious mind, connecting you to your belief system. Universal consciousness makes it possible for you to retrieve information and answers from a source that has no scientific explanation.

ESSENTIALS

The source of universal consciousness is your belief system. You may define it as your contact with God or with whatever power you believe in. Universal consciousness is where you go to ask for help in solving dilemmas that seem beyond your control.

However you define your belief system, it does play a major role in bringing about positive changes in your life. It is the basis for defining the purpose of changes you wish to make. It is often the strength that allows your change to become permanent. Whether you call it the universal mind or the unconscious mind, you will learn how to use it as you progress through this book.

CHAPTER 4
Instant Hypnosis

I n this chapter you will learn more about self-hypnosis, how to develop positive anchors, and how to install them in your unconscious mind by using posthypnotic suggestions. In addition, you will become aware of potential negative anchors that you may be triggering without knowing it.

External and Internal Influences

As you have learned, you naturally move in and out of self-hypnotic trances many times every day. You are constantly bouncing back and forth between your thinking, conscious mind and your unconscious mind, processing and storing information. Incoming information mixes with what is already there and waits, ready to be accessed by the conscious mind. However, you are constantly bombarded with sensory stimulation, which often interferes with your internal processing.

External Influences

Have you ever felt like telling someone to get out of your face, though of course you never actually said it? Many times a day most people experience that something or someone is in their space. How you deal with these situations greatly affects your actions and how you feel during the next few hours, or for a much longer time.

A ripple effect occurs when someone creates a mood or a response or takes an action that is absorbed by others, who then pass it on to more people. It continues on like a ripple in the water. The mood could be either positive or negative—happiness, anger, fear, or doubt. Once you internalize a mood, it acts like a suggestion in a self-hypnotic trance. Then you become the hypnotist who transfers the mood to the next person, who now goes about his business in the suggested mood.

FACTS

Strict rules and regulations, the demands of your job, and bombardment by the media all take their toll on your mood. These influences usually come from outside your family, social institutions or the media.

Internal Influences

You may generate emotions that interfere with your decision-making ability. It is possible that these feelings may be transferred into the moment from some past event. Your conscious mind then has to deal with them, causing you to focus on past memories, pleasant or unpleasant. Or you could have internalized someone else's ripple.

This constant internal interruption can keep you off balance. Every time you attempt to refocus, another message comes up from the unconscious mind. It can be as "in your face" as any external interruption.

If you do not have a place of escape, a place to quiet this internal and external interference, you will continue to be off balance. By creating posthypnotic anchors, you may be able to keep yourself more in balance with life. There will always be interference, but there is always a way to keep in balance through self-hypnosis.

Posthypnotic Suggestions

The most powerful tool in self-hypnosis is the posthypnotic suggestion. As you remember, a hypnotic trance takes place when the conscious mind loses its ability to make critical decisions. During that time your unconscious accepts the suggestion as a reality. A powerful suggestion continues to function after the hypnotic trance has ended, and your conscious mind accepts the suggestion as part of its decision-making process.

The deeper the hypnotic trance, the easier it is to implant the suggestion into your unconscious mind. The more you experience the suggestion as a reality, the more it will actually be a reality in your waking state.

ALERT

When you create a posthypnotic suggestion for yourself, it is important to consider how it could affect others. Actions that you take because of the suggestion could be misunderstood. This subject will be addressed in a later chapter.

The stage show hypnotist seeks out subjects who have fantasy-prone personalities, to ensure that his demonstration will be successful. He wants to have his posthypnotic suggestions accepted as realities. The good subject will dance with a mop, walk an invisible dog, or taste water as vinegar. The audience will enjoy laugh after laugh at the subject's expense.

However, problems can arise when a person's reality is different from everyone else's reality. If the stage show subject were to leave the demonstration and be placed in a public setting, no one would understand what was happening, yet the reality of the posthypnotic suggestion would still be in effect. The person's actions would not be understood. What would you think if you saw someone dancing with a mop or walking an invisible dog down a street? Many people carry out posthypnotic suggestions that they have absorbed without even knowing they were doing so.

Remember that posthypnotic suggestions can be very powerful. In your unconscious mind, they are real, and they can recreate this reality when they are triggered, no matter where you are. When you give yourself a suggestion, always include cautions such as, "The suggestion is only as strong as needed, and I will always be aware of where I am."

Self-Hypnotic Anchors

A self-hypnotic anchor is an action that creates a response. The anchor produces a reaction to a posthypnotic suggestion that was planted in your subconscious mind during a self-hypnotic trance. It may be a word or a touch, a sound or a visual cue, a smell or a taste, or an internal emotion. The stronger the suggestion that you implanted, the greater effect the anchor has in recreating the response.

QUESTIONS?

How can I re-experience a positive state of mind?
Using self-hypnosis and knowledge of your strongest sense modalities, you can create a posthypnotic suggestion to respond to a positive anchor that you plant in your own subconscious mind.

How to Create an Anchor

Let's see how you establish a posthypnotic anchor. To begin, you may use the relaxation induction that you have been practicing in previous chapters. When you reach zero, tell yourself that you will feel very comfortable in a specific place in your mind that is calm and relaxing. This place may be from a memory, a new place, or just a place deep inside yourself, a place where you can have a positive experience through the uniqueness of your sense modalities.

Once you have entered your trance, tell yourself to place your thumb and forefinger together (or, if you wish, you can create your own special word or touch that is meaningful to you). This will be your anchor. The anchor you are creating will instantly remind you of how relaxed and calm you are feeling at the moment.

Every time you use your anchor, you will have this same positive feeling. This feeling will be a little different every time you experience it, and it will be experienced only as much as needed when you use the anchor. Every time you practice self-hypnosis and reinforce your anchor, it will become stronger and stronger in your subconscious mind. Each time you trigger your anchor, it will work better and be more responsive.

Recognize Negative Anchors

You probably have a relationship with someone who knows how to "push your buttons." This person always manages to bring out the worst in you. No matter how many times you tell yourself that you will react differently the next time, you are always pulled back into the same old negative pattern. This person has actually succeeded in hypnotizing you, implanting a negative suggestion in your subconscious mind that influences your critical thinking.

Be Aware of the Moment

It is very easy to lose track of the moment. When you are bombarded with internal and external sensory stimulation, it is easy to become confused. The effect is the same as the flooding hypnosis induction. While you're off chasing around in your head, paying attention to your conscious mind, the unconscious is absorbing suggestions. These suggestions influence your actions.

If you are aware of what is happening in the moment, you are more likely to recognize a negative anchor before it has time to become a trigger. Once something interrupts your thinking pattern, you become open to any suggestion that is being given to you. If you're not aware of the source or of what is happening in that moment, you open yourself up to suggestions that may have a negative impact on you.

Perhaps you have been in a situation where you were focusing on a book or on television. The story was so compelling that you forgot about the time. When you suddenly came back to reality, you still had such a strong connection to the story that you felt out of place with the real world.

Being aware of the moment gives you an edge in escaping confusion. That is the time to trigger your anchor. Triggering it will allow you to step away in your mind for a moment. The big advantage is that no one else knows that you have escaped. From this dissociated position, it is easier to make positive decisions with your conscious mind.

FACTS

Negative subliminal suggestions are implanted when the critical thinking ability of your conscious mind has been disrupted. If you allow someone, something, or a past memory to throw you off balance, you will open up your unconscious to a negative suggestion. Once you learn to recognize the situation, you can counter it by triggering a positive anchor.

Develop Positive Anchors

Now that you have practiced a self-hypnotic trance that included the suggestion to return to a relaxed state by using your anchor, it's time to learn a shortcut. Take a deep breath, exhale, and close your eyes. Slowly count backward from five to zero, telling yourself that you will use your anchor to remember how good it felt in your deep trance. You only need to say the numbers: five, four, three, two, one, and zero.

At zero, trigger the anchor that you gave yourself previously while you were in self-hypnosis, feel relaxed, and count yourself back up to five. Take another deep breath and include your favorite smell image, if you have one. Enjoy your relaxed feeling. Now repeat the same exercise again, but with your eyes open this time. Don't forget to trigger your anchor and feel relaxed.

Next, take a deep breath, trigger your anchor, and go directly to your relaxed feeling. Of course, the longer induction is the most effective form of self-hypnosis, but it is not always possible to do this when it is needed. By using your anchor, you will be able to receive positive benefits anytime you want or need them.

Benefits of Instant Self-Hypnosis

Instant self-hypnosis is a means to step away from the moment, whether you're by yourself or in a crowd of thousands. It can give you the chance to escape mentally and organize your thoughts. It can help get you into the Zone in athletics, and it can also prevent you from taking in someone else's negative suggestions.

The more you practice instant self-hypnosis, the better it will work for you. Soon you will begin to respond to your anchors automatically, giving yourself a chance to step back in your mind for a brief moment. This mental effect can actually carry over into your physical body, and you may find that you feel calmer and more relaxed.

You can use instant self-hypnosis in many areas of your daily routine. It is, however, a good idea to start by identifying one area to begin with. You might think of an occasion when you feel the need to escape for a moment but don't usually have the opportunity to do so. Develop a plan to trigger your self-hypnotic anchor at the moment when you need to escape. Then follow through on your plan.

A Positive Change

Jim was a high school teacher who often encountered situations that required him to take disciplinary action. He had high expectations of both himself and his students. It was difficult for him to maintain his composure when his authority was challenged. He had the reputation of having a very short fuse.

In an effort to become more positive, Jim learned self-hypnosis. He established a daily routine each afternoon when he came home from school, spending fifteen to thirty minutes practicing self-hypnosis. While driving to school, Jim would reinforce in his mind a suggestion that he would remain calm and positive, regardless of the situations he faced.

FACTS

Instant self-hypnosis can become a way of life for you. The more you recognize situations where you can trigger positive anchors, the more you will be able to find balance. Your anchors can come from any of your sense modalities. The more you practice and strive for balance by triggering your anchors, the stronger the response will be.

Self-hypnosis became second nature to him. He began to respond automatically in a much calmer and more positive way when he was faced with a discipline challenge. Over time both the students and the faculty saw Jim in a different light. He was now admired for his ability to bring about positive changes in the lives of students. Life also became much more meaningful to Jim as he continued to use self-hypnosis.

Automatic Response Exercises

Let's examine and identify potential anchors that you can place in your unconscious mind by posthypnotic suggestion. As you do the following exercises, note which ones work best for you. Remember that you will respond differently in each of your sense modalities.

Visual Anchors

Get comfortable, take a deep breath, and exhale. Picture your special, relaxing place, either the one that you have previously identified or a new one (you can always create one from your imagination). Place yourself there. You may feel calm, relaxed, and positive.

Suggest to yourself that you can get a brief flash of this picture whenever you need to relax. The brief flash will not interfere with whatever you are doing at the time, as it is only to remind you to relax. Project yourself forward to future situations where you may benefit from this state. Practice this in your mind. Tell yourself that this brief flash will be your anchor to allow you to feel calm and relaxed.

Auditory Anchors

Your sense of hearing can also be a powerful anchor. You may remember specific songs that have special memories attached to them. Every time you hear one, you are transported back in time to experience that memory again. This is an example of an anchor you have already installed—you just didn't know it.

Get comfortable, take a deep breath, exhale, and turn on a sound in your head. Think of your relaxing music. You may always hear the same song, or you may experience a different one each time. In your mind, set the speed and volume to play at a pace and level that is calm and relaxing. Suggest to yourself that whenever you need to relax and feel calm, you will hear the appropriate song in your head.

Practice projecting yourself ahead in time to a situation where music will help you to be calm and relaxed. If your favorite sound is from nature—the sound of the ocean's waves, birds' calls, or the falling rain—use the same process to practice and install your anchor. The more you practice and prepare to use your anchors, the more they will respond for you when you need them.

Kinesthetic Anchors

Emotion is one of the sensory modality anchors. You anchor the feeling of being calm, relaxed, and positive. Other feelings may also be used to create a calm and relaxed state. Peace, safety, love, and gratitude are some examples. You may identify and install whichever positive feelings you choose.

Get comfortable, take a deep breath, exhale, and feel a positive emotion. Tell yourself that you feel calm and relaxed as you experience this emotion. Suggest to yourself that you will have this feeling at any time when you need to be calm and relaxed. Every time you take a deep breath, you may have this feeling.

Project yourself into future situations where this positive emotion will help you feel calm and relaxed. Practice having this feeling when you need it. The more you practice, the easier it will be for you to bring back the feeling when you need it.

The touch anchor can be physical or a memory. For a physical touch anchor, you might press your thumb and forefinger together or clasp your hands. For a memory touch anchor, you might experience the feeling of a warm bath, a cozy fire, a smooth stone, or a caress. Whatever you choose, suggest to yourself that you will feel calm and relaxed every time you experience these feelings in your mind. The more you practice, the easier it will be to feel calm and relaxed.

Taste Anchors

You may like certain foods that are calm, relaxing, and have a positive effect on your body. Your taste anchor may be tied to a pleasant memory from the past or to something you like to cook. Get comfortable, take a deep breath, exhale, and imagine your favorite positive, calm, relaxing taste. Suggest to yourself that every time you need to feel calm and relaxed, you will remember your favorite taste.

Project this image into the future, and practice situations where remembering your taste anchor provides you with a calm, relaxed feeling. Create a positive feeling every time you experience this taste in your mind. The more you practice, the easier it will be to use your taste anchor to feel calm and relaxed.

Smell Anchors

A smell anchor can be one of the easiest and most powerful to use, as it is closely connected with your breath. Every time you take a breath, you inhale a smell. If you have good smell imagery, all you have to do is remember a calm, relaxing smell and remind yourself to take a deep breath.

You may get comfortable and take a deep breath of your favorite calm, relaxing, positive smell. Suggest to yourself that you will take a deep breath of this smell every time you need to feel calm and relaxed. Project yourself into future situations where you may need this anchor to calm and relax yourself.

Practice this in your mind. Remind yourself that you may use your anchor of a deep breath and relaxing smell anytime you need it. You will automatically take a deep breath, smell your favorite aroma, and feel calm and relaxed. The more you practice, the easier it will be to automatically take a deep breath and feel calm, relaxed, and positive.

Surround Yourself with External Anchors

There are many ways to experience instant self-hypnosis. You can develop anchors that let you use your internal sense modalities as we have discussed. There are also external anchors that you can keep on your person or in your environment to allow you to feel calm, relaxed, and positive.

External Visual Anchors

Many people surround themselves with visual anchors that bring back positive memories from the past. They hang pictures and other items on their walls, take them to their workplaces, and carry them in their wallets and purses. Some people employ more permanent measures, like tattoos.

Think of all the visual anchors that you already have in place. Maybe some of them create a negative response in you. It may be that you are not responsible for many of these negative anchors. Look for negative anchors that you can remove, change, or rearrange. Consider what you might add to give yourself a calm, relaxed, and positive feeling.

Once you've chosen your anchors, use self-hypnosis to suggest to yourself that each time you view your picture or other object, you will feel calm and relaxed. The more you condition yourself to respond favorably to your visual anchors, the easier and stronger the response will be. A view of the outdoors from inside can also work well as an anchor. A shrub, a garden, or a statue can have a calm, relaxing, and positive effect.

External Auditory Anchors

Sounds are a constant part of life. In today's world, it's almost impossible to escape sound. Unfortunately, many of the sounds you experience are not pleasant. Car horns, mechanical sounds, and people's angry voices can destroy your peaceful mood. These sounds may have become negative anchors and create a negative mood that you will carry with you for a while.

SSENTIALS

Think of occasions when sounds interfere with your positive moods, and try to screen out these negative sounds. You might wear earplugs or headphones at work, or play calming music at home.

Sometimes the flooding technique works for sounds. If you hear only one sound, you will focus on it, but if there are many sounds, it becomes harder to focus on any specific one. This sensory overload is often enough to help you direct your attention to your desired focus. If there are a lot of sounds, prepare yourself through a posthypnotic suggestion to be calm and relaxed in the middle of it all.

External Taste Anchors

The risk in using a taste anchor is that the type of food that provides calm, relaxing feelings may not be good for you. For example, chocolates are comforting but hardly a healthy option. You may find you are already using taste anchors that are not in your best interest. Be aware of what the foods you use for relaxation are doing to your body.

If you do decide to use a taste anchor, think of healthy flavors that calm and relax you, and practice moderation in using them. There are wonderful-tasting foods that do not have many calories. You may suggest to yourself that you will look forward to a healthy food that is good for you. As you taste it, you will feel calm and relaxed. The more you practice, the stronger this positive anchor will be in your mind. (Comfort foods will be addressed further in Chapter 9, "Weight Loss.")

External Smell Anchors

The sense of smell provides great enjoyment for many people, but for others it may be a curse. Smells can trigger allergies or headaches. Perfumes, colognes, and deodorants make some people feel ill. If you have a heightened sense of smell, you may experience sensory overload when smelling a strong scent. Strong smells are negative anchors that place you in an uncomfortable state.

Think of your favorite calm, relaxing, positive smell. Can you recreate the actual aroma and carry a small sample with you in a bag or vial? Essential oils work well for this purpose. If you have access to a relaxing smell, you can suggest to yourself to feel calm and relaxed when you smell it.

There are many smells you can keep around as anchors—candles, incense, flowers, or an aroma dispenser. If you find a smell that is calm and relaxing, then you may suggest to yourself in self-hypnosis that you will experience these feelings every time you experience the smell. The more you practice, the easier it will be to use your smell anchor.

CHAPTER 5

Building a Model for Change

You have already identified where your sensory-image strengths lie, and you have practiced using them in self-hypnosis to develop anchors that can help you be calm and relaxed. Now you will learn to construct positive thinking models using your sensory modalities, identify your negative thinking models, and compare the two. You will also examine your comfort zone and learn the importance of continually expanding it.

Thinking Models

There are two types of thinking models: convergent and divergent. A divergent thought process searches for options. When you are stuck, you look for alternatives. A convergent thought process eliminates options until there are none left. When you are stuck, you see no way to move ahead.

Imagine you are going to build a house, renovate an existing one, or redo a room. You'll probably start by examining a model, and you'll usually find something you like and something you dislike about it. You might think of what you'll keep and what you'll change. Then you'll design a new model based on the information you collected.

ESSENTIALS

Thinking models relate to the past, the present, and the future in a similar way. They represent how you remember past experiences and how you imagine future experiences. Your present thinking model is developed through your awareness of your current actions.

You have actual working models to study: people you admire, careers you would like to pursue, and behavior patterns you would like to incorporate into your life. Some models are very rigid; some are very flexible. There are positive models to follow, and there are also negative ones.

Your past thinking model consists of ways you thought and ways you acted in the past. Use insights from these past experiences when you develop your future model. When you feed these insights into your mental computer, you can begin to design your future thought and action models.

What Works for You?

It is difficult to create a change in the way you think. You may make many attempts, but you soon become discouraged and give up. Often, this is because you haven't developed a clear action model beforehand. By building as strong a model as possible before you begin, you will have confidence that you can reach your goal.

Have you ever thought about your natural abilities, or those you have worked hard to achieve? This includes all things that you do well. You may have developed unique abilities through adversities in your life. Because of these hardships you somehow mustered strength to persevere.

At the same time, others may misunderstand the way you think. If you do not fit their thinking model or see things the way they do, they are quick to say you are wrong. When your thinking model is hard for others to understand, it is easy to become frustrated and discouraged. You may have the same feelings when you do not know how to communicate with yourself.

The first step is to examine what you do well by answering the questions that follow. You have completed a similar process with your sensory images. It is possible that you may have a hard time identifying an area of interest in your life at the moment, and that's okay.

What Are Your Interests?

What do you do for fun and relaxation? Does it involve the special place you have already imagined in previous chapters? Why do you enjoy this activity? Is this a hobby or a passion? Is it a way to escape from the pressures of the world?

Do you think about your interest a lot? How much time do you spend on it? Would you spend more time if you could? Do you enjoy telling other people about it or teaching it to others?

Is there more than one thing you enjoy doing? If so, are they related? Are they sports, are they different forms of creativity, or are they in entirely different areas? How do you feel when you're involved? Do you have a love-hate relationship with your interest?

What Do You Believe In?

What is your belief structure? Why do you believe the way you do? Have your beliefs always been the same, or have they changed during your life? Do others believe like you do, or are you different? Are you comfortable explaining your beliefs to others?

Is your belief part of a traditional religion? If so, do you worship with others? If you have a traditional religion, are you comfortable with it? Does it have the flexibility to allow for differences of opinion, or is it rigid and inflexible? Do you believe in religion at all?

Do you spend time each day in contact with your belief system? If so, how much? Do you enter a trance when you communicate with your belief? Can your belief bring about miracles or other unexplainable acts? Do you rely on your belief for help in life situations?

Is your belief system connected to the metaphysical world? Do you look to crystals, nature, guardian angels, spirit guides, tarot cards, the stars, psychics, or other nontraditional aids to help guide you through life? To what or whom do you go when you are in need of a miracle? What do you *really* believe in?

How Are Your Organizational Skills?

How well organized are you? What do you organize best? Do you enjoy the process of organizing things or events? Is your way of organizing the same as other people's, or is it different? Do others ask you for help organizing things? Do others ask you to help them organize their lives?

Do others understand how you organize yourself or events? How well do you work with others in organizing things? Do you enjoy organizing things with others, or would you rather do it by yourself? Do your results meet your expectations? If so, how often?

Do you first organize things in your mind, or do you organize as you go? Do you like to see things, such as your house, organized and in order? Are you happy with the results of your organization? Do you use your organizational skills at work?

Do you organize your schedule? Do you organize your week, month, or year? Do you organize your finances? Do you organize the clothes you wear?

What Do You Do Well?

What do you do well? Are you a good athlete? Are you trained in a special skill? Are you artistic? Do you have a natural ability to do something that others admire?

Do others see something special in you that you do not see in yourself? Are you a natural leader? Do you take on responsibilities? Are you a good listener? Do you take on responsibility for other people's worries?

Are you comfortable with what you do? Are you a good wife or husband? Are you good at communicating with others? Are you good at your job?

When you understand how you process information, you will begin to find it easier to understand other people. These insights should help you become more comfortable with who you are and how you think.

How Do You Treat Others?

How do you treat others? Do you treat them as well as you do yourself, or better, or worse? Are you quick to offer assistance to someone who asks for it? Do you do things for others when they don't ask? Do you expect anything in return when you show someone an act of kindness?

Do you give gifts to others? If so, do you expect them to use the gifts in a certain way, or can they use them as they see fit? Do you expect something in return when you give a gift? Do you try to control others?

How do you treat people at your workplace? How do you treat friends, family, and strangers? Are you a good teacher? Do you have patience with others? Are you a good follower?

How Do You Treat Yourself?

How well do you treat yourself? Do you get upset with yourself when you do not achieve what you expect? Do you expect more of yourself than of others? Do you expect less of yourself than others do? Do you treat yourself in the same manner you treat others?

Do you feel that others give you all the recognition you deserve? Do you look for praise or other forms of reinforcement from others? Do you give yourself rewards or other incentives for doing a good job? Do you talk positively to yourself? Are you patient with yourself?

Do you give yourself second chances when something goes wrong? Can you find something positive in a negative situation? Do you put yourself down, or do you feel that you do everything perfectly?

How Do You Solve Puzzles?

Do you enjoy solving puzzles? Do you solve them as you go, figuring out the next piece as you try it, or do you analyze it in your mind first? Do you use your intuition when solving a puzzle?

Do you enjoy watching or reading mystery stories? Do you try to figure out the conclusion before it is revealed? Can you put yourself into the mind of one or more of the characters in the story? Can you make up a story in your own mind and write it down?

Do you like metaphysical mysteries or stories of experiences about the unknown? What do you think of the mystery of life? Do you think there is more in the world than what we normally see? Are there other worlds in the universe? Do you believe in what you think?

What Is Your Comfort Zone?

Sometimes your greatest gift or ability can be a curse, if you misunderstand it or use it improperly. It is important to recognize this and be aware of how a particular ability or skill may be an asset to you and others.

How comfortable are you with your interests, with your beliefs, with the way you organize, with your abilities, and with the way you treat others and yourself? How comfortable are you with the way you feel, deep inside? Are you comfortable with your problem-solving skills?

Are you comfortable with the past, with the present, and with how the future looks at this moment? Can you develop a positive model of your mind through the exercises you have completed? This model is not expected to be perfect; in fact, you may see many flaws in it. If everything in life were perfect, there would be no reason to seek improvement in yourself or in the lives of others around you.

We all have our zones of comfort and discomfort. People who spend their lives trying to stay in the comfort zone will find this zone shrinking, and they may never allow themselves to grow. If you know your comfort zone, however, you can take small risks, with the confidence that you can always go back to where you were. In order to grow, you need to use your current knowledge to help push yourself to the next level. Through self-hypnosis you can examine what you don't now know how to change.

What Doesn't Work for You?

So far, the model of yourself that you are developing has been focused on the integrity of your structure and on what works for you. But you also need to know and understand what, why, and how things don't work for you. Once you know this, you have two choices: you can continue to do what doesn't work, or you can consider changing.

FACTS

Just as you look for the flaws in a building plan, you may also look for the flaws in yourself. If you spend all your time looking only at what is right, you will never see what is wrong. Like the shrinking comfort zone, eventually there will be less and less that is right. Your confidence about making positive changes in your life will continue to decrease.

Once you have identified what you want to change, your strengths can help bring the change about. To accomplish this, you need to understand the difference between what works and what doesn't, so that you will have two models to compare. Placing yourself in a comfortable self-hypnotic trance, you can look rationally at the positives and the negatives.

Where Did It Begin?

Imagine going into your memory bank to examine the origins of the model you want to change. When and where did it begin? What was happening around you and to you at the time of its inception? It is possible that you may not be able to identify when it began.

Can you follow the progression of this negative model from early on to where it is now? Can you note any significant places during this process that help you understand how the negative model has progressed? How clear an image of the progression can you get? What internal feelings and external experiences have influenced this negative model?

Were you responsible for creating this model yourself, or did you have help? Was the development of the model out of your control? If so, who or what had control? Is there anything good about your negative model? Is there any part of it that you want to keep?

How Do You Feel about It?

Once you have examined your negative thinking model from a distance, let yourself experience how you feel about it. Give yourself the suggestion that you need only feel enough of the emotions to get the idea of the real experience. What kind of feelings do you get from the image? What don't you like? Is there anything positive about your negative model?

Can you both watch and feel yourself experiencing your negative model? How do you feel about yourself? How do you feel about others in the model? How do you think they feel about you? What kind of emotions do others in your negative model have?

Can you get a clear image of how you feel in this model? Can you go back and forth between different images of the model? Can you follow the emotional path of your model, from your early memories until now? Can you get a clear understanding of how the model developed into what it is today?

Comparing Negative and Positive Models

Once you have a fairly clear understanding of your negative model, compare it to your positive model, to the things you do well. It's best to do this in your comfort zone, your self-hypnotic trance. Find a comfortable place, loosen your clothing, take a deep breath, exhale, and feel calm, relaxed, and positive. Use your anchors to help trigger a comfortable and relaxing self-hypnotic trance. When you have finished, bring yourself back to the level of your conscious mind, calm and relaxed.

Suggest to yourself that you can see the differences between the two models. Using your positive-strength model, determine if there is something different you can try in the negative model that would bring about better results. Did you find anything you might try? It might be something very small, but it is a beginning.

Consider the conversations that take place in your negative model, and look for better ways to communicate. How do others communicate with you? Ask yourself whether you created this negative model or whether others created it around you. Did you and someone else both contribute to the development of the negative model? Now that you are aware of the differences between the two models, how might you now try to create a model with positive changes?

ESSENTIALS

"Try pretending! This is another word for positive thinking. The subconscious mind sees pretending as a valid part of eventual accomplishment. When we pretend something will happen, it has a far better chance of happening than when we don't."
—Henry Leo Bolduc,
Your Creative Voice

How do you feel about making a change in your model? Is it possible for you to make this change? What are the positive aspects of the change? What are the negatives? Who will benefit from the change?

Other Self-Hypnosis Tools

If you have a difficult time receiving answers to your questions while in self-hypnosis, you may want to try a couple of other methods. The first is the pendulum technique addressed in Chapter 1. The second is automatic writing. Both methods allow you the opportunity to receive answers to your questions without prior knowledge of the response.

The Pendulum

A pendulum can help you get answers from the unconscious mind without using sensory recall. If you want to try this, draw a circle on a blank sheet of paper and divide it into four sections by adding two lines that cross in the center. Take a deep breath, exhale, feel calm and relaxed, hold your pendulum over the paper, and ask it to show you a *yes*. It will move either back and forth or from side to side. It will move the other way for *no*.

If you choose not to draw a circle, just ask the pendulum to show you *yes*, then ask it to show you *no*. If there is no answer to your question, ask it not to move at all. Now you are ready to ask questions.

Begin by asking yes-or-no questions about the model that you want to change. You might ask if the negative model began at a certain time. You can use this method to hone in on time sequences, emotions, and other facts regarding your negative model. Through the use of the pendulum you may receive self-hypnotic insights that you would not have gotten otherwise.

Automatic Writing

To try this method, all you need is a piece of paper and something to write with. You may seat yourself at a computer or typewriter instead, wherever you are most comfortable. Place the writing utensil in your hand at the top left-hand corner of the paper, or place your fingers on the keyboard. Take a deep breath, exhale, and let your positive anchors help guide you into a comfortable hypnotic trance that is calm and relaxing.

Suggest to yourself when you enter your trance to let your hand or fingers begin to write. Suggest that the information that comes from your unconscious mind be helpful to you in understanding the negative model you want to change. You may ask that this information give insights that can be used positively in the future.

Once you've reached a comfortable trance level, you can let your mind go where it likes. Your unconscious will work on its own, giving information to your fingers or hand. Be patient, as you may not get much of a response at first. Like other techniques in self-hypnosis, the more you practice, the easier it is to have positive results. After a comfortable amount of time, allow yourself to come back to the surface of your mind, calm and relaxed.

FACTS

It is possible for some people to enter a deep self-hypnotic trance with the suggestion that automatic writing take place. Music has been written this way, too. Mozart once received a whole symphony that took days to transcribe.

You can use your pendulum regularly for guidance. After determining *yes* and *no*, always ask permission to ask your questions. Automatic writing can be used to channel information from the universal mind. Perhaps you'll find a book waiting to come through if you use this method of writing.

Big Picture, Little Picture

Your sensory-image modalities come into play as you make comparisons between your thinking models. There are two ways to approach each model: one is the large, detached view, and the second is the up-close-and-personal view.

Using your strong sensory imagery, you will examine your two models, the negative and the positive. You may step back in your mind as if watching a video of yourself, and you may also step into the picture to experience the feelings.

First find a comfortable place, loosen your clothes, take a deep breath, and count yourself down from five to zero, to a calm and relaxing self-hypnotic trance. To help yourself go deeper, use one or more of the positive anchors you identified and learned to trigger in the last chapter. When you reach a comfortable trance level, suggest to yourself that you are now ready to examine the model that you want to change. Remember, anytime you feel the need to do so, you may always open your eyes, end your trance, take a deep breath, and feel calm and relaxed.

ALERT

It is always advisable to maintain a firm grip on reality. Your good imagination can have the potential to distort the truth. Remember that any action you take creates a reaction someplace else.

What is it that you want to change? Identify the big picture first. Take a step back in your mind and consider your question from a detached state, as if watching yourself in a video or on television. Using your five senses, study the whole picture. Can you see yourself doing what you want to change? If there are conversations with others or sounds taking place, can you hear them?

Which of your other senses do you experience in your study of the big picture? Are there smells, tastes, or feelings? If there are other people involved in this image, what are their effects on you? How clearly can you bring up these images without experiencing negative emotions? If you feel discomfort with these emotions, you may tone them down or shut them off.

Tale of Two Ministers

The following story demonstrates the advantage of being pushed out of the comfort zone every once in a while. In the story, both ministers are new to their profession—one is young and the other made a recent career change.

Sean, a young minister with a strong background in NLP imagery, wrote visual sermons for his Sunday morning parishioners. His kinesthetic sense was very strong, and no matter how hard he tried to focus on his sermon while he was speaking, something would always break his concentration. This interruption would make him uncomfortable, and he would lose his thought and say something out of context. His congregation would laugh and so would he. These little awkward moments actually brought the minister and his parishioners closer together.

Fred entered a career in the ministry after teaching in college. He was used to making scholarly presentations tailored to the high academic level of his students. Even though his first church was a very small rural congregation far from any university, he spent many hours preparing lofty sermons for his polite but unresponsive listeners. One day he forgot his written text, and he apologetically muddled through his topic. The congregation thought it was his best sermon ever.

QUESTIONS?

What is the ultimate question I should ask myself?
"What is best for the whole?" If you feel responsible for lugging the world around all by yourself, it will soon become too heavy. You can ask for help with your burden, however. It's all according to what you believe—is your thinking model positive or negative?

Sometimes people forget to be aware of what they are doing. They get so involved in the little picture that they cannot see the effects they have on others. The minister who keeps his eyes on his notes will never see how he affects his listeners. If you do not watch where you are going, you are likely to wind up in a collision.

Permission to Treat Yourself Positively

It is not unusual for a person to be much harder on himself or herself than on others. The exercises in this chapter are meant to give you the opportunity to understand your strengths and weaknesses. Your weaknesses are often directly related to your strengths. Your strongest sense is often too finely tuned; it takes in more than is needed and the waters of your conscious mind get all roiled up.

When this happens, you now have the opportunity to use self-hypnotic trance and take a step back, letting the waters settle. In a calm, relaxing trance state, you can develop, examine, and compare your mind models.

CHAPTER 6

Changing a Bad Habit

This chapter will cover what habits are, how you develop them, and how your unconscious mind relies on the habit's benefit to you. You will experience a technique of self-hypnosis that involves a picture within a picture, and you will use this to push through, creating a clear image of your new habit.

What Is a Habit?

We are all creatures of habit, most of them good and some bad—but is your life consumed by your habits? People often use certain speech patterns without realizing it. "Ah" is a good example. Many people say "ah" as a way to reorganize their thought patterns and make time to choose their next words. This can be such a habitual part of their speech that, until they hear a recording of themselves or are reminded by others, they are oblivious to their "ahs."

QUESTIONS?

What is it like to see a video or hear a recording of yourself?
If you are not accustomed to hearing or seeing yourself, your first reaction may be embarrassment. What you actually said or did may turn out to be completely different from what you thought you were saying or doing.

Physical movements are part of your mannerisms. You may move your hands when you speak, or you may feel the need to clasp them together. You may play with your hair or rock back and forth when you are seated. You may grit your teeth or bite your nails. It's only when you are reminded of what you're doing that the habit comes into consciousness.

But what, exactly, is a habit? It is an action, either mental or physical, that you consciously repeated at first, until it was absorbed by your unconscious mind. But now you continue to repeat it, with little or no conscious awareness.

How a Habit Can Affect Others

Do you know someone who has an annoying habit? Sometimes it is so bad that you try to avoid that person as often as you can. Some people have a habit of using profanities, which may be appropriate in certain situations and totally inappropriate in others, but the words always seem to pop out of their mouths at the wrong time. It makes you want to disappear, to claim you do not know these offending people.

Do you know people who laugh loudly, or those who stammer or stutter? Do you know people who go around humming all the time? They usually think these sounds are only in their heads, where no one else can hear them. Then there are people who find the wrong time to belch.

"Have a good day." How many times have store clerks said that to you as you pay your bill? If they meant it, it would be one thing, but most of the time they don't even look up to see whom they are talking to. They may not even be aware of what they are saying. The words just automatically come out at the end of the sale.

You may know someone who has good habits. She is always polite, finds the right words to say, is always calm, and genuinely cares about others. She may always send you a card or give you a call at a specific time. Her home and garden are immaculate. Sometimes a person can develop habits that are too perfect, which makes everyone else feel uncomfortable.

Identifying Your Habits

You have habits that you don't even know about. Your habit patterns began to take shape at a very early age. They could have started when your mother or another family member reminded you over and over again to do something: "Brush your teeth," "Clean your plate," and "Close the door." You eventually did these things without being reminded.

ESSENTIALS
For a habit to become established in your unconscious mind, you must consciously practice it for a period of time. This time period is between three and six weeks, depending on your effort.

As you grew older, you may have learned to ride a bike, skip rope, or play a sport. Each one of these activities takes time to learn. Eventually, many of these skills became automatic, and you didn't have to think about them consciously.

If you were to teach someone to drive a car, you would find that there are a lot of steps involved that you don't think about anymore; you just do them. These may include opening the door, putting the key in the ignition, or checking the mirrors before you drive off. When your student takes the wheel, you may find your directions are lacking some steps.

Many of your habits continue day after day, without your being aware of their existence. It is only when you discover a habit, or when someone reminds you of it, that it comes back to your level of awareness. Once you are aware of a habit, you have the choice of letting it continue the way it is or changing it.

Your Habits Are Old Friends

Many of your habits are content right where they are; they have become part of your life. It's sometimes difficult to perform normal, daily functions without being accompanied by your habit. Your habits may be providing you with many benefits other than their primary or original functions.

Problems arise when a habit outgrows its usefulness. While part of you doesn't want it around anymore, another part may not be ready for it to go. Your conscious mind is saying, "Go." Your unconscious mind is saying, "I need you."

A conflict between your two minds erupts, and you are caught in the middle. You want to get rid of that habit, but something sabotages your good intentions again and again. The battle between your conscious and unconscious minds can keep you totally off balance.

Many habits are very enjoyable, and yet you know they are bad for you. Some, if continued, could drastically impair your well-being. You want to stop, but something keeps pulling you back. When you're experiencing your habit, you are in a trance state. Your conscious mind is unaware of what is happening to you. At the same time, your unconscious mind believes it is doing something positive for you.

Identifying the Benefits of a Habit

Unless an understanding can be negotiated between your two minds, you haven't got much chance of changing the unwanted habit on a permanent basis. You may succeed for a while, but the need is still there, and the old friend, the habit, waits until it's time to return, often when you're under stress. The habit wears down your resistance and you give in, only to be back where you were before, off balance again.

The first step in bringing about permanent change is to examine what the habit is doing for you, which is often something you are not even aware of. Think of a habit you want to change, and put your self-hypnosis to work.

Find a comfortable place, loosen your clothes, take a deep breath, exhale, and count yourself into a trance. Suggest to yourself that you will go back in your memory and use sensory imagery to examine the habit you want to change.

ESSENTIALS

Notice and experience whatever you find that is positive about your habit. You may ask yourself some of the questions on this page, and when you are finished, count yourself back to the surface of your mind, feeling calm and relaxed.

When did I first start the habit, where was I at the time, and who was with me? What did I look like when I first started, and how did I feel? Where and when do I use my habit now? How often do I use it? What do I like about the habit?

Reasons to Change a Habit

There are many reasons for changing a habit. You may want the change for your health, for work, to eliminate stress, for your self-esteem, for financial purposes, or to benefit someone else. Once you have determined that you need to change a habit, begin by examining it, in order to understand it. When both the benefits and the negatives are determined, a new habit goal can be established.

Study Your Habit

After you have identified what you like about your habit, perform a self-hypnotic exercise to determine what you do not like about it. Use the exercise you learned in the last chapter to compare what does work and what doesn't work. It contains, as you have experienced, positive and negative model building.

The pressure to change a habit can come from within you, or someone or something else can motivate you to change. Your habit may be something you do that you don't want to do anymore. If that is the case, think of something you want to start doing in place of the habit. What you want to do instead is called your new habit goal.

When you compare positive and negative models of your habit, it can help you determine your purpose for the change. The more clearly your five senses can image the positives and the negatives, the stronger your comparisons can be. Here is a questionnaire to help you make comparisons:

- What do I like best and least about my habit?
- When I experience my habit, what are my best and worst feelings about it?
- How did I feel about my habit when it started, compared with how I feel today?
- How has my habit changed over time?
- What part of me wants to keep my habit, and what part of me doesn't want it anymore?

Benefits of a Change

How will changing your habit benefit you? It is important to identify how your life will improve when you change your habit. You might see a benefit to your health or self-esteem, or a financial gain. The change may help open the door to a career change or an advance in your present career. Build the clearest image you can by experiencing it through your sense modalities.

After you have determined what good the habit change will do for you, ask yourself what good your change will do for others. Most people put others first and themselves last. Imagine, for a moment, someone else who wanted to change a habit similar to yours. If he asked you for advice, what will you tell him? Wouldn't you encourage him to treat himself positively and patiently as he works to change the habit?

When you communicate with yourself, do you use the same manner you use with others? Or are you are harder on yourself than on others? Wouldn't it be better if you treated yourself the same way as you do others? If you have patience and take it one step at a time when you change your habit, will this benefit others?

If you change, will this have a favorable impact on the lives of other people? Even if you do not want to change this habit, would doing so be good for someone you care about? Deciding to change a habit for someone else can be a stronger incentive than just doing it for yourself. You can give yourself permission to change, knowing that a lot of good can come out of it, especially for others.

ALERT

Some habits can be very destructive in nature. When you attempt to change these habits without proper counseling, the results can be as negative as the habit, or more so. Seek professional, qualified help when you want to change a serious and potentially destructive habit.

Imagine Yourself without the Habit

Now that you have developed models of what you don't like about your habit and what you do like, it's time to construct another model. This is a future image of what it will be like when you change your habit. Your negative and positive models help provide part of the information needed for the change. You may turn to your self-hypnotic techniques to help you develop your change model, experiencing it through all five of your senses.

Picture how you will look, imagine how you will feel, and think of how others will feel about you after you have changed. Hear what others will say about your change. Experience your change using the most powerful image you can develop.

As you build your model, consider how strongly you believe in the change. If others are a factor, feel positive about what you're doing, even if you don't really want to do it. Relate the integrity of this change to something you do feel very strongly about. Ask yourself whether you would treat something or someone you care about the same way as you have been treating yourself. Ask yourself if you are living by a double standard, working to build something special and at the time trying to destroy it.

Run this new image model of your change through your entire day and evening. Check to see if there are places where you experience resistance to your change. The resistance might come from you, or it might come from someone else. Look at options that might help you overcome resistance.

Examine the Resistance

Here is a self-hypnotic technique that can help you resolve resistance inside yourself as you construct your habit change; it is sometimes called *parts therapy*. In a hypnotic trance, suggest to yourself that you will communicate with your mind and with different parts of your body to see how they feel about your habit change.

The part of you that likes something that is bad for you must be willing to compromise before an acceptable image for change can be installed through self-hypnosis. One dissonant part can sabotage the whole habit change. The more clearly you understand any resistance to your change, the better chance you'll have for a successful change.

FACTS

Sometimes it may take more than one try to determine all the parts that are resistant to your habit change. When something sabotages you, examine what happened, and then develop and install changes for next time. Your desire and patience will help you work toward and be successful in your habit change.

The key to parts therapy is to come up with a compromise, so that each part feels it has something to gain from the change.

If you bring about the change by sheer willpower, you'll always have a tendency to slip back into the old habit when your conscious mind is not paying attention. If you, and all of your parts, feel that installing a new habit is desirable, the change will be much easier and more lasting.

Mental Holograms

Mental holograms can help strengthen your imagery; they work well for implanting subliminal suggestions in your unconscious mind. A hologram occurs when there are two different images in one picture. When you hold a hologram at a certain angle, you see one picture, and when you change the angle you see another picture; when you move the picture back and forth you alternate between the two images. In hypnosis, a hologram happens when you go back and forth between two or more mental images.

You can create mental holograms while you are experiencing self-hypnosis. Suggest to yourself that you will move back and forth between your negative and positive images and the image you have developed for your habit change. The more vividly you can compare models, the clearer the image you produce for the habit change will be.

ESSENTIALS

Holograms can be experienced in all five senses. If you feel a certain way about something that is positive, you can compare that feeling with something you thought was positive but then found out was negative. The goal is to flip the view, to see the same image from a different angle.

A hologram is similar to a mirror: it is a way of reminding yourself of something you are doing that you don't notice until you see it. When you see the image in a different way, it can help your conscious mind become aware of the habit. Once you are aware, you can continue doing it, or you can make a change.

The Ecology Check

All the information has now been gathered, and there is only one more step before the reframe is ready. It is called the ecology check. Now is the time to ask yourself, "What kind of an effect will this change have on me? What will I be like after I have changed?"

FACTS

A reframe is the installation of a new habit into the unconscious mind. The unconscious is like a computer: it runs the programs that have been installed on it. To change, a new program must be installed on the computer of your unconscious.

How Will the New Change Affect Others?

Your change may have a big impact on someone else. This person may not think the change is positive to your relationship with him. Your change may be very threatening to your partner, and it is possible he may try to sabotage your habit change.

Imagine how your partner or relative might be convinced that he is helping you change, even though that may not be the case. It's sort of like saying, "Thanks for staying out of my way." You can provide updates and make an effort to help your partner feel good about what you're doing for yourself. However, it is possible that certain people contributed to your old habit and may not be compatible with your new one.

Installing the Change

A self-hypnotic trance presents the imagery of the new habit to the unconscious mind, which will accept this change as a new reality. Then, when the mind sees that you need something that was provided by the old habit, it will turn instead to the new habit you installed in your self-hypnotic trance.

The first step, as usual, is to find a comfortable position, loosen your clothes, take a deep breath, exhale, and count yourself back into a hypnotic trance, feeling calm and relaxed. When you reach a comfortable trance level, suggest to yourself that you will get as clear a picture of the old habit as you can, and experience it through all five senses. Once you have completed this, do the same with your new habit change model. Experience the change with all five senses.

Now go back to your old habit, and imagine it as big, dark, and negative. Next, insert a small image of your new habit into part of the negative image. Let the new image be much brighter and more vibrant than the negative one. Push the new image right through the old, dark one. Feel the energy of the change as you push it through.

Let your screen go blank, and bring back the old image again. Let it be darker and dimmer. Put the small positive change image back into the big negative image. Make it even brighter and more vibrant than before. Push it through again, even more strongly this time.

Keep doing this. Each time, let the old, negative image become darker and dimmer. Each time you push the positive change through, let it be brighter and more vibrant. Keep doing this exercise until the old image is completely gone, and you can't bring it back anymore. All you can see is the new habit image, bright, clear, and vibrant.

Reinforcing the Change

The pushing-through technique can be very powerful. Once you have completed the reframe, however, plan to repeat this exercise as part of your daily self-hypnosis routine. Each time, feel the strength of the new habit grow stronger and stronger, and let any recall of the old, negative habit become weaker and weaker. It is very important to reinforce habit change through self-hypnosis.

Don't forget that you can also develop feeling or verbal anchors that strengthen your positive response to the habit change. You can trigger these anchors whenever you need to give yourself a boost. The more you use positive anchors, the more firmly your new habit will be installed in your unconscious mind. It sometimes takes a few weeks to install the new habit completely. Remember to encourage yourself, just as you would another person.

If you are visual, create a mental image of the change in your mind. If you relate to the sense of hearing, repeat words of encouragement, or hear them in your head. If you rely on your feeling sense, feel the positive energy of your progress. If you respond to the sense of smell, enjoy scents that represent a positive attitude and success. If you work best with your sense of taste, taste healthy, positive tastes.

A Case Study: Changing a Habit

Karen was a high school senior who looked forward to going on to college. As a little girl, she loved to sit in her mother's lap, twisting her own hair with her fingers. It became her version of a security blanket. She loved her hair's silky, smooth feeling.

By the time she went to elementary school, she was too big to sit in her mother's lap. She was, however, still shy, and unconsciously she continued to twist and twirl her hair with her fingers. It became a habit that she carried with her into high school. The more stress she felt at school, the more she pulled and twisted her hair. She even began pulling some of it out of her head.

Karen and her family were anxious that she overcome this habit before she went to college, but she had tried before with little success. They decided to try hypnosis, so they found a hypnotherapist in their area who specialized in habit change.

Getting the Information

First the hypnotherapist asked a series of questions to help understand Karen's mental makeup. Together, they developed a model of what she did well. She was not very visual, but she had a strong sense of touch. Feeling was important to her, especially the feeling of comfort: she loved the feeling of something soft and fuzzy.

To build a model of what she didn't like, the hypnotherapist asked what foods she didn't care for, and he watched her mouth pucker up as she told him. He asked what she hated to touch and feel in her hand. She hated the feel of anything slimy, from wet noodles to live fish.

Model for Change

Now, for the first time, the hypnotherapist addressed Karen's habit. He had her go back to when she first started her habit as a small child and experience how it felt. Then he had her experience the negative ways her habit currently embarrassed her. Finally he took her forward in time to experience both how it would feel if she changed her habit, and how it would feel if she didn't.

Then he told Karen to ask her mind and her hands what would be acceptable if she didn't twist and pull her hair anymore. She felt her hands needed to have something reminiscent of her hair to play with. She thought of warm and fuzzy, and she remembered that she had a very small cloth doll. She had always liked the way it felt when she played with it, so she thought she could carry it with her.

The hypnotherapist asked Karen to ask if this would be acceptable to her whole self, and the feeling was yes. He then asked if she would be willing to imagine how her hair would feel if it were all oily and slimy. Karen cringed at the thought. Her hair was a little oily, so she focused on that feeling and she didn't like it.

Her last step before hypnosis was to run the program of her habit change to see where there might be resistance. She still felt a little insecure when she was under a lot of pressure to produce. She decided she might do some deep breathing to help her feel calm and relaxed when she felt pressure. She ran the program again, and this time she felt more positive about its potential for success.

Using Anchors for Change

Now the hypnotherapist put Karen into a deep trance. She experienced what it would be like to feel her cloth doll and be calm and relaxed. She experienced what it would be like if she continued to play with her oily, slimy hair. It was very unpleasant. She experienced this image as dark and unpleasant.

Next she felt the image of a calm and relaxing feeling as her fingers played with her little cloth doll. She was asked to place this image into her negative image. She was asked to push her new feeling through the old, clear her mind, and do the process over again several times, until the old hair-playing image was gone from her mind.

She practiced this imagery each day, and her new habit grew stronger and stronger. She also used her anchor to trigger calm and relaxed feelings. She taught herself to say the word *fuzzy* to feel relaxed and calm without needing her doll. Karen graduated from high school and used her new confidence to be successful at college.

CHAPTER 7

Hypnosis and Stress

I n this chapter you will learn about stress and its immediate and long-term side effects. You will examine internal and external stresses and learn to identify their sources. You will learn self-hypnosis techniques to deal with stress, and you will see how stress affects the connection between your body, mind, and soul.

What Is Stress?

Stress is an evolutionary function that originated because early humans had to be aware of danger and be prepared to enter the fight-or-flight mode. In this mode, the heartbeat quickens, the muscles tense up, the senses become hyper-alert, and the body is prepared to engage in combat or retreat.

Today, your ancient fight-or-flight warning system is still on guard. Whenever you feel emotions such as fear, anger, anxiety, or frustration, you trigger this warning system.

The business of dealing with stress impacts almost every product on the market today. Items are marketed as being stress-free, relieving stress, or providing escape from stress. There are many over-the-counter and prescription stress medications and therapies to help you deal with stress: there are sound, color, aroma, and smell therapies, and relaxation techniques.

The Effects of Stress

How much stress do you have in your life? How long have you been under stress? Do you experience angry or anxious emotions daily, emotions that linger within you and never seem to be resolved? Do you catch a lot of colds, experience lingering tiredness, or find it hard to set and accomplish goals? If you often feel the effects of stress, self-hypnosis can help you resolve it.

Short-Term Effects

When you begin to feel stress, your blood pressure starts to rise, your heart starts beating faster, you tense up, your stomach may feel like it has a rock in it, and you may even start to sweat. These physical reactions to stress can be triggered by a memory, by something taking place in the moment, or by anticipating a future action. The hypothalamus gland can trigger as many as nine different hormones, which all put your body into the readiness mode.

If your body is not in good condition, this sudden surge can put a tremendous strain on the heart, as the increased force of blood surges through your veins. This pressure can also affect the brain and lungs. The less prepared you are for the stress, the more you are threatened with serious consequences. If your arteries are already partly clogged, for example, something has to give when the pressure builds too high.

QUESTIONS?

What does the hypothalamus do?
The hypothalamus gland, the size of a grape and centered in your brain, produces hormones that signal most of the other glands in the body to go on high alert or to calm down.

The sudden need to release internal stress may also result in sudden external outbursts. You might find yourself saying things you had not planned to say, or you might do things that lead to confrontation. You may smash something, throw something, break down in tears, or take some other action that could be very hard to undo. Many people deal with stress by using destructive habits. Smoking, drinking, overeating, or drug abuse may all be used incorrectly as stress relievers.

The Holmes-Rahe Stress Scale

It would be ideal to live a stress-free life. Unfortunately that is not possible for most of us. Once you acknowledge that stress is a part of your daily life, you can take positive steps to help resolve it. Left unresolved, short-term stress turns into long-term stress. The Holmes-Rahe Social Readjustment Scale shows the potential effects of long-term stress. (For more information, visit ✍ *http://my.webmd.com/encyclopedia/article/1674.52493*)

The Holmes-Rahe stress scale measures life change units. It was devised by Dr. T. H. Holmes and Dr. R. H. Rahe as a scoring system for stressful events that might occur during one year of a person's life. If the stress score adds up to 300 or more, the individual may be under significant threat of illness.

The top seven stresses in the scale include:

1. Death of a spouse   100
2. Divorce   73
3. Marital separation   65
4. Imprisonment   63
5. Death of a close family member   63
6. Personal injury or illness   53
7. Marriage   50

Long-Term Stress

The psychological effects of long-term stress include nervousness, anxiety, moodiness, depression, frustration, and sadness. If you are under long-term stress, you might have trouble thinking clearly, making decisions, focusing, learning, or remembering. You might find it hard to sleep or become prone to accidents or be consumed with negative thoughts. You may take up negative habits or develop nervous tics.

Physical effects of long-term stress can include headaches, muscle pain, back pain, chest pain, upset stomach and diarrhea, constipation, and shaky, sweaty, or cold hands. Stress can lead to hives, skin rashes, tooth grinding, ringing in the ears, or lingering colds. College students or schoolteachers may focus so hard on their work that they don't take time to rest and relax. Then at semester break or vacation, the first thing they do is let their guard down and get sick.

ALERT

The longer that stress goes unresolved, the greater the chance that you will develop a serious illness. If you are experiencing any of the psychological or physical symptoms of stress, the sooner you seek professional guidance, the better the chance that you will find relief.

If you have the opportunity, position yourself where you can watch people entering and leaving a store, a post office, a workplace, or a public transportation depot. Watch people's physiology: the way they carry themselves and their facial expressions. Watch how they wear their stress, and think about how you wear yours.

The effects of long-term stress are usually easy to observe. A person may have a painful walk; she may be bent over or have a slow, confused, awkward gait. She may look as if she has no self-confidence and would have trouble making a decision. Her face may show signs of stress, and she may look older than her age. She may be overweight, have high blood pressure, or explode in anger at a moment's notice.

Internal and External Stress

There is stress everywhere. We constantly create it within ourselves, and we are bombarded by it from other sources. It is quite possible to experience stress and not be sure where it came from. Identifying the roots of stress is a step toward resolving it.

Internal Stress

Internal stress is generated by your mind, both unconscious and conscious; it may be triggered by past experiences, present conditions, and expectations of future situations. Memories of unresolved stressful situations from the past consume the lives of many people. A negative memory image is played and replayed in your mind, and you continue to relive a negative experience or series of experiences again and again. It is like being caught in a time warp that never ends.

These images come out of your unconscious mind and are remembered in one or more of your five sense modalities. A visual image gives you the opportunity to see the situation over and over. If your hearing sense is strong, you may rehear old conversations. The emotional sense is linked to your other four senses, so when you experience past stresses, you will relive their emotional content again and again. Taste and smell can also trigger stressful memories.

Emotional stress can come from powerful feelings that may not immediately have an identifiable source. It can paralyze you, create depression, and even require therapy. It can relate to specific times of the year such as holidays, or it can be tied to the length or shortness of daylight. The change of seasons can also trigger internal stress for no apparent reason.

External Stress

A lot of stress is created by external situations. It can be related to work, school, or relationships. External stress can manifest in a split second—highway rage is a good example. You can be driving down the highway minding your own business, when another driver suddenly swerves into your lane, causing you to maneuver quickly to avoid an accident and creating an angry response in you that could lead to confrontation.

Situations like this often do not end peacefully. If you are not prepared to step away from a stressful situation, the consequences can be disastrous. External stress happens all the time. You may see something that upsets you, or it could be something said to you or overheard.

Loud noise or music can cause external stress. Your ability to feel another person's emotions can overwhelm you with painful feelings. External stress may be caused by a bad smell or an unpleasant taste. Even a pleasant situation can suddenly trigger an unpleasant memory.

Identifying Stress

Much of the stress you encounter is easy to identify. You can relate it to something that just happened, something that is happening now, or something you expect to happen in the future. But is your identification correct? Is the situation really the root of your stress? Or is your stress part of a recurring pattern?

Lingering feelings of extreme anxiety and stress may be a sign of chronic depression. If you experience these types of symptoms, it is advisable to seek professional counseling as soon as possible.

To help yourself identify a recurring pattern of stress, you may try a self-hypnosis technique known as the calendar method. Find a comfortable position, loosen your clothes, take a deep breath, exhale, and count yourself down into a calm and relaxing trance. You may trigger your anchors to help you go deeper into trance.

Suggest to yourself that you only need to experience a small amount of a stressful feeling to help you get a clear image of where it came from. You may always open your eyes and end the trance anytime you want.

When you have reached your comfortable trance level, focus on a current stressful feeling. Once you have identified and experienced a small amount of the stress emotion, go back to an earlier, similar stress emotion. Keep going back until you find your earliest image of this stress. Once you have done this, ask yourself if there are any other images in your unconscious mind that relate to your present stress emotion.

Stress Transference

It is possible that you may transfer one stress emotion to another without consciously realizing what you are doing. If you overreact to something, it can be an indication of this. You might suddenly be consumed with an emotion for no apparent reason, but it was triggered by something that brought the stress image out of your unconscious mind. That emotion might take over, and then you are just along for the ride.

FACTS

Transference occurs when a person has an emotional feeling about something and refocuses the feeling onto something or someone else. Psychoanalysts use observations of transference to help arrive at the emotional roots of a patient's problem.

Affect-Bridge Regression Technique

The affect-bridge regression is a technique you can use to look for the root of a stressful emotion. It goes backward in time like the calendar technique, except that it uses the kinesthetic sense of emotions. To try this technique, find a comfortable place, loosen your clothes, take a deep breath, exhale, and count yourself down into a calm and relaxing self-hypnotic trance. Remember, you can always open your eyes anytime you want, and come back relaxed and calm. You may trigger your anchors to help you go deeper.

Suggest to yourself that you will feel just enough of your stressful emotion to help you go back to times in your memory when you experienced the same feeling. As you go backward, examine the pattern of your stress. Once you are at the root of the emotion, ask yourself what other early experiences or emotions may be related to this emotion.

Continue backward into your unconscious mind as far as you can go, examining your memories. Collect as much information as possible, without questioning what comes to you. After the session is over, you can examine the information you have collected and compare it to your current stress situation. You may gain some new insights into your past through this process.

ESSENTIALS

Whenever you are collecting memory images through self-hypnosis, try to keep your conscious mind from analyzing the information until after the trance. The lighter the trance, the easier it is for the conscious mind to intrude. Once you have finished your trance, you will have time to digest what you have experienced.

Unknown Sources of Stress

It is possible that you may experience stress in your life that cannot be readily linked to any specific source. Your earliest memories may contain feelings of stress or distress, as if you were born with it. That is possible: you may have absorbed someone else's stress at a very young age, or it may have come from a past life (see Chapter 17).

Resolving Stress

It would be nice to say that you can live totally free of stress. However, the truth is that there is stress around you, no matter where you live, work, or play. The key to healthy living is the ability to resolve stress each time you encounter it. One of the first steps is to take care of yourself: your mind, your body, and your soul.

Take Care of Your Body

Taking care of your physical self is very important. You have learned the effect that stress can have on your body. A body that is out of condition is at risk, even under normal stress. If your doctors approve it, a daily routine of exercise, such as walking, swimming, jogging, or working out at a gym, can have positive benefits in resolving stress. The activity helps disperse any nervous energy that has built up inside you.

Proper eating habits are a plus for the body. Too much of any one thing can be bad for you. Moderation is the key to balance. Excessive amounts of salt, fat, sugar, or alcohol can throw your system off balance. Combining proper foods and exercise can make you feel much more in tune with your body.

Another key ingredient for the body is to get enough sleep. When you're tired, stress can build into frustration. It is also good for the body to play a sport or experience a creative activity. Painting, playing a musical instrument, singing, acting, or some other hobby can keep you occupied and active. A healthy body is a great asset in resolving stress.

Take Care of Your Mind

Self-hypnosis can be a great help in resolving stress to the mind. When you use the dissociation techniques that you have learned in previous chapters, you can step away from stress for brief, refreshing moments. These methods include the relaxation induction, instant hypnosis with triggered anchors, and the flooding technique.

Here is a variation of an image induction that may help you escape to a safe place in the clouds. Find a comfortable spot, loosen your clothes, take a deep breath, exhale, and count yourself backward from five to zero. Suggest to yourself that when you reach your calm and relaxed trance state, you will be surrounded by a beautiful white cloud. This cloud will feel calm, relaxing, and safe. It will be as if you have drifted far, far away from all the things that made you feel stressed.

This beautiful white cloud is a safe place where you can look down on your stress and examine it without negative feelings. From here you can get a clear view that will help you make positive decisions for resolving your stress. When you come back to the surface of your mind, you will be calm and relaxed, and you'll have new insights from the visit to your beautiful white cloud. You may count yourself back from zero to five when you are ready, knowing you can always go back to this beautiful white cloud.

You can take yourself any place you want to go: it could be a vacation spot, the ocean, or the mountains. The object is for you to mentally get away from your stress for a few minutes or a few seconds. When you come back, you may have a new perspective to understand and resolve your stress.

Take Care of Your Soul

The universal mind is an important part of your soul. It is the place where you enlist the unknown to give you strength and produce miracles. Your belief system can be a source for spawning new ideas and hope. The universal mind helps you continue when you feel you are at a dead end.

If you believe in something positive, whether it is explained by a religious tradition or is your own individual belief, you may ask it for help. You can look for guidance on your life's direction. You can even ask that the right words come out of your mouth in times of stressful communication—just a brief moment of turning to your belief could help you respond in a positive, nonconfrontational manner. The power of prayer is very strong.

Self-hypnosis is a good way to contact the universal mind. Count yourself down into a trance state, and suggest to yourself that you will communicate with your belief system. Ask that the right answers come to you or that you will take a positive action, especially relating to stress. You may ask for strength to move beyond a certain mood or to make the best decision for all concerned. If your stress is about others, you may ask for help for them.

If your soul has past life memories that cause stress, self-hypnosis can help with their resolution. It is always good to remember that because you are on earth at this time and place, this is where your current assignment is. If you believe there is such a thing as a life map, ask that you may be open to the direction, free from the stress of worry.

Unresolved Past Stress

If you have unresolved past stress, which you are continually reliving in your memory, you are actually putting yourself in a negative trance. The suggestion of past stress is planted in your unconscious, and it never leaves. Until the stress is resolved, you will constantly be under its influence. Understanding it will help you develop a positive model to resolve it. The situation that caused the stress has already happened, and as soon as you resolve it, you'll get on a positive track for the future.

To examine a past unresolved stress, find a comfortable place, loosen your clothes, take a deep breath, exhale, and count yourself down from five to zero, to a calm and relaxing trance. You can observe the past from a positive place in your mind, stepping into the image to feel just enough emotion that will help you understand the stress situation. You may open your eyes anytime you want, and come back to the surface of your mind calm and relaxed.

ESSENTIALS

You might consider asking your belief system to send love to the other person, regardless of the conditions that started the stress. The more positive energy you send out, the less old, negative energy you will hold in. In the current moment, you can begin to make changes that will enable you to believe in the best for the whole universe in the future.

When you are ready, suggest to yourself that your unconscious mind will provide the correct information in clear images from your memory. Ask yourself: Did I create the stress situation, or did someone else create it? What dialogue took place, if there was any? What could I have said or done differently? What, if anything, could I do now that will improve the situation?

Once you have gathered as many insights from the past as possible, develop a positive stress resolution model. If the situation involved someone else, imagine what you might do or say to give that person the opportunity to find resolution.

Current Stress

Current stress can be caused by an internal image from the past. The push method is a good way to deal with internal negative images. After you have examined your negative model, you'll develop a positive model to run over the negative. In your relaxed trance state, create a small positive image inside of the bigger negative one. Fill the positive image full of universal love, positive color, inspiring sound, and whatever you experience as good, and push that image right through the darker, negative one.

Feel the love, and believe in the possibility that things will work out for the best for everyone. Believe that your universal mind, your religion, your angels, or whatever gives you strength is working with you. Ask that resolution take place in the best way possible. Keep pushing the new image through the old image until the old image will not come back. When you have completed this exercise, watch for miracles.

You may create instant anchors that continually run this positive mind model. The more you practice, the more these positive feelings will become an automatic part of your life. This technique can be used for any stress that suddenly pops up.

Instant self-hypnosis can help you step away in your mind from a stressful situation. When you do this, you have an opportunity to resolve stress before it gets out of hand. Instant self-hypnosis can help you step aside and let the negatives roll on by. At this moment, you can also interrupt another person's thought pattern. You do this by saying or doing something different than the other person expected. It is a way of showing the person his negative actions without pointing them out directly.

Future Stress

Not knowing can be stressful. If you are not sure how a situation will work out, this can cause a lot of anxiety. When you expect something to go perfectly, it seldom does. You may worry about many things related to the future: health, work, the weather, unpaid bills, or relationships. You can be so focused on the future that you are not aware of the present moment.

FACTS

You may use your self-hypnotic trance to ask your belief system for guidance and that the future will work out in the best possible way. You may continually ask for protection and strength. You can push positive feelings through negative ones. You can ask your angels for help. You can trigger your instant self-hypnotic anchors whenever you need to communicate with the universal mind.

It is not unusual for people to imagine the future without considering the options. You may be able to see only the one way you want things to go. If something interrupts your image, you may not know how to create another one; you did not consider the possibility of unforeseen circumstances. But if you were taking a trip, you would prepare the best you could for whatever you might encounter.

When you have planned as much as possible for the journey of life, it's time to have faith that you have done the best you can. That doesn't mean that you could not do better the next time. Fear of failure can hold you captive. When you give yourself permission to do the best you can, it may open the door to success. The more you use self-hypnotic suggestion to do your best, the more you will relax, free from the stress of the fear of failure.

Keeping Stress Under Control

To help you keep stress under control, you may want to try the flooding technique while exercising. It is good for the mind, body, and the soul. You can work on resolving past stress, current stress, and future stress all at the same time. While you are exercising, you may use headphones and play sounds, music, or a self-help message.

Suggest to yourself that you may find answers or hope for resolving any stress you may have now or will encounter in the future. Let your mind go where it will. Enjoy your exercise while your conscious, unconscious, and universal minds communicate with one another. When you finish, feel calm, relaxed, and open to the answers that may come up to the surface of your mind.

The more you practice self-hypnotic techniques for stress resolution, the more your positive suggestions will automatically become part of your unconscious mind. Once you have established a routine of self-hypnosis, it will soon become a new, positive habit in your life. Don't be surprised if friends and family begin to notice a difference in you, commenting that you seem less stressed and more positive and focused.

CHAPTER 8

Stop Smoking with Hypnosis

In this chapter you will examine the history, effects, addictiveness, benefits, and problems of smoking cigarettes. You will develop a negative model of your habit and a positive one for change. Finally, you will learn how your new, non-smoking habit will allow you to get in tune with your mind, body, and soul.

The History of Tobacco

The nicotiana plant has been a part of the Native American culture for as long as 2,000 years. Native Americans smoked dried tobacco leaves in a stone pipe called a *tabaca*. They used tobacco for medical purposes, for religious ceremonies and offerings to the spirits, and as incense. Europeans incorporated the tobacco plant into their lifestyle after Christopher Columbus brought it to Europe.

By the 1600s, tobacco was in widespread use throughout Europe and was thought to cure many illnesses. In the American colonies the tobacco industry grew rapidly, soon establishing itself in both the northern and the southern states. (It is now a multibillion-dollar industry.) Over time, people found various uses for tobacco, making snuff, pulverized tobacco, and chewing tobacco, and smoking it in pipes and cigars. In the early 1900s, cigarettes became the most popular form of tobacco; the height of their popularity was during World War II, when they were included as part of the soldiers' daily rations.

In the 1930s the concept that tobacco had medicinal benefits began to change, but it took decades for the general public to take notice. An article in *Reader's Digest* from the 1950s, entitled "Cancer by the Carton," is credited by the publication *The History and Impact of the Tobacco Plant* as having had the first major impact in publicizing the hazards of tobacco use. Over the last fifty years, the battle between tobacco companies and health advocates has been waged in every kind of public forum and in the courts. Despite high prices, evidence of tobacco's deadliness, and a multitude of new products to help you quit, people still continue to smoke.

Addiction

Is smoking an addiction? It is said that Mark Twain once quipped, "Quitting smoking is easy. I've done it a thousand times." The drug nicotine is highly addictive. To stop smoking, you must deal with both the physical and the psychological needs it develops. Until you do, you will ride the same roller coaster as Mark Twain did.

Once nicotine has been inhaled into your lungs, it is absorbed by your bloodstream and reaches the heart, brain, liver, and all the rest of your body. Nicotine is considered to be as addictive as heroin and cocaine. Even though over two-thirds of all smokers want to stop, only an estimated 6 percent are able to quit. With all the negative information regarding the effects of smoking, you may wonder why someone would start in the first place.

FACTS

Nicotine can be either a stimulant or a sedative. The first smoke of the day often provides a rush of energy for the user. Over the course of the day, as the level of nicotine in the system rises, the nerve cells become desensitized and the sedative effect kicks in. By the next morning the body is ready for another jolt.

The Word *Quit*

The word *quit* by itself is very negative; it implies that you are going to have to give up something that you enjoy. It is even worse when someone else tells you that you have to quit. When you hear those words, it's only natural that you respond, "Oh yeah? You can't tell me what to do. I will do what I want."

Smokers seem to have embraced this philosophy: it is their right to smoke. As long as they have the desire to smoke, they will continue to do it, regardless of the consequences to themselves or others. Hypnosis is powerless to stop a determined smoker. The rebel in him will win every time.

Rather than thinking about having to quit, having to give up smoking, or giving up on yourself, imagine that you give yourself permission to be smoke-free. This takes a lot of courage. *Courage* is one of those words that implies a lot of self-strength and willpower. The strength and resolve can be there, but it doesn't have to be a struggle. It can be a natural transition, especially when you use the powerful imagery of self-hypnosis.

The Benefits of a Smoking Lifestyle

You might not think there are any benefits in smoking, but all smokers are getting some sort of benefit or they wouldn't keep doing it. For some it provides a safe place, for others a way of escaping, and for others a way to organize the day. Cigarettes may be the only friends a person has. It may be hard to imagine a life without smoking.

Keep a Log

The first step in becoming smoke-free is to understand the benefits you are now getting from smoking. If you want to stop smoking, you probably don't think you are getting any benefit from your nasty habit. Your unconscious mind disagrees, however, and it will create a smoking trance, taking control from the conscious mind. When the smoking trance has ended, your conscious mind gets upset with your unconscious for failing to keep you smoke-free. Both minds have your best interests at heart, but they are at odds over what is best, smoking or not smoking.

As you go about your daily routine, take note of where and how often you smoke. Are you smoking the entire cigarette, pipe, cigar, or whatever you smoke? Do you sometimes smoke all of it and sometimes only part? If so, why? You may want to keep a diary or log for a few days to help you become aware of your smoking habits.

As you are about to have a smoke, ask yourself why you want it. Keep track of the different reasons that you smoke. Ask yourself how you feel while you're smoking, and how you feel afterward. Do you smoke alone, or do others smoke with you? Is smoking part of your social life?

Use Self-Hypnosis

You can also review your smoking habit using self-hypnosis. Find a comfortable place, loosen your clothing, take as deep a breath as possible, exhale, and count yourself down from five to zero, into a calm and relaxing trance. (If you need to refresh your memory on how to get into a trance, review the information in the first few chapters of this book.) When you get to your trance level, review your smoking activities during the day and at night, to understand how often and how much you are experiencing your habit.

Review Your Smoking Habit

When you have done your review, start to build a model of what benefits smoking has for you. Imagine your first smoke of the day. Just before you light up, what part of yourself is asking for it? Is it your mind or your body? If so, which part wants you to smoke?

Do your lungs want to smoke, or is the need in your head? Is it for the rush that goes through your body, is it something for your hands to do, or is it something else? How does the first puff feel? What are its benefits? How did it feel as you inhaled it? How was the taste, and how was the smell? What were you doing as you smoked?

Follow your smoking activities through the day and night. Identify all the ways that smoking gives you a benefit. Does it allow you time to take a deep breath and relax? Do you escape in a cloud of smoke; is it an outlet for frustration, anger, boredom, or some other emotion? Does smoking provide a chance for you to be with friends; is it a social outlet? If you were smoke-free, would you have to give up these people, or would you have to stop going to certain places that you enjoy?

A L E R T

If you truly want to stop smoking, there is always a way to accomplish it, and it comes down to your beliefs. If you believe you will be addicted for life, you may be. If you believe you really can eliminate smoking from your life, it can happen. It is your right to be smoke-free if you choose.

What Do You Dislike about Smoking?

Now that you have developed a positive model of why you smoke, it's time to develop a negative model of everything you don't like about smoking. Is there a difference between the way the smoke feels in your lungs when you first start a smoke and when you end it? Is there a change in how smoking feels as you continue to smoke during your daily routine? If there is a change in feeling, when does the worst feeling occur? What is the worst feeling you have ever had from smoking?

What is your visual image of yourself when you smoke? What don't you like about it? How does the smell of smoke make you feel? What is your worst smell memory of smoking? Are there any unpleasant sounds or conversations you can relate to smoking?

Think of unpleasant memories that relate to smoking. Feel them as strongly as you can, with as many of your sense modalities as possible. Imagine how other people who do not smoke view your smoking. Create a negative picture of yourself smoking. Calculate how much money you spend on smoking: every day, every week, and every year.

Going Back to the Roots

Now use self-hypnosis to go back and examine the roots of your smoking habit. When did you first smoke? What did that first smoke feel like? Did it make you feel older? Did you smoke to fit in with the crowd or to rebel against authority? Was it exciting?

How did that first smoke taste? Was it pleasant or unpleasant? Did it make you want to have more? Did you have to smoke in secret so your parents wouldn't find out? Did other members of your family smoke: parent, grandparent, brother, or sister?

Now look at yourself when you first started smoking and compare it with where you are today. If you could talk to yourself back when you began, knowing what you know now about the health issues, what would you say to yourself about smoking? Would you encourage yourself to smoke, or would you try to convince yourself to stop before it's too late?

What about the people you started smoking with? To the best of your knowledge, are they still smoking today, and if so, what is their health like? Has smoking impacted any of their lives? How about your relatives who smoked: did it impact their lives? Have there ever been any health issues related to smoking in your family or in your friends' lives?

Begin to Change Your Habit

You have now developed a model of all the benefits that smoking gives you, and a model of all the things you find negative in the habit. What other negatives can you relate to smoking? Imagine a food you can't stand; there may be more than one. Do you dislike it because of the taste, the smell, the feel, or the appearance?

Add Some More Negatives

Anything you can put into your negative image will help. Imagine the effects smoking has on your body, on your lungs, on your throat, on your circulation, on your blood, on your heart, on your mouth, and on your brain. Imagine what it would be like if you continued to smoke. What would your condition be in a year, in five years, in ten years or more?

Focus on each puff, each time asking yourself, "What is this smoke doing to my body? How is it affecting my lungs? Can I feel it spreading throughout my body and depleting the oxygen in my blood? Is it filling my lungs with sediment and making it hard for me to breathe? Can I create an image in my mind of what the insides of my body look like when I smoke?"

Transfer Some Negatives

Think of the most unlikable food you know. Do you eat it every day, or would you eat it if someone served it to you? Relate this food to your smoking habit, and transfer the strongest negative that you can onto your habit. Feel, taste, smell, hear, and see yourself experiencing the food image in a very negative way, and put your smoking image right in the middle. Think of how you wouldn't eat that food if you were not smoking, but you will have to eat it if you smoke.

Does Your Smoking Affect Others?

Is there anyone else in your life who is impacted negatively by your smoking? Do you smoke around friends or family who don't smoke? Do you smoke where no one can see you, and then brush your teeth or use a mouthwash before you come in contact with anyone? Do you smoke in your car, with or without other passengers? Do you teach, work with customers, clients, or patients, or hold your children after you smoke?

Do you think your habit does not impact others as long as you don't smoke around them? Think again! Remember your five senses? Everyone else has them, too. Anyone who has a visual imagination will picture you smoking when he smells smoke on your breath, your skin, your hair, or your clothes. You may think people aren't watching, but they are, really, in their minds.

Think of all the people who worry about your smoking habit. Every time they smell smoke on you, they worry about you, and as you remember from the last chapter, stress can have a negative impact on health. Do you enjoy causing others to worry at the expense of your habit?

Imagine children who look up to you and admire you and may want to be like you someday. You don't smoke in front of them, and yet they know that you smoke because they can smell it on you. Imagine some day in the future when they remember you and all your good qualities at a time when they are a bit stressed. Their unconscious minds will remember that you used smoking to relax, and so they may start to smoke. You might just as well start them smoking right now.

The Cost of Smoking

For some people money is no object, and the cost of smoking is not important to them. However, for most people the amount of money wasted to support a smoking habit is significant. Have you ever figured out how much you spend on smoking? What is the cost per day, week, month, year, ten years, or over your lifetime? Imagine what that money could become if you invested it in an interest-bearing account.

Are you losing money because of the cost of your health insurance? Do you pay more in premiums than a nonsmoker does? Could you be getting other benefits from your insurance, such as a health club membership? How much would that add up to on a yearly basis?

ESSENTIALS

Consider starting a savings account or an investment fund with the money you used to spend on smoking. Ten dollars a week adds up to over 500 dollars in a year, while 20 dollars a week comes to over 1,000 dollars. Imagine how that would add up in twenty years.

Have you ever had health problems related to smoking? Has smoking ever contributed to your missing work? It might be just have been a day or two with a cold or a cough, but it could become something more serious. It could be pneumonia or emphysema or heart or circulatory problems. How much might these costs add up to on a yearly basis?

How about other people who might be impacted by the loss of your earning power? Does every day you miss work have an effect on your family? How much would it cost if someday you couldn't work at all, as a result of your smoking habit? How about others who may get sick as a result of your secondhand smoke? How much money would they lose?

Examine the Benefits

Examine all the benefits of being smoke-free. How much better off will you be immediately, in five years, or in ten years from now? How much more will you be able to taste, to breathe, or to smell? Imagine having the lung capacity and strength to walk, play with your children or grandchildren, or do other things that you will have to stop doing if you continue to smoke. Imagine how good your skin, your hair, and your clothes will smell when you become a nonsmoker.

Imagine how good your car or your house will smell. Imagine all the people who had to smell your smoky breath, who won't have to smell that anymore. Think of how your habit change will benefit you at work or in other environments. Imagine how healthy and fresh you will feel. Imagine being free of the stress you now feel as a smoker.

Think of the monetary savings. What will you do with all the money you'll save as a nonsmoker? You might invest it, take a vacation, or buy a car or some other big item. You might set it aside for a college education, the down payment on a home, or a retirement fund. You might purchase clothes or gifts or just enjoy spending it.

The Model for Change

Now it's time to ask the parts of yourself that like smoking what they would accept in order for the whole of you to be smoke-free. Concentrate on the negative smoking model, and ask the resistant part of yourself to accept something that is much better than what smoking has provided.

ESSENTIALS Go back over all the places in your day and night where smoking is a benefit to you, and ask the part of you that experiences a benefit if it would accept something else, something that would be better for the rest of you.

It may be that you are a shallow breather, and the only time you take a deep breath is when you smoke. Compare the taste, smell, and feel of smoke with fresh air or a favorite smell. It may be that you hold a cigarette while thinking, and your hands need something else to do. It may be that you need to escape for a moment. This is a great place to use your instant self-hypnotic anchors.

Imagine socializing with smokers and feeling glad that you are no longer trapped. Run through all the scenarios you can think of that might interfere with your being smoke-free. Might unseen stress or a life change throw you off? Imagine an old friend whom you trusted, and whom you later found out wasn't trustworthy. Guess what, that old friend is still there as your smoking habit.

Once you have developed the strongest smoke-free model that you can, run it into the future to see how it is going to work. Are there any places in your smoke-free image that you think may present obstacles to your habit change? If there are, examine these areas again to see what else you may develop to complete a successful change. When you feel that the smoke-free habit change model is ready to install, find a comfortable place for self-hypnosis.

Installing the Model for Change

Loosen your clothes, take a deep breath, exhale, and count yourself slowly from five to zero, into a calm and relaxing trance. In between numbers you may suggest to yourself that you will go deeper and deeper into self-hypnosis, feeling more and more calm and relaxed with each count. You may feel yourself sinking deeper and deeper into your trance. When you reach zero, suggest to yourself that you will experience your habit change with all five senses, and you will look forward to a positive habit change of being smoke-free. You may allow yourself to count down into a calm and relaxing deep trance.

Imagine your smoking habit in as unpleasant a way as you can, using your sense modalities to experience all the negatives. Suggest to yourself that you will experience the worst of the tastes, smells, feels, pictures, and sounds. Make your image dark and foreboding. Now experience your smoke-free image in the brightest way you can make it. Feel and experience with your five senses how good it is to be smoke-free, for yourself and others. Experience the difference in tastes, smells, feelings, visual images, and sounds.

Now run both the negative and positive models into the future: a month, a year, five years, ten years or more. See and experience the difference in the two outcomes: the first showing what would happen if you continued to smoke, the second being your smoke-free future. Feel how good it is to finally be free of this negative friend. Experience with all five senses how your health will deteriorate if you do not make the change.

Now bring the negative image back, dark and foreboding. Place a small, positive, smoke-free image in one spot on the negative image. Push the smoke-free image right through the old negative one, feeling how good this new image is as you push it through. Now let your mental screen clear, and continue this same process several more times, until the old image is gone and you feel the freedom of the new one. Anchor this smoke-free image and trigger it so you can retrieve it by instant self-hypnosis several times a day.

When you have finished, count yourself up slowly to the surface of your mind, from zero to five. When you arrive, open your eyes and feel calm and relaxed. Take a few minutes to enjoy the benefits of your new habit, of being smoke-free.

Once you have installed your smoke-free habit, carry at least one physical anchor that you can touch or see to reinforce your new habit. It could be a picture showing your goal for the money you save, or a picture of someone special. Or it could be something that has a pleasant smell.

You may continue to repeat this process to make adjustments in your program. It is a good idea to practice this smoke-free self-hypnotic induction once a day for the next three to six weeks, and use your instant self-hypnotic anchors many times a day to help reinforce your suggestions for being smoke-free.

CHAPTER 9

Weight Loss

Self-hypnosis can be very useful in reaching and maintaining goals for your eating habits. This chapter is designed to help you use self-hypnosis in conjunction with a proper diet program that you have received from a doctor, dietitian, or other health specialist.

The Word *Diet*

The word *diet* has as little appeal as *quit*. It implies that you have to give up a food that has brought you a lot of pleasure. Once you commit yourself to a diet, you expect to miss the enjoyment that your friends and family have when they enjoy your favorite foods. You find yourself feeling left out, different, and penalized for your love of food. Why couldn't you have been given a body that would not gain weight, so you could eat as others do?

You probably resent being on a diet. You look forward to a time when you will be free of the punishment you must endure. You patiently step on the scales, watching and waiting until you can reward yourself for your sacrifices with a special meal, and you imagine it so strongly that you can almost taste it. Finally the time comes and you reward yourself, only to start the weight gain all over again.

The Eating Trance

You have probably heard this story before: A guy starts out with a plate of chicken wings, and the next thing he knows, it is just a pile of bones. He ate the whole thing and can't even remember doing it. Many people actually trigger a self-hypnotic anchor when they start to eat. Once the trigger is activated, the eating trance begins. Their conscious minds focus attention on something else, and they are not aware of how much, what, or how often they are eating.

ESSENTIALS

Food can create a trance all by itself. Simply enjoying a favorite food can bring back memories, and off you go into a remembrance trance. Food can invoke sad memories as well as pleasant ones. Some people eat to help relieve stress, while others eat because they are bored. Many people eat to put off doing something they don't want to do.

If you eat for companionship and comfort, it may be because you don't have much but food to keep you company. If you eat for emotional support, you may eat when you're happy, when you're sad, when you're depressed, or when you're mad. It might not make any difference what you eat—you just need to eat *something*.

Once the eating process has begun, you are powerless to stop yourself. You have put yourself deep into a trance, and you're not worried about the results of your actions. Once you come out of the trance, you realize what just happened; you are confronted with what you just ate, and the argument between the conscious and unconscious begins again.

As you remember, one definition of a trance is that your conscious mind is open to suggestion and loses its ability to make critical decisions, so the unconscious mind takes over. The unconscious is now taking care of your needs, and it doesn't care how or what you eat, as long as the need is satisfied. When you are in an eating trance, you are busy fulfilling your need—but when you finish, you find out that the real need wasn't satisfied after all. You might want to take a few days and write down when, where, and what you eat. Also examine why—what the need was before you ate and how you felt about what you ate.

Examine Your Eating Habits

The first step to understanding your complex relationship with food is to examine your eating habits. You may have done this many times before, but perhaps doing it again will help you find one new clue or idea to make a change for the better.

The more thorough you are, the easier it will be for you to understand your eating habits. What is your first food of the day? Do you eat in the morning? It is also important to keep track of the types of food you eat. What are their fat, sugar, calorie, and salt contents?

If you have coffee, do you use cream and sugar? If so, how much? Do you drink other beverages? What is the size of your serving, and do you have seconds? Do you add things, such as bread, butter, jelly, maple syrup, or other condiments to your food?

As you have already learned, no one has the same mind, body, or soul as you do. Many of your eating habits are a result of the way your mind functions. They are just another extension of your mental makeup, which contributes to your uniqueness.

Who Controls the Food You Eat?

You do, right? But is that really the case? We are often only partly in control over the food that ends up on our plates. Much of the food we eat is tied into relationships with other people.

Love, family, and food go hand in hand. Remember the old-fashioned custom of the family meal, where the mother prepares a sumptuous feast with at least enough food to fill all the plates twice? Someone else often heaps the servings onto your plate. If you don't eat it all, you are rejecting the love shown in the preparation and serving of the food. It is hopeless for you to resist, and you end up consuming much more than you had planned.

You may remember being told as a child, "Make sure you clean your plate. You know there are starving children in other parts of the world. Be thankful that you have something to eat." That old guilt about not cleaning your plate still haunts you like a ghost from your childhood.

Food can have a lot of control issues connected to it. Even when you summon the courage to go on a diet, there is usually someone who is waiting to try to tempt you to go off it. This person tries to overfeed you and then complains about the fact that you are too fat or too thin. It becomes an endless cycle of control and entrapment, with no way to break the cycle. In frustration you turn to food to escape your feelings.

Understand the Food You Eat

An excellent way to assess what and how much you eat each day is to keep an accurate log. When you understand what ingredients are in your food and what they do, you can begin to develop a model of your eating habits as related to your weight. Each person digests food a little differently. Once you have tracked your food intake during the day and evening, it is time to really take a look at the ingredients that are in those foods.

How Much Salt Do You Eat?

If you have a poor sense of taste, adding salt helps give flavor to what you eat. Do you add salt to your food? If you do add salt, how much does it total up to? Total the number of shakes from the saltshaker, then shake a day's worth of salt into a measuring cup to see how much you've eaten.

Take note of all the salt that is listed in the ingredients of packaged foods you eat. Include canned items such as soups, frozen items such as entrées, snacks such as chips and nuts, and hotdogs and luncheon meats. Count everything that you can find an ingredient list for, and if you can't find out, make an honest estimate of the salt content. If you eat out at fast-food restaurants, ask if they have a list of contents for the foods they serve. This table will help you compute your daily totals.

MEASUREMENT CONVERSIONS		
1 pint	=	2 cups
1 ounce	=	2 tablespoons
1 tablespoon	=	3 teaspoons
½ ounce	=	15 grams
1 teaspoon	=	5 grams
1 teaspoon of salt	=	2,000 grams of sodium
1 ounce	=	30 grams
1 gram	=	1000 milligrams

Perhaps salt is not a problem for you. If it is, though, the amount of salt you use, coupled with stress, can add up to high blood pressure. Knowledge of how salt is affecting your health can help when you develop a self-hypnosis model for your eating habit change. Remember, when you are in your eating trance, you are probably not aware of how much salt you are putting into your body.

FACTS

"When there is too much salt in the body for the kidneys to handle, it is reabsorbed into the bloodstream. The bloodstream then absorbs water to maintain the right balance of sodium. This increased flow puts pressure on the vessels and the result is high blood pressure or hypertension."

—Patty Bryan,
Food Values: Sodium

How Much Sugar Do You Eat?

There is probably a lot of sugar in many of the foods you eat, and it has a special place in eating habits. A piece of candy can be a reward for something special. A piece of chocolate may actually be your piece of comfort. Sugar can give you an energy lift for a brief time before it makes you feel sluggish.

Take a look at the sugar you consume. How much do you add to your food each day? Do you use it in your coffee, in your tea, on your cereal, or on other foods? Once you have totaled up the amount of sugar you add to food each day, measure it out to see what it looks like. Is there as much as you thought there'd be, or is there more?

Now check the ingredient list to find how much sugar is in the packaged foods you eat on a daily basis. Include all the foods you eat that come from a container. They may be canned, such as soups or jellies, frozen, such as berries or ice cream, or bottled, such as soft drinks or juices. Once you have totaled the amount of sugar you eat in packaged food, add all that sugar to the amount you add to your food.

Now total up the sugar content of all the other foods you eat during the day. Include muffins, candy, and meals eaten out or at home, anything that does not have an ingredient list. Determine the size of your portions so you can estimate the sugar content. If you are eating in a fast-food restaurant, ask for a food content list. It would be a good idea to have a calorie chart to take with you to restaurants that do not have printed information about their food contents.

How Much Fat Do You Eat?

It's time to determine how much fat you consume on a daily basis. Start by adding up the amount of milk or cream you add to foods such as coffee or cereal. How much butter do you use each day? Do you add oils to your food, such as olive oil or vegetable oil? If so, how much a day?

Do you eat deep-fried foods such as French fries, onion rings, and doughnuts? Do you eat home fries or other foods that are cooked in grease? How much fat is in the packaged food you eat on a daily basis? Don't forget to look at food ingredients and lists of food contents.

ESSENTIALS

There are three types of fatty acids in food. Saturated fats predominate in meats, dairy products, and some vegetable fats such as palm and coconut oils. Monounsaturated fats are found in olive, canola, and peanut oils. Polyunsaturated fats are found in soybean, corn, sunflower, safflower, and cottonseed oils, and in some fish. Saturated fat can raise the blood's cholesterol level.

How much fat do you eat per day in fast foods? How much fat do you consume when you eat in other restaurants or at home? What types of fat are you eating: saturated, monounsaturated, or polyunsaturated? Now add up all the fats in the food you eat during the day.

While you are making totals, also count up the number of calories in your food. The Consumer Information Center recommends 1,600 calories a day for inactive women and older adults, 2,200 calories a day for children, teenage girls, active women, many sedentary men, and women who are breast-feeding, and 2,800 calories a day for teenage boys, active men, and very active women. How does your daily total compare with these recommendations?

What Foods Do You Like?

What are the foods you enjoy most? How often and when do you eat them? Do your favorite foods fit into a daily pattern, or do you eat them less frequently?

Are these foods good for you? Do you eat certain foods for stress release or when you need to feel comforted? Are there foods you eat to reward yourself, to punish yourself, to protect yourself, or to delay doing something that you don't want to do?

Do you eat certain foods because you like their texture—their smoothness or their crunch? Is there a particular spice, seasoning, or herb you enjoy? Do you like foods that are warm, cold, leftover, or right out of the oven? Do you like certain foods because of their smell?

Do you enjoy hearing certain foods cook? Do you like special foods for different seasons, temperature changes, or types of days? Are there foods you enjoy eating because they bring back special memories? Are there foods that give you a special energy or a sense of wellness? Are there any other benefits you receive from food besides those mentioned in this section?

What Foods Are Bad for You?

Which of your favorite foods are bad for you? List them according to their ingredients and the impact they have on your health. Remember that you are different from everyone else in the way you digest food. A food that would pose a health risk or cause weight gain in one person might be all right for another. Your doctor can advise you on the foods that are right for you.

What type of food do you have the biggest problem avoiding? What are the ingredients of the bad foods you like? Do they have a lot of salt, fat, or sugar? Are you eating more of the enjoyable, bad food than you need to?

Are you eating the healthy foods you like occasionally, or more often? Do you feel healthy, fulfilled, or satisfied when you eat healthy, good foods that you enjoy? Are these foods available to you all the time?

Does someone prepare or control the food you eat? Is it harder to make a choice between good and bad foods when someone else is with you? Do you feel pressure from someone else to eat foods that are unhealthy for you? Does it make you feel trapped, or do you enjoy having someone else make food decisions for you?

What Foods Do You Dislike?

What foods do you dislike? Is it due to the taste, smell, feel, appearance, or sound of the food? Does the color of certain foods discourage you from eating them? Are there foods you find unappealing when they're served one way, but which are more enjoyable if served another way? What is the least enjoyable food you can think of? Is that because of its taste, feel, smell, appearance, or the way it sounds when you eat it?

What food would you positively never eat, even if nothing else were available? Is there more than one food that is distasteful to you? If you could eat only one food, what would it be? Do you associate any food with bad memories and never eat it anymore? If a food made you ill once, that could be enough for you never to want it again. Are there any foods that you feel neutral toward—foods that you don't care whether you eat or not?

The more positive you are about your healthy food, the more in tune with yourself you will be. The more you trigger your positive self-hypnotic anchors, the easier it will be to get into a positive mood.

Reframe Your Eating Habits

Self-hypnosis can help you change your eating habits. You can reframe your image of the foods that are your weakness. Almost every food has something negative about it. When you are unaware of this negative aspect, you'll eat the food. Reframing your eating habits will provide a different view of the foods you now find irresistible.

Develop a Negative Eating Habit Model

Find a comfortable place, take a deep breath, exhale, and count yourself down from five to zero, suggesting to yourself that you will feel calm and relaxed as you experience your self-hypnotic trance. Suggest that you will respond to the following questions, using imagery in as many of your senses as your mental makeup provides for you.

What is the worst picture you can imagine from your past or current eating habits? Do you have any negative memories of conversations with others or with yourself about the way you eat? If so, how do they make you feel? Were other people trying to control you, or did they accuse you of something having to do with food? Did these conversations affect your self-esteem?

What negative experiences can you remember having to do with food? What is the worst-feeling food you can imagine? Are there foods you simply can't stand to have in your mouth or to touch? Are there foods that you can't even look at without feeling something negative? Are there foods that you can't stand to smell or taste?

Imagine what it would be like to take all the salt out of the foods you eat daily and eat the salt all by itself. How would that taste or feel as it went into your body? Now picture a big spoonful of pure fat. Taste it and feel it as it goes into your body. Do the same thing with the sugar you eat every day.

Develop a Positive Eating Habit Model

Now imagine what it would be like to eat healthy foods and be at an ideal weight. Can you picture what you would look like? How would you feel about this change in your eating habits? Would it be good for your health, for your job, for your self-esteem, and for your relationships with others? Can you imagine what friends and family will say as you work toward and reach your goal?

Can you imagine how good someone else might feel when you change your eating habits? Imagine how someone else might be inspired to make positive life changes as a result of your changing your eating habits. How would you feel about yourself, knowing you were making a positive change to help someone else? Imagine being able to fit into clothes you haven't worn for a while; imagine wanting to do more physical activities.

Imagine how it will feel to escape from the old relationship with foods that were holding you prisoner, not allowing you to get beyond their grasp. Imagine having the freedom to choose healthy foods to eat.

Imagine all your positive feelings about healthy foods, and look forward to the enjoyment of eating them. Imagine how you can enjoy feeling full of good, healthy food without feeling guilty. Think of your worst negative food image, and feel how good it is not to have to eat that way anymore. How does this new image fit with the way you feel about life? Feel good about your new, positive food habit change model.

Your New Eating Habit Model

Imagine your old eating habits. Think of the bad food you liked, and separate the ingredients in your mind. Experience as negatively as possible the taste, feel, and smell of plain salt, pure fat, and straight sugar. Imagine that every time you begin to eat these bad foods, you experience all the things you don't like in the first bite. Consider these foods in relationship to other foods you can't stand.

ESSENTIALS Look for any areas that might be a problem: certain times of day, occasions when you eat with others, times of stress, times of loneliness, or other unforeseen situations. If there is resistance, ask what would be an acceptable substitute. It might be a positive food or another activity.

Now imagine your new, positive eating habit model. Run through it in your mind, experiencing how it will be. Run through your new change program again, then bring up your old program, making it as dark and foreboding as possible. Imagine what your life will be like if you don't change. How would you be in a year, two years, ten years? Feel this old, negative image, and place a bright little positive image in one corner.

Install Your New Eating Habit Model

Find a comfortable place, loosen your clothes, take a deep breath, exhale, and count yourself down from five to zero into a calm and relaxing self-hypnotic trance. When you are ready, suggest to yourself that you will push your new, positive eating habit image through your old, negative habit image, feeling the change with all your five senses. When you have done this once, clear your mental screen and do it over again several times, until the old, negative image disappears. Let your unconscious mind experience the benefits of this change. Count yourself slowly back to the surface of your mind, feeling this new image become stronger and stronger every time you experience self-hypnosis.

Balance Your Mind, Body, and Soul

Now that you have installed your new eating habit, use your instant self-hypnotic anchors to help reinforce this new image. You are now aware of the negative tastes of salt, fat, and sugar in the unhealthy foods you once liked. There is nothing enjoyable about these foods anymore. On the other hand, remind yourself how enjoyable the new, healthy food is. When you see someone else eating your old favorites, let yourself feel happy that you don't have to eat them anymore.

Now that you have addressed healthy foods for the body, consider what else you might do. Can you start an exercise program? You don't have to start big. Perhaps you could take a walk or a swim, or begin an exercise program at a gym or fitness club. You may meet new friends with similar healthy interests. Every little extra movement you do will help you on your habit change path.

Eating healthy can be a meditation in itself. There is a theory that the mood you are in when you eat directly impacts how you digest your food. If you are not in a good mood when it is time to eat, consider taking a walk or meditating first.

The more you believe in having healthy eating habits, the more you will be in tune with your total self. If you believe that there is a reason beyond yourself to eat in a healthy way, it will be even easier to stay in tune. The more you use self-hypnosis to assist your mind, body, and soul to be in tune with your life's purpose, the more successful you will be in achieving this purpose. A body that is taken care of with healthy food and exercise is better prepared for the journey of life.

CHAPTER 10

Improving
Your Health

In this chapter you will see how incorporating self-hypnosis into your wellness program can get you started in the right direction, you will examine hypnosis for pain control, surgery, and oncology, and you will have a chance to experience a hypnosis depth test to learn how deeply you can go into a trance.

Establish Your Wellness Habit

Creating the habit of good health is a process that you may be inclined to push to the back of your mind. Stress can creep into your life at any time, and if you are not prepared to handle it, it stays with you. It is time to use self-hypnosis to establish your wellness habits.

QUESTIONS?

How should I regard my body in my total wellness program?
Treat your body with as much care as you would give a piece of machinery: like a car, which is given regular maintenance such as oil changes, tire rotation, and lubrication. Do you keep up the maintenance on your body, or do you drive around hoping nothing will break?

How do you maintain your health? Do you have a regular maintenance program for your body, mind, and soul? Or do you let yourself become distracted by stress and bad habits, hoping that the vehicle of your body, mind, and soul will stand up to the speed at which you're driving yourself?

Self-Hypnosis and a Healthy Body

Are you currently on a regular exercise program, eating a balanced diet that is right for you, and are you free of any destructive habits, such as smoking? If not, you may want to take steps as soon as possible to establish goals that are good for your body. How would you imagine your body responding to a wellness program?

Find a comfortable spot, loosen your clothes, take a deep breath, exhale, and count yourself down from five to zero into a calm and relaxing trance. Suggest to yourself that you will review your daily maintenance of your body, using your five senses.

If you are able to exercise, when do you exercise each day? Do you have a set routine, or do you exercise only occasionally? How does your body feel when it exercises and when it doesn't? How does it feel now?

Even if exercise is impossible, imagine it in your trance. You could walk to a favorite place in your mind, imagining your physical movements and feeling the healthy effects of the exercise as you move in your mind. Remember the story of Milton Erickson, who mentally practiced getting out of his bed. Your mind can actually create an experience of reality for your muscles and other parts of your body. If you are able to exercise, mentally experience the wellness benefits that it can give your body.

Self-hypnosis creates a mental reality that can cause your body to react to the experience that is being imagined. If you have a health condition that does not allow you to exercise, check with your doctor before engaging in this type of mental imagery.

Now imagine your eating habits and other wellness habits during your daily schedule. How do they fit in to your body's wellness program? Examine any situations you encounter daily that may have a negative impact on your physical health. Develop negative and positive models of your wellness habits, and construct a positive model for change. While in your trance, give yourself a posthypnotic suggestion that you will constantly let your mind be aware of your body's physical health, and that you will feel your body responding positively to each healthy thing that you do.

Self-Hypnosis and a Healthy Mind

Do you practice any form of mental relaxation on a daily basis, such as meditation or self-hypnosis? What other positive relaxation techniques do you practice? Some of these may be linked with physical activity: martial arts, running, or other sports. If you do any of these activities, how do you feel after you have completed them? Are you able to find mental escape and relaxation during the day?

Do you have habits that are negative for your physical body, but have positive benefits for your mind? For example, do you smoke, overeat, or something similar? Do you go about your day calm, relaxed, and in balance, or does the slightest little thing throw you into turmoil? If you are mentally out of balance, you may want to use self-hypnosis to help bring your mind back in tune. Use self-hypnosis to examine your daily mental habits, identifying the times when you become stressed or otherwise out of sync with yourself.

Once you have identified these times, think how and when you can use self-hypnosis for positive change. A good time to use self-hypnosis might be when you awake in the morning or before you go to bed at night. Feel calm and relaxed, and let your stress float out into space or wherever you allow it to go. Imagine your mind and your body responding in a positive way to your relaxed, calm feeling.

Imagine your mind and body feeling peaceful and healthy. If there is a color that you associate with good health, imagine it flowing throughout your body and mind. If you feel tension, imagine your body and mind relaxing, and feel calm and positive as you relax. Give yourself a posthypnotic suggestion that your body and mind will respond positively each time you allow yourself to relax and feel healthy and in tune.

Self-Hypnosis and Your Soul's Health

How you feel about your life can have a major impact on your wellness. Do you believe that life has a purpose, something beyond your daily existence? Do you believe that something or someone is watching out for you? Do you believe in the possibility of miracles, predestination, or other unexplainable happenings? Do you believe you have a life map to follow? Is your outlook on life optimistic or pessimistic?

Self-hypnosis, combined with a positive belief system, can truly bring about unexplainable medical miracles. Prayer trances, which put you in touch with your belief through the universal mind, may provide you with the mental and physical strength to overcome seemingly insurmountable obstacles. The more you believe that your life's goals are in harmony with those of the universal mind, the more your life will have a sense of flow and purpose to it.

In your relaxed trance, ask yourself how you feel about your life's purpose. Are you in tune with it, or do you feel you are off course? Are there parts of your life that you wish were more in harmony with your beliefs? If so, how would you start to resolve them? Are you in tune with other people in your life?

Now imagine that your conscious, unconscious, and universal minds are in harmony with one another. Imagine everything you do during your life is being done for the total whole. Everything you eat, all your habits, all your thoughts, and all your actions are done for the best of all concerned. Everything you do is working in harmony with your body, your mind, and your soul's purpose, and your good health and wellness are a part of being in tune. Count yourself back up to the surface of your mind, feeling in tune and knowing that your life has a purpose, even if you do not yet understand it.

Hypnosis and Pain Control

Hypnosis can be helpful in controlling chronic pain, pain that never completely disappears. Chronic pain can be the result of a medical condition, or it can be caused by physical damage, perhaps from an accident. Pain can take an emotional and physical toll on you; it can cause stress that, in turn, amplifies the pain.

Anxiety and worry often accompany medical conditions that cause pain. You may fear a yet-unknown illness, or you may fear a recent diagnosis. The moment you become aware of the pain, you focus on it. As long as your focus remains on the pain, you are not focused on wellness.

QUESTIONS?

What is pain amnesia?
Focusing on pain keeps it in your mind constantly. If you acknowledge that there is pain and then turn your focus to something positive, it is possible to forget the pain for a period of time. Pain amnesia moves the awareness of pain to your unconscious mind, so your conscious is not aware of it.

Before designing a self-hypnotic pain control program for yourself, you need to have a complete understanding of the reason for the pain. Discuss the pain with your doctor and work with her to develop your wellness model. Your doctor may not be familiar with how hypnosis works, and you may need to furnish her with information about the benefits of self-hypnosis.

There are several techniques that use self-hypnosis for pain control; these include diminishing the pain, dissociation from the pain, and transference of the pain. You can also develop an image of the pain and build a positive model to push through it.

The Dimmer Switch Technique

The dimmer switch technique gradually turns down the intensity of the pain. You can use a knob or a slider control, whichever works best for you. This induction will use a dimmer scale from ten to one, but you can change the count, making your own adjustments.

Find a comfortable place, loosen your clothes, take a deep breath, and exhale. Take a couple more deep breaths, exhaling in between, and then take a deep breath and hold it for a few moments before exhaling. Let your eyes go out of focus, and when you're ready, close them. You may be aware that you are beginning to relax your muscles. Some of your muscles may tighten from time to time, and when they do, you may relax them and go deeper and deeper into self-hypnosis.

ESSENTIALS

When you count yourself down, allow plenty of time at each number. Continually suggest to yourself that you are going deeper and deeper, and that the pain is getting dimmer and dimmer with each movement of the control. Repeating the suggestions helps to reinforce them in the unconscious mind.

Now imagine your dimmer switch. Picture it, if you can, and feel your fingers ready to control it. Set the dial on ten. In a few moments you may start counting slowly backward, from ten to one. Before you begin to count, focus on the dial, and feel your fingers ready to turn it down one click each time you say a number. If you are ready, begin.

Ten: you feel your fingers on the knob, and you feel the pain as you breathe in and out, relaxing more and more with each breath.

Nine: repeat to yourself that you are relaxing and going deeper into hypnosis every time you turn down your pain control. Anticipate each number as you count down to one, and as you turn down the pain control switch on each count, the pain becomes dimmer and dimmer, just as lights get dimmer when you slowly turned them down.

When you reach one, suggest to yourself that the pain will be completely diminished. If you are going to sleep, suggest that you will sleep, calm and relaxed. If you are doing something active, suggest that you will go about your activity calmly, relaxed, and with the pain diminished.

The Pain Dissociation Technique

Pain dissociation techniques may work well if you are confined to bed or immobile. They can also be used before going to sleep or during a longer self-hypnotic trance. In pain dissociation, you use self-hypnosis to escape pain by mentally leaving your body.

You may use any destination for this purpose: a favorite remembered place, an imagined place, a place up in the clouds, or a place deep inside yourself. You can use the mind model you have created of your five senses to locate the best place for you.

Find a comfortable place, loosen your clothing, take a deep breath, exhale, and let your eyes go out of focus. Suggest to yourself that when you reach zero, you will be in your favorite place, and you will feel its positive healing energy with all five senses. You may be aware of the muscles in your body: some are stiff and some are relaxed. Each time you feel a muscle relax, you will go deeper and deeper into self-hypnosis. When you're ready, slowly count yourself backward from ten to zero.

As you count down, suggest to yourself that you will relax more and more, and go deeper and deeper into hypnosis with each number. Also suggest that when you reach zero, you will be in your favorite place, experiencing its healing energy with all five senses. Think of a healing smell as you breathe in and out, allowing it to become stronger and stronger with each count. Take your time, and feel yourself going deeper and deeper into hypnosis with each count.

When you reach zero, you can suggest that you may fall asleep in your special place, far away from pain, or you can spend as long as you want there, free of pain. Suggest to yourself that you can visit this place anytime you want by giving yourself a special word, phrase, or touch as an anchor. You may also suggest that when you come back to consciousness, you will continue to be free of pain. When you are ready to come back, you can count yourself upward, or you can slowly drift back to the surface of your mind.

The Pain Transference Technique

Pain transference techniques can help move a pain from one part of your body to another. Headaches, for example, can be addressed by this method. From a comfortable position, do your relaxation exercise, counting down from five to zero. Suggest to yourself that you will go deeper and deeper into self-hypnosis with each number.

Tell yourself that when you get to zero, you will focus on your pain, and you will move it to one of your little fingers. When you transfer the pain, its original location will feel normal and healthy. You will send all the pain to your little finger. Once all the pain is in your little finger, suggest that when you wiggle your little finger, the pain will float off into the air.

FACTS

If you experience migraine headaches, you can use heat transference through self-hypnosis to move the heat you feel in your head just before the headache begins. If you can cool down your head and send the heat to your fingers, you can avoid the headache. When the heat reaches the ends of your fingers, you can send it out into space.

Hypnosis and Surgery

Hypnosis can be used in many aspects of surgery. It can help relieve your stress and anxiety before an operation, it can serve as a total or partial substitute for anesthesia during surgery, and it can help with pain control and healing imagery after surgery.

Preparing for Surgery

You probably feel a lot of anxiety and stress just before surgery. You might worry about the outcome of the operation, the prognosis for your well-being, the time involved in recovery, and how your illness is affecting friends and family members. Chapter 7, "Hypnosis and Stress," can help you develop positive self-hypnosis models to use during presurgery.

Your belief system can be a major source of strength for you as you face surgery. If you believe in a positive outcome and turn your fears and anxiety over to the universal mind, you will be prepared mentally and spiritually for the operation. Consider how the improvement in your health will benefit others. Your positive attitude can be an inspiration for others: doctors, nurses, friends, family, and other patients.

FACTS

There are several different hypnosis depth tests, including the LeCron-Bordeaux, which has fifty levels, the Davis-Husband (thirty levels), the Stanford Scale (twelve levels), and the Arons Depth Scale (six levels). Only 10 percent of patients who wish to use hypnosis for surgery are suitable candidates.

When you develop a presurgery self-hypnosis induction, you'll include relaxation, calming, wellness, and positive belief suggestions. Give yourself a suggestion that your body will work with the surgeons, and that you will begin healing immediately, feeling positive about your wellness. Develop an image of what the healing looks and feels like, and use your senses of smell, sound, and taste to strengthen your wellness image. Give yourself posthypnotic suggestions that your body will continue to respond positively to these suggestions. Practice your self-hypnosis right up until your operation.

Hypnosis During Surgery

Today, many hospitals have an anesthesiologist or nurse who is trained in both anesthesia and hypnosis. Hypnosis for surgery is called *hypno-anesthesia.* Some people are allergic to chemical anesthesia, and others may want to cut down on the use of chemicals. Before you use hypnosis for surgery or other medical procedures, the doctor must determine how deep into a trance you can go. The deeper into hypnosis you can go, the more effective it will be in surgery—but not everyone can reach a level that is deep enough to be suitable for surgery.

Depth Testing

To test your hypnosis depth level, you may want to record and play back the following induction, or you may have someone read it to you. Find a comfortable position, loosen your clothes, take a deep breath, and exhale. Let your eyes go out of focus, as you continue to breathe slowly in and out. You may feel your muscles relaxing, and you may notice from time to time that one stiffens a little. When you feel a muscle stiffen, you may relax it and go deeper and deeper into hypnosis.

QUESTIONS?

How do I assess my hypnosis depth test?
If you were going to use hypnosis for surgery or another medical application, you would want to have someone trained and certified in hypnosis to assess your trance level. You may be able to go deeper into hypnosis when you work with a specialist than you did doing the exercise in this book.

You may now close your eyes and relax. In a moment you will feel your eyelids getting heavier and heavier. With each breath, your eyelids are getting heavier and heavier; in fact they will become so heavy that you will not be able to open them. You can try, but you notice that they will not open, and you need not try anymore as you go deeper and deeper into hypnosis. You are going deeper and deeper into hypnosis, relaxing and feeling very calm and comfortable.

Going Deeper into Hypnosis

Now you may notice that your arms are getting heavier and heavier. With each breath, your arms are getting heavier and heavier as you go deeper into hypnosis. In fact your arms are now so heavy that you cannot lift them. Try if you want, but your arms will not lift, and now you don't need to try anymore as you go deeper and deeper into hypnosis. You will continue to go deeper and deeper into hypnosis, relaxing more and more.

Now you will count from one to ten, and you will notice that there is no number between six and eight. As you count slowly—one, two, three, four, five, six, eight, nine, ten—you will go deeper and deeper into hypnosis. Each time you count one, two, three, four, five, six, eight, nine, ten, you will go deeper and deeper. You do not need to try again. You are relaxing more and more as you go deeper and deeper into hypnosis.

You will notice that your right hand and arm are beginning to feel numb. You are aware of your right hand and arm as they get very, very numb. Even though you are aware of your right hand and arm, you will have no feeling in them at all. It is a comfortable sensation, and you will go deeper and deeper into hypnosis. With each breath you will relax more and more and go deeper and deeper.

Deep Enough for Surgery

Now you will notice that your right hand and arm have lost all sensation. You have absolutely no sense of your right hand and arm, and it will seem as if they are not even there. You may also open your eyes and see a large clock on the wall. You will watch its second hand go around and around as you go deeper and deeper into hypnosis. With each movement of the second hand, you will feel more and more relaxed as you go deeper and deeper into hypnosis.

You will notice that your right hand and arm are slowly beginning to disappear. They are fading and fading. It is all right with you, and as they disappear, you will go deeper and deeper into hypnosis. Your right hand and arm have now totally disappeared. You may close your eyes and go deeper and deeper into hypnosis.

You have now reached the deepest level of hypnosis, and in a moment you may begin to count slowly from zero to five. As you count back to the surface of your mind, you will be aware of your right hand and arm as they come back to full feeling. The imaginary clock on the wall will be gone, you will feel your right hand and arm, and you will remember the number seven between six and eight. Your arms and hands will feel normal again, and when you reach the number five as you count upward, you will open your eyes and be wide awake as you end your hypnotic trance. You are feeling relaxed and comfortable.

Hypnosis and Oncology

Hypnosis can be very valuable for the treatment of cancer when used in teamwork with doctors. It can help with stress, anxiety, and pain, as well as with healing imagery. For this, you develop a mental image of what your cancer looks and feels like, and an image of what your healthy body looks and feels like. Once the two images have been created, you push the wellness image through your mind, forcing the negative one out.

One very effective image is to visualize gray cells and healthy cells. The healthy cells chase the gray cells out of the body. As the healthy cells chase the gray cells out, feel your body getting healthier and healthier, and feel the cancer shrinking smaller and smaller. If you respond to colors, select a negative and a positive color, and run the positive color through the negative until the negative one is gone.

Any of your five senses can be used in a wellness image. You might use a healing smell, healing sounds, a healing picture, a healing feeling, or even a healing taste. You can give yourself a posthypnotic suggestion that your positive, healthy image will continue when you are in a waking state, and that it will become stronger and stronger.

Hypnosis and Other Areas of Medicine

With the ever-increasing interest in alternative health care, hypnosis has been integrated into many areas of traditional medicine. It is used in obstetrics, surgery, oncology, dermatology, pain control, and dentistry, to name a few. Many hospitals now have personnel trained in hypnosis on staff.

Hypno-birthing is becoming very popular. Many hospitals now employ nurses or hypnotherapists trained in this technique, who teach expectant parents how to use hypnosis for childbirth. Hypnosis can be used for stress, anxiety, pain, and to help muscles relax during delivery.

Hypnosis is also used in dentistry, where it is especially helpful with anxiety. Because of the dentist's time constraints, you may be hypnotized before going to the office and given a posthypnotic suggestion that you will experience when you are in the dentist's chair. You can numb a finger and rub the tooth to be worked on, and the tooth will become numb.

Remember, self-hypnosis cannot effect a medical cure. It can help supplement and reinforce your doctor's good health goals for you. Self-hypnosis can be very effective when used in conjunction with traditional medicine for better health.

Hypnosis is also used in many other branches of medicine, including gynecology, dermatology, pediatrics, and orthopedics. Ask your doctor or a certified hypnotherapist if you have questions about hypnosis and health. The sooner you start to use self-hypnosis as part of your wellness, the sooner you may begin to see positive results.

CHAPTER 11

Overcoming a Fear or Phobia

Many people have fears and anxieties, but these do not disrupt their daily lives. If a fear becomes so intense that it causes a person to avoid situations or objects, it is labeled a phobia, a disease classified as an anxiety disorder. Phobias are often caused by traumatic events in a person's childhood, which are re-experienced in stressful situations later on.

Social Phobias

A social phobia is often triggered by the fear of failure. If you have a social phobia, you have an intense fear of being embarrassed or humiliated by other people. You may have low self-esteem and see everything you do wrong as a major catastrophe. You are easily embarrassed and blush when your anxiety is exposed to others. The more you experience the phobia, the more you may withdraw from life.

You may remember that shy student in the back of the class who hoped he was invisible to the teacher. (Perhaps you were that person.) He made it all the way through school without ever having a social relationship with other students. Eventually someone found something unique about him, brought him out of his shell, and encouraged him to discover his own sense of self.

SSENTIALS Physical symptoms of a social phobia include heart palpitations, rapid heartbeat, or tightness in the chest or stomach or muscles. They also include sweating, hyperventilation, diarrhea, blushing, tremors, rapid thinking, and confusion.

Do you or anyone you know have the symptoms of a social phobia? Do you avoid situations that could cause embarrassment? Do you have a fear, anxiety, or worry that holds you back from advancing in your career or social life? Does your fear of failure keep you from trying?

Specific Phobias

A specific phobia is an irrational fear of a certain object or situation. It can be directed toward almost anything; well-known phobias include fear of flying, heights, bridges, water, highway driving, dogs, cats, mice, or other animals. Some people have an uncontrollable fear of insects, snakes, injuries involving blood, escalators, or a different race of people. The fear of crowds, of being alone, of being poor, and of being successful may also be classified in this category.

Do you or someone you know have a specific phobia? The phobia is always there under the surface of your mind, and the smallest hint of it causes you to react in unexplainable ways. Most adults are aware of their phobias, but they are powerless to stop them once they have taken over the critical-thinking ability of their conscious minds. The unconscious mind has sent a message to react to the situation, regardless of whether the reaction is rational or irrational.

The mere thought of the phobia can trigger anxiety and cause both physical symptoms and emotional responses. Fear is one of those emotions, and it can trigger anxious thoughts that lead to excessive worry and possibly to panic. The more the stress of worry consumes an individual, the greater the chance he'll experience health complications.

The Phobia Habit

In Chapter 6 you learned how to discover the roots of a habit. You went back in your mind through self-hypnosis to find out when, where, and how you learned your habit. Once the habit was learned, it was planted in your unconscious mind, and now when the need to experience the habit is triggered, the habit automatically starts its progression without interruption from your critical, conscious mind.

Phobia Trance

One of the first principals of hypnotic trance is the loss of critical thinking by the conscious mind. While you are in a trance, your unconscious mind receives a suggestion and accepts it as reality. This perceived reality creates a response, and your unconscious mind does not differentiate between an appropriate reaction and an inappropriate reaction. When a phobia is triggered, you are powerless to stop its progress, even though you know your phobic reactions are irrational. Doesn't it seem as though a habit and a phobia have a lot in common?

The stage show hypnotist creates phobias in subjects as part of her act. The hypnotist can then have the subject stand at the edge of an invisible cliff, experience fear when encountering an invisible snake, or shrink with embarrassment over a situation that never really happened. The audience loves it, and yet the imaginary phobia isn't funny to the subject experiencing it. Real-life phobias aren't funny either, and the person experiencing them is in the same type of trance as the stage show subject. The phobia trance experience is completely out of proportion with reality.

ESSENTIALS

Although it can be very funny and entertaining to watch, when a subject on-stage is confronted by a fear, it can be dangerous. The stage show hypnotist must maintain constant control and be ready to end the phobia trance at a moment's notice.

Habit trances can become intricately woven into the unconscious mind, as you have seen in the chapters on smoking, weight control, and stress. Your ancient internal warning signals of fight or flight come into play with a phobia. The body and mind go on a state of high alert, and the phobic danger trance is so strong that it can actually cause you to panic.

Roots of a Phobia

Self-hypnosis can be used to understand a phobia by helping you search for its beginnings. You can use the affect-bridge technique, the calendar technique, or both of them to provide information to help you resolve the phobia. If you can dissociate from the emotions of the phobia, it may help provide a clearer image of its roots. Television, video, movie, or book regression methods can also be an effective way to produce regression results. (You can find out how to use these methods in Chapter 17.)

Affect-Bridge Regression for a Phobia

The affect-bridge regression technique uses sensory recall to go back over events in your life, to find the beginnings of a phobic trance. The images can be recalled in one or more of the five senses. You may be able to experience the images directly, to dissociate and watch the experience, or you may possibly do both. The purpose of the regression is to determine, as best as possible, when, where, and how the phobia began.

ALERT

Whenever you experience self-hypnosis, always give yourself the suggestion that you may end your trance at any time. This is especially important when you are revisiting unpleasant or traumatic situations in your life. Contact a certified professional if you want help dealing with any overwhelming feelings you might experience.

When you are ready, find a comfortable location, loosen your clothes, take a deep breath, and exhale. Continue breathing slowly, allowing yourself to relax more and more with each breath. Let your eyes go out of focus, and when you are ready, let them close and allow yourself to go deeper into self-hypnosis. You may be aware of many of your muscles, some of which are tight and some relaxed. As you relax each tight muscle, let yourself relax more and more, going deeper and deeper into self-hypnosis.

In a few moments, count yourself down from five to zero, telling yourself that your unconscious mind will respond to your suggestions. Suggest that you may end your trance anytime you want to by opening your eyes or moving your body. You may feel calm and relaxed in your trance regardless of the images you experience. Suggest to yourself that when you get to zero, you will be able to experience just a very small image of your phobia, the way it was the last time you experienced it. You will feel just enough so the image will be nonthreatening, and you may feel positive about beginning to understand your phobia.

Count Backward

As you count slowly down from five to zero, suggest to yourself that you may go deeper and deeper into self-hypnosis with each number. You may go at a pace that is comfortable for you. If you are ready, you may begin slowly counting. Very slowly, relaxing more and more, go deeper and deeper into self-hypnosis with each count. You may look forward to going deeper and deeper until you reach zero.

When you reach zero, you will be able to end your trance anytime you want by opening your eyes or moving your body. At zero, experience a small image of the last time your phobia was present. You may see a picture, hear voices or sounds, and feel, taste, or smell anything that helps you get a clear and accurate image of your phobia.

If you can watch yourself experiencing your phobia, do so, but only to a point that is manageable for you. If you can feel your emotions while you experienced your phobia, only do so to an amount that is manageable for you. Develop as clear an image of your last phobia experience as possible.

Find Your Phobia's Beginnings

Now that you have a clear image of your last phobia experience, go back to a similar one within the last month or two. Experience that situation the same way you did the more recent one. Now go back to an earlier one, perhaps six months ago. Experience this image in the same manner as the other two. Go back a year, and do the same thing.

Go back to a similar experience two years ago. Then go back three years and then five, always experiencing the images at a level of intensity that is manageable for you. Keep going back until you have gone as far as possible. Always remain open to other images that might come from your unconscious mind; these may be different but somehow related to your phobia image.

Go back to the very first phobia image that is in your mind:

- How old were you when you first experienced the phobia?
- Where did this experience take place?
- How did it happen?
- Who was with you at the time?
- Can you feel a manageable amount of the emotional image?

If you can watch yourself experiencing this early image, notice whether your emotional experience matches your visual image. Does the image match the fear that currently accompanies your phobia? Can you compare two different images?

What is actually taking place as you watch the image of your first experience of the phobia? Watch it as you are now, as an adult, and then experience the emotional image of the situation you had when you were a child. What is the same in both images, and what is different?

Compare Information

Once you have gathered as much information as you can about your phobia, suggest to yourself that you will slowly count up from zero to five. You will come back to the surface of your mind, relaxed, calm, and refreshed. You will have a new, positive understanding of your phobia that may help to resolve it. Slowly count back to five, open your eyes, take a deep breath, and exhale, feeling calm, comfortable, and very relaxed. Take a few moments and assess the information your have just received from your unconscious mind.

ESSENTIALS

Usually a child's view of a situation is very different from an adult's perspective of the same situation. To a child, everything is bigger than life. Adults often look back at their childhood memories and wonder why similar experiences seem so different now.

What was the comparison of your experiences like? You may not have been able to develop comparable images, or you may have had images that made no sense to you at all.

You may have gotten images related to different and seemingly unconnected situations in your life, or from a different period of history. You could have pictured symbolic imagery, like in a dream. Do not dismiss the things that you do not understand; you need not make them fit. You are, in a sense, putting together a puzzle. The pieces that do not fit at the moment may be useful later, as you focus on larger aspects of the puzzle.

Resolving a Phobia

To resolve a phobia, you have to understand why you need it; then you can develop a model for positive change. The affect-bridge regression technique can give you the how, where, and when of the phobia's origins. Once the roots of the phobia are understood, you may be able to resolve the irrational fear and anxiety connected with it. That does not mean you will never experience this fear again, but now you can take action to go beyond the feeling of fear.

It is always advisable to recognize the potential danger involved with activities you may take to resolve a phobia. For example, if you lose all fear of heights, you may take risks that could lead to injury.

ALERT

When practicing pain control, part of you acknowledges the pain so that the rest of you doesn't need to focus on it. If you try to block or fight the pain, it will always be in your consciousness. The same goes for the anxiety and fear connected to a phobia. If you try to fight the fear, it consumes you, and you will never be free of it. Knowing where, how, and why the anxiety and fear began provides you an opportunity to acknowledge it and go beyond it.

Cognitive Behavior Therapy

Cognitive behavior therapy is used to desensitize an individual who has a phobia or a strong anxiety. You start the therapy by receiving a very slight exposure to your phobia. When you have become accustomed to the exposure, it is increased slightly. Each time you accept the amount of exposure, it is increased, until full exposure is possible without triggering the phobia.

Cognitive behavior techniques can work well with self-hypnosis. While in a hypnotic trance, you can remain calm and relaxed as you desensitize the phobia. The more you experience a positive outcome when experiencing the phobia in your mind, the more it becomes a posthypnotic suggestion to be calm and relaxed when you are actually in the situation. With this therapy, it is helpful but not necessary to know the roots of the phobia. If the roots cannot be determined, you can work with your present fears.

To experience cognitive behavior therapy, find a comfortable position, loosen your clothes, take a deep breath, and exhale. Let your eyes go out of focus, and when you are ready, close them, and slowly count yourself down from five to zero, to a very comfortable place in your mind. You will always be able to open your eyes or move your body whenever you feel the need to end your trance. Suggest to yourself that you will experience only a small amount of exposure to your phobia, and you will remain calm and relaxed.

Spend a suitable amount of time with your phobic emotions, seeing them from several different angles—be both the experiencer and the observer as you get accustomed to your emotions. When you're ready, count yourself slowly from zero to five, back to the surface of your mind, feeling calm and relaxed. Each time you use self-hypnosis, suggest to yourself that you will experience a little more of your phobia. When you feel you are gaining confidence during self-hypnosis, you may want to find a safe, controlled environment and try a small amount of real-life exposure to the phobia.

Self-Hypnosis and Cognitive Behavior Therapy

Martha was terrified of driving. Somehow she had managed to get her driver's license, but she would only go a mile or so from her home; after that, she had to rely on her husband. She wouldn't venture to any of the shopping centers because they were too far away. Her husband worked during the day, and Martha was stuck at home unless a friend picked her up and drove her someplace.

She was tired of her dependence on others, and decided to go to a hypnotherapist to get help. Through regression she learned that once she had gone to a neighboring town with her mother, and they had been in a minor car accident with no injuries. Her mother had become so upset that she vowed never to drive out of town again without her husband along. Even though Martha's mother was able to resume her regular driving habit a short time later, the suggestion had been planted in Martha's unconscious mind.

Shortly after she was married, Martha unconsciously repeated her mother's experience. She nearly had an accident while driving several miles from home, was very shaken, and vowed not to travel any distance away from her home unless her husband was with her.

Martha began using self-hypnosis to imagine herself driving to the limit of her comfortable driving range. Then she imagined going one street further, turning around, and driving back, suggesting to herself that she would feel calm and relaxed and enjoy the experience. After a few mental rehearsals, she drove her car the extra distance, and returned to her comfortable area.

She continued to expand her comfortable driving zone until she could drive about in confidence. She also got herself a cell phone, so she knew she could contact her husband if she needed to. Martha was no longer held prisoner by her fear of driving. Her story demonstrates how the combination of self-hypnosis and cognitive behavior modification can be very successful in resolving phobias.

Interrupting the Phobic Trance

A habitual phobic reaction is triggered by the unconscious mind; the conscious mind is often powerless to stop the action. Once a phobia has been triggered, the conscious mind ceases to think rationally, and the phobia continues until it runs its course. Classifying a phobia as a habit shows us how the principles used in self-hypnosis for habit change can be applied to changing a phobia. With a habitual phobia, the unconscious mind is trying to warn the conscious mind of impending danger or potential embarrassment.

Just as with any other habit, the unconscious mind wants to make sure the conscious mind is aware and won't take a dangerous action. With a phobia, the unconscious wants the conscious mind to recognize the feeling in its earliest stages so there is plenty of warning for an alternative, positive action to be taken.

You may use self-hypnosis to practice making positive responses in situations where your old fear and anxiety once ruled you. You may suggest to yourself that you will respond to any feeling coming from your unconscious mind in a way that is calm and relaxed for your whole self and for the situation. No matter what happens, you will remain calm and in control. The more you practice positive imagery and give yourself posthypnotic suggestions, the better you will be prepared to handle the old phobia situations.

ESSENTIALS

Self-hypnosis can help you prepare yourself for situations that once triggered your phobias. Your belief structure can also play a large part in resolving a phobia, especially a social phobia. If you believe that you are giving your best, then that is enough. If someone criticizes you, ask yourself how *you* would treat another person in this situation. Would you encourage her or make fun of her?

The Benefits of Fear

Fear is not all bad. Sometimes it comes from a source inside you that you may not recognize—your intuition. The unconscious mind processes a lot of information that is constantly being provided through your senses, and you may not consciously know about all this information.

When you get an intuitive signal, all you know is that you have a feeling. Many people who work in dangerous occupations have learned to listen to their intuition when it sends a warning signal. Those who don't may not survive.

Everyone is faced with fear. How you respond to it and how you resolve it afterward may affect you for the rest of your life. If you are able to resolve it, you return to a sense of normalcy. If you cannot resolve it, your fear might turn into a phobia.

CHAPTER 12

Improving Your Sports Performance

T his chapter examines the use of self-hypnosis in sports. You will learn how your mental and physical makeup affect your relationship with sports, how to use self-hypnotic mental imagery to prepare yourself for your favorite sports, and how to develop anchors that help you get in the Zone.

Hypnosis and Sports Psychology

Sports psychology has developed into a well-respected profession, which is used by all types of athletes, from high school to professional. Both sports psychologists and coaches use visual imagery with athletes to help them achieve maximum athletic performances. Visual imagery is a form of hypnosis.

Whether you participate in sports occasionally or often, whether you are an amateur or a professional, part of the enjoyment is challenging yourself to do your best. That challenge can turn into a love-hate relationship, however. A sports fanatic will push to achieve more and more until it is no longer enjoyable, and then she may have to walk away from the sport for a while.

The potential earning power of a professional athlete is limited only by her ability, and the pressure to achieve starts at an early age. Some parents hope to live out their own dreams through their children, wanting, and sometimes demanding, that their children reach performance and success levels that the parents may never have been able to achieve. These issues are for the sports psychologist to deal with, not the hypnotist.

ESSENTIALS

Self-hypnosis can be an excellent tool to help you improve your sports performance. You should have the right mental perspective when using it, however. If you feel a lot of anxiety or other stress when trying self-hypnosis, consult a competent sports psychologist.

A sports psychologist may use hypnosis as a tool for the total development of an athlete. It may not be called hypnosis, but it will probably involve guided imagery while in a relaxed state. (Many specialists create their own terms for the techniques they use.) The goal is to teach the athlete how to develop his own self-hypnotic techniques to enhance his performance. The practitioner makes suggestions to the unconscious mind that aid mental training and gives posthypnotic suggestions that trigger positive performance anchors.

Working with Your Natural Abilities

You may be a natural athlete, born to play sports: perhaps you can't even explain how you do what you do. Or you may have to work extremely hard for every little improvement, putting in many more hours of training than a natural athlete and yet never reaching the same performance level. Perhaps you are the type of person who will never be an outstanding athlete because you lack coordination or are too short, too tall, too heavy, or unfit in another way for the sport you are attempting.

Find the Right Sport

To a certain extent your inherited physical and mental traits determine your potential for a particular sport. You may have been born with physical characteristics that are just right for a specific sport. The shape of your skull may give you the excellent side vision that would be a benefit in basketball, or you may have a small body that would be perfect for gymnastics. If you search, you will probably find at least one sport in which you might be competitive.

Even with the right build for a sport, you may have some handicap that would prevent you from being able to participate fully, or there could be something in your mental makeup that prevents you from reaching your physical potential. With patience you should be able to find a sport that is right for both your mental and physical attributes.

Whether you are an active sports enthusiast or someone who occasionally participates in a sport, it is very important to have a physical checkup before engaging in strenuous exercise. It may also be advisable to consult a sports trainer for advice.

Sports come in two categories: team and individual. Many individual sports are labeled "life sports," as they can be enjoyed throughout your lifetime, whatever your performance level. Individual sports can be either competitive or noncompetitive, and include skiing, running, biking, rowing, bowling, and golf. (If you are not competing against someone else, however, you are probably competing against your own past performance.)

Team sports, as a general rule, are most popular with children, teens, and young adults. By age forty fewer people participate in team sports, although better conditioning and better health habits may change this pattern. The real purpose of sports should be to find an outlet for built up energy and stress, and to keep your body in good physical condition.

Your Mental Makeup

Your natural mental makeup is very important in the development of your athletic performance: you may be visual or kinesthetic or have excellent hearing. These senses all play a role in sports, and so, to a lesser degree, do taste and smell. They are important for imagery and to put you in the Zone. Although the senses have been discussed at length in earlier chapters, we will review their relationship to sports applications. Your mind creates images in three different time frames: past memories, the experiences of the present moment, and future situations.

Visual Imagery

Most athletes are visual. They rely on their eyes to provide information so they can respond rapidly and accurately. Winning and losing depends on it. How well do you see? Is your field of vision wide or narrow? How good is your visual imagination? Can you see pictures in your mind with your eyes open, or with them closed?

If you play a sport, can you visualize yourself playing it? Can you watch yourself from different angles or positions? Can you visualize as if you were actually playing the sport rather than watching yourself play? Can you slow down, speed up, stop, or rewind the action? Do you visualize in bright color, dim color, gray, or black and white?

Can you visualize yourself playing your sport in different situations? Can you imagine situations when things are going well in your sport? Can you imagine things not going well? Can you split your visual screen and see the two pictures at once: one where things are going well and one where they aren't?

Tactile and Auditory Imagery

Can you imagine what it feels like to play a sport? Can you feel your muscles move, the grip of a club, a bat, a ball; can you feel the weight of your uniform? Can you imagine when your breathing changes, when your pulse rate quickens, and when you begin to sweat? Can you feel the excitement of the crowd, the highs of victory, and the lows of defeat? Can you imagine the temperature, the wind, and the texture of the playing field or floor? Can you imagine the feeling of your environment: the snow, the track, the water, the grass, the wheel, the speed you are going, or the power of the apparatus you may be riding or driving?

Can you feel the emotions of the crowd or of the other participants in the sport? Can you imagine how you'll feel when you are winning, and when you're loosing? Can you imagine how your opponent feels? Can you experience pushing yourself to your limits, giving all you have?

ESSENTIALS Crowd noise can have a major impact on both teams and individuals playing a sport. In college basketball, fans try to break the concentration of foul shooters by waving towels and yelling. In sports such as golf and tennis, the organizers try to keep the crowds quiet so the athletes can concentrate on the game.

What do you hear when you play your sport in your imagination? Can you hear the sound of the bat hitting the ball, the engine, the blades on the ice, or the skis on the snow? Can you hear the sound of your own voice: are you encouraging yourself to do the best you can or blaming yourself when something doesn't go as well as you planned? Can you hear the voice of your coach praising or criticizing you?

Do hearing and feeling work together in your imagery? When you imagine hearing the crowd, the coach, your teammates, friends, family, or yourself, do you feel pumped up? Do you hear and feel the energy of an opposing team's cheering crowd? Does this drag your energy down? Do you feel excitement when you imagine the sounds involved in your favorite sport? When you imagine yourself in competition, do you hear any sounds at all, or is your focus totally on your game?

Taste and Smell Imagery

Tastes and smells also can be useful when you do self-hypnotic imagery training for your sport. Both senses can put you deeper into the Zone.

Can you imagine any smells involved with your sport? Can you smell the locker room, the equipment, the supplies, the gymnasium, or the out-of-doors? Are there any pleasant smells, unpleasant smells, or smells that energize you? Can you change the smell as you move around in your imagery? Can you intensify or decrease a smell?

Can you imagine any tastes involved with your sport: an energy beverage, chewing gum, or something else you chew? Can you imagine feeling the energy from something nutritious such as fruit or energy bars? Can you also imagine tasting or smelling this nutritious food? Can you taste or smell victory or defeat?

FACTS

Your five senses—sight, hearing, touch, taste, and smell—define your mental sports imagery. They all play a part in preparing you through the use of self-hypnotic imagery. The stronger the image that you have, the more realistic your sports imagery will be.

Self-Hypnotic Imagery Relaxation Exercise

Now that you have assessed your sports imagery in the five senses, it's time to experience a basic self-hypnotic relaxation exercise. You may want to record the following script and listen to it as you experience self-hypnosis. You may also have someone read it to you, or you can memorize it and talk to yourself as you experience the exercise.

Begin the Self-Hypnosis Exercise

When you are ready, find a comfortable place, loosen your clothes, take a deep breath, and exhale slowly. Do this a couple more times, just as you do when you prepare to concentrate on playing your favorite sport. You will always be aware of other things, such as the sounds around you, when you experience self-hypnosis. You can always open your eyes or move about whenever you want to end your trance. As you breathe in and out, you may allow your eyes to go out of focus and the muscles in your body to relax.

If a muscle stiffens up, you may relax it and go deeper into your trance. In a few moments you will begin to count backward from five to zero. You may suggest to yourself that with each number you will go deeper and deeper into your trance. You may also suggest that when you reach zero, you may mentally experience participating in your favorite sport. You may relive a positive experience from your memory, or you can imagine participating in a future event.

When you get to zero, you may experience imagery with all five senses. It will be as if the experience is live. You may feel your muscles move, hear the crowd, clearly see the image, and experience any smells or tastes that belong to the image. You may experience all the emotions, visualizing the brightest pictures.

Count Down

When you are ready, begin slowly counting down to zero.

- **FIVE.** After each number, suggest to yourself that you are going deeper and deeper into self-hypnosis. Breathe in and out slowly, relaxing and going deeper.
- **FOUR.** You may feel yourself relaxing more and more, and looking forward to reaching zero where you can enjoy imaging your favorite sport.
- **THREE.** You are feeling calm and relaxed, going deeper and looking forward to experiencing your favorite sport. You may feel yourself beginning to enter the focus of the sports Zone.
- **TWO.** You are getting closer and closer to entering the sports Zone.
- **ONE.** You are almost there. You may go deeper and deeper. You look forward to experiencing your sport, and you prepare to be in the Zone, where you are very aware of all five of your senses. Now prepare to enter your sports Zone as you reach zero.
- **ZERO.**

Experience the Zone Imagery

Now that you have reached zero, you may experience a special situation in your sport. You may see the visual imagery in bright colors as you hear the sounds. You may feel the adrenaline start to build in your body as you prepare to participate in your favorite sport. Focus in on one image. What do you see, what do you hear, what do you feel, what do you taste, and what do you smell?

Take as long as you want, and enjoy the experience of playing your favorite sport. You may stop the action at any time, or rewind it and play it again. You may visualize it from different angles, up close, and at a distance. You may watch yourself as if you were on video, or you may experience your sport firsthand. This will be a positive and relaxing experience for you, as you enjoy playing your favorite sport.

When you are ready, you may slowly count yourself back up from zero to five, feeling very relaxed and positive about your experience in self-hypnotic sports visualization. You may give yourself a key word, a phrase, or a physical touch that will help you find the Zone automatically anytime that you would like to. You may now count yourself back up to the surface, suggesting to yourself that you will feel calm, relaxed, and refreshed.

ESSENTIALS

Mental training is used in many different sports. In shooting, rifle team members practice entire 400-shot matches in their minds. Mentally, they perform every movement of each shot as they actually would during a match, including the scoring. The process can take a couple of hours.

How was this experience for you? Were you able to experience the hypnotic suggestions? Could you see, hear, feel, taste, and smell your sports image? Which was your strongest sense? Which was the weakest? The way you image through your senses is different than anyone else's, and now you are beginning to understand and become comfortable with the way your own mental imagery works.

Self-Hypnosis Mental Training Model

Now that you have experienced a sports relaxation exercise, it is time to learn how to use self-hypnosis to help with your mental training. Just as in most hypnosis applications, you will build positive and negative models of what works and what doesn't work for you in your sport. You may be able to understand how to improve your athletic ability by comparing the two models at once. If you are ready, find a comfortable place, loosen your clothing, and prepare to begin.

Building Models

Take a deep breath, exhale, and let your eyes go out of focus. Suggest to yourself that when you get to zero, you will be able to image in all your senses. As you continue to breath slowly in and out, count yourself down from five to zero, allowing yourself to relax more and more, and go deeper and deeper with each number. You may go into your athletic Zone when you reach zero. You may count down at a speed that is relaxing and comfortable for you.

When you reach zero, choose a sport in which you want to improve, and see or experience yourself performing an action from the sport very well. Focus in on your muscle movements, on the internal and external feelings you have, and on any sounds that go with the experience. Watch yourself if you can, and then experience the inner feeling of what you visualized. You may repeat the visualization several times if you wish. If there are any tastes or smells involved in your image, you may experience them, too.

When you have thoroughly reviewed this image, choose a similar action that you do not do as well. Focus in on your muscle movement, on your internal and external feelings, and on any sounds that go with the experience. Watch yourself in the activity, and then experience that you are actually doing it. Replay the image as many times as required to get a clear concept of what didn't work for you. You may also imagine tastes and smells that are a part of this image.

Compare Models

Now split your visual image screen, and see if you can run the negative and positive models at once. While you run your two models, compare the differences. Take your time, stopping the movement if necessary, and compare as many details as possible. Run the negative and positive together or separately, as many times as needed.

Can you see any difference between the two? Which parts of both images are the same, and which parts are different? What feels the same and what feels different in the images? Can you feel and see yourself doing something wrong in the image that doesn't work? Make sure you examine each image from just before the action starts to just after it ends.

Compare your emotional feelings and energy. In the two images, was there a difference in the location or in other physical conditions; was there a difference in the crowd, in the temperature, or in the climate? Was there a difference in sound, taste, or smell? Compile as much information about your comparisons as possible. How did your feelings change after you finished comparing these two models?

Build a Mental Practice Model

If you now have a good comparison showing what you are doing right and wrong in your sport, imagine a new, positive model in your mind. Run the new image several times, experiencing it in as many of your senses as you can. Feel your muscles responding correctly with each move you make during this sports imagery.

ESSENTIALS

Golf is a good example of a sport where mental corrections are made right on the spot. When a golfer hits a shot that doesn't meet his expectations, he often stands in the same place, swings his club, and mentally erases the previous shot. This serves to correct the image in the golfer's mind, preparing him for the next time he faces a similar situation.

Now go back to the image that didn't work well, and experience correcting the things that were wrong. Feel and watch the corrections. Use as many of your senses as you can to experience the changes. Run this change model as many times as you want, stopping it or slowing it down whenever you need to.

Now run a series of images of similar plays with various scenarios. Change the factors: the conditions, the crowd, the sounds, the emotions, the opponents, or anything else that may apply to your sport. Each time you run your imagery, practice making corrections so that you experience responding correctly to a variety of conditions. The more you practice making corrections in your mind, the more automatic it will become when you are actually playing your sport.

Make a Habit of Mental Training

Now that you have learned how to build a mental training model by identifying and making corrections in your sport, pick a time each day when you can use self-hypnosis for mental practice. You may wish to practice during your normal training schedule, if you have one, or you may practice at another time. Even if you are a "weekend warrior" or if you just play occasionally, you can still train mentally on a regular basis.

Establish Your Habit

Establish a time each day, or several days a week, where you can devote half an hour or more to practicing mental sports imagery. Look for any resistance that may sabotage your sports imagery training: friends or family, business, or even your own energy or mood. If you are taking time away from others, they may feel you are shutting them out. The more you make them feel a part of your mental training, the more they may encourage you to practice self-hypnosis. You may want to make yourself a tape or memorize a script to help you reach a good trance level.

Find a comfortable place with as little outside interference as possible. Loosen your clothes, take a deep breath of air, exhale slowly, and let your eyes go out of focus, relaxing more and more with each breath. You may let your muscles relax, and when you're ready, let your eyes close and slowly count yourself down from five to zero. Suggest to yourself that when you reach zero, you will be able to experience your sports mental training image with all five senses, creating as strong an image as possible. Your imagery may be a little different each time you practice, and you can always make corrections and change the images anytime you want.

You may suggest that you look forward to experiencing this imagery. Anytime you feel the need, you may always open your eyes or move your body and end your mental training trance. You may practice the same situation several times, or you may run different images. As you practice, visualize the scene, feel your muscles responding, hear positive sounds of encouragement, and taste and smell the experience of working to the best of your sports potential.

Develop Zone Anchors

Now imagine yourself responding to your mental training when you are actually participating in your sport. Give yourself a mental or physical anchor that helps you enter a sports Zone trance when you're ready to play. Imagine yourself using this anchor, and feel the experience of focusing and performing as you did during mental practice. Suggest to yourself that anytime you play your sport, you will be prepared to respond in many different situations to the best of your potential.

FACTS

Athletes use physical and mental anchors all the time to help them get into the Zone. In baseball, each batter has a ritual of movements he uses before approaching the plate. The foul shooter in basketball often takes a deep breath and exhales or dribbles the basketball a certain number of times.

Now suggest to yourself that when you are playing your sport, you will always be prepared to respond at your highest potential. Practice triggering your anchors by feeling the words or actions you use when you are preparing to play your sport. Practice this several times in your mind.

Suggest to yourself that after you have counted yourself back up from zero to the surface of your conscious mind, you will automatically respond to your positive sports anchors. Suggest that when you use your triggers, you will go into your athletic Zone, very aware of everything you need to do to work to your highest potential. Suggest that you will be able to focus on the positive things you need to do to reach your potential, and when you're ready, count yourself back up to the surface of your mind from zero to five.

In the Sports Zone

Now when you are preparing to participate in your sport physically, remember to trigger your self-hypnotic anchors. Feel yourself going into hyper-focus, totally aware of everything that helps you reach your athletic potential. Be prepared to make corrections if something is out of balance or is different than expected.

The more you suggest to yourself that you enjoy participating in your sport, not only for yourself but for others, the greater your opportunity will be to reach your maximum potential. When you believe in the positive side of sports, this can be reflected in many other aspects of your life: it can benefit your relationships and your career. The right amount of athletic activity, coupled with mental and spiritual activity, can keep you in tune and fit for your life's journey.

CHAPTER 13

Developing Your Creative Abilities

In this chapter you will learn to recognize your creative potential by assessing your creative imagery in all five senses. You will identify your natural creative strengths and weaknesses, find out how to use self-hypnosis to determine creative goals and establish anchors that help trigger creative trances, and examine the connection between creativity and the unconscious and universal minds.

Creativity: A Gift or a Curse?

Natural talent is as much a curse as it is a gift. You probably know someone who is a natural musician or a self-trained artist or a gifted writer, but who does very little with her talent. You may wish that some of her talent had been given to you. The naturally gifted person rarely sees her own talent as others see it. For her there is nothing special in what she does, and she may not value her abilities very highly.

FACTS

A closet musician is someone who learned to play without lessons, and who does not consider what he does good enough to share with others. When he is alone, he finds great enjoyment and stress release playing his music, but the moment he thinks someone is listening, he stops playing, very embarrassed at being overheard. He has little confidence in his ability.

What Are Your Talents?

Do you consider yourself to have natural artistic talents? Have you worked hard to perfect the ability to do a craft or to perform? Sometimes a person will spend years developing an artistic talent, only to see someone else, who has put very little effort into developing this ability, receive recognition and praise.

Natural Talents

Do you have at least one natural artistic talent? You might have more talent than you think. Do other people tell you that you have superior abilities? If so, are these in areas where you do not consider yourself above average? Do you wish that your friends or family wouldn't try to push or manipulate you into doing something creative that you are not interested in?

Do you feel that you are not being recognized for a talent that you do have? Do you get frustrated easily when you try to perform with others or teach? When you start out at a similar level of ability as someone else, do you soon get way ahead and become bored by the pace?

Do you get frustrated at trying to explain what your creative work is all about? Do you feel you know things others don't know, and although you try to explain, they never understand? Do you wish you lived during a different time when things weren't as modern, and do you use older methods and techniques to create your art whenever you can? Do you have a love-hate relationship with your creative self; do you sometimes find that what you once enjoyed doing has become mentally painful?

Do you hope to discover in yourself a natural talent that has remained dormant? Do you feel deep down inside that you *do* have a natural talent, but you have always been afraid of taking the risk of developing it? Have you always wanted to do something creative, but family members or friends blocked or discouraged you? Do you have a passion to bare your soul by doing something creative? If you answer yes to any of these questions, you may have a natural-born creative talent waiting to break through.

Developed Talents

Do you try to do something creative that is not natural to you? Have you spent countless hours practicing and training hard to make up for a lack of natural talent? Did you ever work hard to accomplish something creative, and when you finished you weren't sure how you did it? By some miracle it worked out, but you knew you were fooling people because you really didn't know what you were doing.

When working on your talent, have you often felt stiff or awkward with the results? Have you ever watched or listened to someone perform who knew all the notes or moves, but who lacked emotion? The results may have seemed mechanical and stiff or may have been unpleasant and even painful.

Have you had a parent, teacher, or coach who expected you to duplicate his or her directions exactly when doing something creative? Did you get frustrated at not being able to meet your mentor's expectations? Many teachers and coaches teach creativity in a mechanical way, which can block the student's creative ability. The key is to identify what you do well and use that as a model to help build confidence in your creative gifts. Everyone is born with a natural creative gift of some type, and now it's time to examine your natural-born talents.

Your Creative Strengths

Your five senses are very important to the way your creative gifts have been shaped. Your mental makeup is different from everyone else's, and so is your creative talent. The first step in developing your creative talent is to become comfortable with what you *can* do instead of what you *can't* do. Finding your comfort zone is the beginning of getting in tune with your creative gifts.

Visual Creativity

Do you imagine in pictures? Are they in color or black and white? Can you hold a picture in your mind and examine different sections, as you might do with a photograph or a painting? Could you project a picture from your mind onto a piece of paper and trace around the outline? If you can do any of these things, try sketching something that you visualize in your mind.

Can you look at a person or an object and hold the image in your mind after you look away? Can you paint or sketch that image? When you see a color or a shadow, can you see many different shades of color in it? Can you imagine yourself in a picture in your mind? Could you sketch yourself?

Do you see energies or auras when you look at things or people? Can you imagine pictures in your mind from a different time period, past or future? Can you look at a piece of wood or stone or even an undeveloped landscape and see what could be created from it? Can you imagine a piece of fabric as a completed sewing project? Do you use your visual sense in any other way that might help you be more creative?

Have you ever dreamed an idea for creating something artistic? Do you enjoy decorating, or creating appetizing and colorful meals? Can you imagine stories in your mind that unfold like a motion picture? Have you ever done something creative but can't remember actually doing it? Can you change a visual image in your mind and reproduce it on paper?

Auditory Creativity

Can you imagine sounds, voices, or music in your head? Can you reproduce sounds that you hear in your mind or in reality? If you can, is your pitch accurate? Can you hear a song in your mind and reproduce it perfectly, vocally or on an instrument? If you play a musical instrument, can you play by ear?

Are you more sensitive to out-of-tune music than other people? If you play an instrument, was it hard for you to learn to read music? If this is the case, your ear may have been trying to overrule what you read. Can you both read music and play by ear? Have you ever tried composing music?

Can you imagine a story taking place in your mind that includes voices or other sounds? Can you visualize and hear the story at the same time? Can you write it down? If the information comes too fast, can you slow it down or rerun the action and dialogue? Do you enjoy writing poetry or letters, or do you keep a diary? Have you ever dreamed story plots, and if so, have you written them down?

If you push a child to develop a talent before he is ready, he may rebel when he gets older and never reach his creative potential. A slow, steady progress at a comfortable pace could help him continue to grow.

Emotional Creativity

If you can create stories in your mind, do you experience any emotions connected with them? If you imagine several characters in your story, can you experience the emotions of each one? Can you imagine what it would feel like to become one of the characters, experiencing his thoughts and emotions? Do you enjoy acting out or imagining what it would be like to be a certain person, real or made up?

Can you imagine what it would feel like to live in a different time or in a different culture? Can you imagine the emotions of animals, either wild or domestic? Can you imagine and describe the feeling of different textures and temperatures? Could you imagine how you'd look wearing different items of clothing and then describe how each one feels?

Do you like to work with your hands? Can you imagine a picture in your mind and then build it or create a model of it? Do you enjoy making crafts, knitting, or sewing? Do you use ready-made plans, create your own, or combine the two? Do you feel relaxed when you use your hands to do something creative? When you work with your hands, do you get lost in time?

If you play music, do you feel the emotion or the soul of what you are performing? When you are acting, dancing, or reciting poetry, do you feel the emotion of the work you are performing? Do you sometimes feel that the music has taken you over, and you are not controlling the performance? When you have completed a creative act, do you feel emotionally exhilarated or drained? Do you feel so passionate when you are involved with your creative outlet that you begin to find the experience overwhelming and painful?

Creativity in Taste and Smell

When you imagine a picture in your mind, can you also experience the smells or tastes? Could you move around the picture describing the different smells or tastes? Can you compare tastes or smells with different sense images, such as sounds, feelings, or colors? Can you imagine a picture or story from a different time and describe what the foods taste and smell like?

Can you imagine a motion picture in your mind and experience the tastes and smells that go with it? Could you describe them as you write the story down? Can you imagine and describe the smells of certain scenes, animals, or people? If you paint, can you imagine the smell of the paint thinner or linseed oil?

Can you create a recipe in your mind, experiencing what the taste will be like as you blend certain ingredients? As you create this recipe, can you imagine what it will smell like? Can you use all your senses to imagine creating a meal, experiencing the sights, sounds, emotions, texture, tastes, and smells? Can you prepare the meal in reality the same way as you imagined it in your mind?

Can smells or tastes help you to imagine stories or pictures in your mind? Could you imagine emotions that are related to smells and tastes, and then describe them accurately so that others might experience them? Do you find that certain smells or tastes can help put you in a creative mood? Do you have any other creative interests that you relate to taste, smell, or any of the other senses?

Your Creative Weaknesses

Were you able to image creatively in one or more of the five senses? It is best to identify your more creative senses before looking at those that are not as strong. Working with what you know and do naturally provides the comfort of being assured that you *can* accomplish something creative. When you expand your creative comfort zone, you can draw on the knowledge and ability you already have.

ESSENTIALS

A weakness cannot weaken you if you use a strength instead. The goal of this chapter is for you to get comfortable creating something that is artistic and enjoyable, to satisfy both yourself and other people who come in contact with your work. Give yourself permission to do the best you can.

Which of the senses did not produce strong imagery in your mind? Can you visualize well? If not, then your strengths may be in sounds or feelings. Is your ability to image with sound strong or weak? Are you interested in musical activities, either vocal or instrumental, or do you have a poor ability to reproduce sounds? Do you draw on emotions when you are creative, or do you attempt to do everything mechanically or scientifically?

Are you comfortable in front of people, or do you prefer to be in the background? Are your senses of smell and taste good or poor? Do you imagine stories in your mind, or do you prefer to be active rather than absorbed in thought? Do you like to imagine? Are there creative situations in which you never seem to be able to do what others can do?

Develop Your Creative Gifts

You may already excel in one or more creative area. You may be looking to find a creative outlet for yourself. Whatever your level of development, if you want your natural abilities to grow, you must cultivate them. Sadly, many people with natural creative gifts never give themselves the opportunity to reach their potential. To develop that potential, your mind, body, and soul need to be in tune with your three minds: conscious, unconscious, and universal consciousness.

Choose Your Creative Outlet

Even if you don't consciously know what your creative gifts are and how they can be used, your unconscious mind may already know. Self-hypnosis can help you communicate with your intuitive, unconscious mind. To experience self-hypnosis, find a comfortable position, loosen your clothing, take a deep breath, exhale, and let your eyes go out of focus. Let the muscles in your body relax, close your eyes, and in a moment count slowly down from five to zero. Suggest to yourself that when you reach zero, you will feel calm and relaxed, and you will let your unconscious mind evaluate the creative gifts you have been given, so you can understand how they may be developed and shared.

QUESTIONS?

How can I find my natural creative ability?
Take note of the creative activities that you do automatically. Maybe you doodle, sketch, hum, whistle, drum with your fingers, imagine stories, write letters or poetry, arrange flowers or furniture, study people, cook, or surround yourself with healing smells. These are all natural creative abilities.

Suggest that you will go deeper and deeper into hypnosis with each count. When you reach zero, allow yourself to feel calm, relaxed, and open to your unconscious mind's communication. Suggest that even after you count back up to the surface of your mind, you will remain open to the messages from your unconscious mind. When you're ready, count yourself back up to five, then take a deep breath, open your eyes, and feel comfortable and relaxed. Now allow yourself to be open to the creativity of your unconscious mind.

You may try self-hypnosis just before going to sleep, and suggest that when you wake up, you will have answers about how to develop and share your creative gifts. You can also call on your belief system for help. Suggest that when you are in your trance, the universal mind will provide inspiration and direction about how to develop and share your creative gifts. Tell yourself that you will always be on the lookout for the universal mind's directions. Once you start asking your belief system for guidance, answers can come from anywhere, such as a conversation with a friend or even a chance meeting with someone you don't know.

ESSENTIALS

When you are thinking about or immersed in a creative project, always have a means of capturing the ideas that pop out of your unconscious mind. Keep a pad of notepaper, a sketchbook, or a tape recorder near you at all times, even after you have gone to bed at night.

Self-hypnosis works hand in hand with your belief system. The more you use your trance to ask for help and guidance, the more you will be amazed at what materializes around you to help you find your direction. As you have previously learned, you develop a habit by constant repetition of an action. Instant self-hypnotic anchors can help you develop the habit of constantly being in touch with the unconscious and universal minds. The more you are open to this communication, the easier it will be to stay in tune with your creative gifts.

Set Your Goals

Once you know the kind of creative ability you want to develop, it is time to set goals to help it grow. Start with small, realistic, and reachable goals. The first step is to practice self-hypnosis to create a communication link with all three of your minds. Next investigate how to begin to nurture your creativity. You may want to check the Internet, read a book, take a class, or join a group of like-minded individuals.

What materials do you need to get started? What will it cost to begin and sustain your development? Can you afford to spend what you need to develop your creative abilities? If not, you may seek financial aid or scholarships, or investigate bartering or trading work for your studies. The more you can believe that your creative gifts are meant to be shared, the more you will be open to the miracles that can make it happen.

When you make a commitment to develop your creative talent, it is possible that friends or family may feel left out. It does take time and hard work to strive toward your goal, so make your journey easier by asking for permission from others and keeping them up-to-date on your quest. To establish your creative habit, you will need time, space, and a regular routine. You will need patience and an understanding that the creative flow is never quite the same from one day to the next. Through self-hypnosis, suggest to yourself that you will have a positive and unique experience every time you are open to your creative gifts.

Where Does Creativity Come From?

Where does your creative talent come from? If it comes from your unconscious mind, is the process of creativity actually a form of trance? Many times an artist will paint a picture or a writer write a story, and he will have no memory of actually doing the work. The greatest work often seems to come at a low or vulnerable point in an artist's life, when his conscious mind is in a state of confusion. At that point his soul seems to open up, and he is caught up in the creative flow until something interrupts or the work is finished.

Now the artist has a beautiful, creative work, but he may not be sure how it was accomplished. The great dilemma is, can he create another work? Can he really take credit for something he doesn't remember doing? His ego cries out for recognition, and he may feel his work has great value. This dilemma can manifest itself in an artistic block that can last until the artist reaches another low point in his life, when he becomes open to the unconscious flow again.

If creativity is, in fact, a self-hypnotic trance, why not use hypnosis all the time instead of waiting until you are at a low point? The more you use self-hypnosis to suggest to yourself that you will be open to the unconscious mind to help you create, the more automatic your creative flow will become. You may want to develop a routine of self-hypnosis before attempting any creative project.

FACTS

Some of the world's greatest artists had physical or mental conditions that gave them a different view of the world than most people have. As a result they developed unique styles that set their work apart. Painter Edgar Degas had myopia; Claude Monet had cataracts; and van Gogh suffered from depression.

The universal mind is the other major factor involved in creativity. When you are in a self-hypnotic trance, you might suggest to your belief system that ideas and enhanced creative abilities be sent to you for the purpose of inspiring others. The more you recognize that you, personally, are only part of your creativity, the easier it will be to accept help from the universal mind. When you count yourself down to zero, you might ask the universal mind for the right guidance, ideas, or visions to help in whatever creative project you are doing. When your project comes together in ways that you can't explain, it's a miracle—and miracles can become part of your creative work.

Enhance Your Creativity

Now it is time to create self-hypnotic anchors to help you reach and use your creative trance. To establish your anchor, find a comfortable place, loosen your clothing, take a deep breath, exhale, and let your eyes go out of focus. Let your muscles relax and your eyes close, and slowly begin counting down from five to zero. Suggest to yourself that when you reach zero, you will be calm, relaxed, and in touch with your unconscious and universal creative minds. Suggest that you will be open to the information and inspiration that is needed to let your creative self work to the best of its abilities.

The creative hypnotic trance can be hazardous to your health. Many gifted artists enter a self-induced trance when they are involved in a creative project. They may remain there until the project is finished or until they are forced to stop because they have failed to pay attention to their health or other life conditions.

Self-Hypnotic Creative Anchors

Once you reach zero and are in touch with your unconscious mind and universal mind, suggest to yourself that you will be able to use a special word, touch, or feeling to put yourself instantly back in touch with these creative minds. Select your anchor and practice it several times while in your trance, feeling it getting stronger and stronger. Also give yourself a posthypnotic suggestion that every time you begin a creative activity, you will automatically be in touch with your unconscious and universal conscious minds. Suggest to yourself that you will automatically enter a creative trance by triggering your creative anchor.

When you're ready, count yourself back up to the surface of your mind, feeling relaxed and positive. Once you have emerged from your trance, trigger your anchor and experience the connection with your creative minds. Select a time each day when you can practice self-hypnosis to reinforce your creative suggestions and anchors.

You might do this exercise after going to bed at night, suggesting that your minds will communicate creative ideas while you sleep. Always be ready to capture the creative inspiration when it rises to the surface. The more you give yourself permission to remain open to and accept the guidance and creativity of your unconscious and universal minds, the more you will become aware of this communication.

How to Begin the Creative Process

1. Determine your creative goal.
2. Define your creative goal's purpose for you and others.
3. Develop an action plan to reach your creative goal.
4. Determine a series of small goals that you can easily achieve on your way to the big goal.
5. Determine what your creative goal will cost in education and materials.
6. Determine when and where you will create.
7. Have patience and flexibility as you work toward your creative goal.

Strike a Balance

It is very easy to develop a love-hate relationship with your creative gifts. Even with the use of self-hypnosis, the creative flow can't be expected to run like tap water. Each time you open the faucet in your mind, the flow is different. Sometimes it runs so fast that it is impossible to capture all the information, and at other times it is only a slow drip. Either way, it is important for you to retain a proper balance between your three minds and your mental, physical, and spiritual self.

Receiving creative energy from the universe is like acting in a play. Once the curtain falls, the actors go back to their regular lives, and once the creative trance has ended, it is good for you to step back into a normal life. It is good for your creative self to eat right, exercise regularly, and stay in touch with your beliefs.

The first step in beginning your creative journey is to establish a daily time for self-hypnosis. The very soul of your creative ability waits under the surface of your conscious mind, ready to flow up through your unconscious and universal minds. Your creativity originates from the center of the universe, and it brings something to your conscious reality that is beyond normal, everyday human experience. It is there, waiting to be tapped when you are ready.

SSENTIALS

Whenever you are involved in a creative project that takes time away from friends or family, always let them feel they are helping you with the project somehow. Keep them informed and thank them for their support, even when they don't seem to be supporting you as you'd like.

CHAPTER 14

Becoming a Better Student

In this chapter you will examine the changing role of education in today's world and understand your natural mode of learning through the five senses. You will identify your ideal learning situations; look at the role of the parent, teacher, and student in establishing a positive and productive learning trance; and finally, you will experience a self-hypnotic trance to help you with your learning skills.

How Do You Know What You Know?

How is it that some students figure out how to learn while others lose confidence in their abilities? If you apply the concepts used in self-hypnosis to learning, you can assess your abilities as a student by looking at how you learn and recall information through the five senses. Begin by identifying your comfortable learning zone. You'll come to understand your level of knowledge and also how you naturally assemble and recall knowledge.

Motivational Learning

When you are doing something you enjoy, you are more apt to apply yourself. When you see no reason to learn certain information, you will be less likely to learn it. You also need to have a positive learning environment. Even if you are motivated, it may not be possible for you to learn because something or someone interrupts your focus. Sometimes you may be thrown off by your own sensitivity.

ALERT

If a student has behavioral problems, is constantly forgetful or disorganized, cannot stay focused, and has low self-esteem, she may have a neurological disorder such as ADD/ADHD. If you feel this might be the case, consult your child's doctor.

If you are working with a student, pick a nonthreatening environment and a subject that he is interested in, and help him to share how he learns. When you communicate with the student on a comfortable level, you lay the groundwork for establishing future self-hypnotic anchors that can create learning trances. You can ask yourself or a student the following questions to assess how information is learned and recalled. The questions are directed toward any subject that you or the student may be interested in. You may change or add questions as necessary.

- What do you enjoy doing, and how did you learn to do it?
- When you do something you like, how and why do you enjoy it?

- Can you describe how you do what you do?
- Why did you learn to do it?
- Is it fun to do it, and has the level of enjoyment been the same or has it grown or diminished since you began?
- Do you enjoy talking about it, teaching about it, or demonstrating it to other people?
- Can you remember how you began and how you have progressed?
- What else do you enjoy doing?

Visual Learning

When you choose to learn something, how much do you rely on your visual sense? Do you learn by watching, or do you use actual or mental pictures? Can you store visual images in your mind and recall them when you want to? In other words, if you learn through watching or picturing in your mind, can you accurately remember what you saw? Can you describe, either orally or in writing, what you can picture in your mind?

Can you picture the image in your mind and move around in it, gathering information? Can you see it from different angles? Can you see yourself in the image? Do you see it in color, black and white, or gray tones? Is the picture in your mind clear or fuzzy?

Do you remember information through pictures in your mind? Can you read a description of something and create a picture of it in your mind? Can you picture what someone else describes? Can you remember what you read or what someone else describes by recalling a picture in your mind? How much do you rely on pictures in your mind to recall information?

Auditory Learning

Do you remember by recalling sounds or conversations that took place around a certain situation? Can you listen to something mechanical, like an engine, and tell what its working condition is? Do you hold conversations in your mind to help yourself recall information? Can you remember a relaxing sound that helps you feel calm? Can you mentally change the volume of sounds, making them louder or softer?

When you study, can you concentrate if there is music playing or other sounds in the background? Do you learn better with music or other sounds as part of the background? Are there certain styles or tempos of music that help you to focus on your learning? If you hum or sing to yourself when you study, can you recall the information you were studying when you remember the tune you were humming as you learned it?

ESSENTIALS

Some attention problems, especially those in a young student, may be caused by a sensory overload. If a student has extremely good hearing, the smallest sound can break her focus. Sensory overload can be experienced in any of the five senses. You may be able to teach the student to tune out the overload.

Is it easier for you to concentrate when things around you are quiet? Do you play music or sing? If you do, how do you remember music? Do you prefer loud or soft sounds? How else does your hearing help you learn and remember information?

Kinesthetic Learning

Do you enjoy being active when you learn? Do you move your body or wiggle your fingers or feet? When you are listening, do you like to doodle, move your hands, play with your fingers, or make other movements? Is there something in particular that you like to hold in your hands when you are learning? Do you like to tap your feet or wiggle your fingers to music when you are learning?

Is it easier for you to learn something when you get hands-on experience? If so, how do you remember the information? Do you remember by recalling what something feels like? Would you rather learn in an informal setting or a formal classroom? Would you rather learn outdoors or inside?

Do you learn better in certain moods? Can you create a learning mood in yourself? Do you enjoy learning by yourself or with others? If you learn better in a group, how do you remember the information you learned at that time? Are there any other feelings that help you learn?

Learning Through Smell and Taste

When you learn, do you like to be surrounded by special smells? Do you burn incense or candles when you study? Does the smell of food help you study? Do certain places where you study have smells that help you feel comfortable and make it easier to learn? If smell is important to your learning process, can you remember a smell that helps you recall information?

Is it easier to learn when you are enjoying food, drink, or gum? There may be a special food you enjoy eating while studying. Can you recall information when you remember a certain taste? Can you think of any other situation where taste is important to you for learning and recalling information?

Do you ever combine the senses of taste and smell to create a positive learning environment? Can you think of combinations of tastes and smells and remember information that you have learned? Do you combine tastes and smells with any of your other senses to recall information? If so, what are they?

Learning Environment

The proper learning environment can make the difference between a good student and a poor student. Your optimal environment might be in a classroom or it could be at home. You may be comfortable in class and unable to focus at home, or the situation could be reversed.

What Makes It Difficult to Learn?

Where is it the most difficult for you to learn—at school, at home, or someplace else? Why is it hard for you to learn there? Is it the physical location, is it the time of day or night, or is the problem with the teacher or other students? Is it hard for you to focus because of something that you see, hear, feel, taste, or smell? What other things make it hard for you to learn there?

Is it the subject you are studying that makes it hard to learn? If it was something you really liked, could you learn it in that location? Do you focus for a certain amount of time, and then lose focus? If so, what makes you lose your concentration? Is it the way you are studying that stops you from learning?

Would it be easier to study the same subject if it were presented to you differently? If so, what would be the best way? If you could change your learning environment, how would you do it? In your life, have your learning experiences been mostly negative or mostly positive?

What Makes It Easy to Learn?

Where is it easy for you to learn? What helps you focus—is it the place, the time, the teacher, or something else? Does a positive learning environment rely on something visual, on sounds or silence, or on the right feel, taste, or smell? Can you remember and feel what it is like to be in your most comfortable learning environment? Can you picture it?

Are there subjects that seem to be easier to learn than others? What teaching methods make a subject easy to learn for you? Which most facilitates your learning—reading about a subject, hands-on experience, watching a video, listening to a lecture, or watching a demonstration by the teacher or other class members? Are you more comfortable learning by yourself or in a group?

ESSENTIALS

Try to figure out what would be your most comfortable learning environment. Can you describe this place? What does it need to have for you to see it as comfortable?

Do you enjoy listening to music or other sounds when you study? Do you enjoy having the freedom to move about, or do you like a more controlled environment? Is there a subject that you lose yourself in when you study? Have you ever focused so hard that you didn't hear others talking to you?

Compare What Works and What Doesn't

Now compare environments where you enjoy studying or learning and where you do not. Is the difference in the physical location, or does it involve different situations within the same location? Does the difference involve visual factors, such as lighting, decorations, or views? Is there a difference in sound between the locations; does one have more noise or louder music? Is there a difference in feelings or emotions, in smells, or even in tastes?

If the difference is not in the physical location, what is different about times when you can focus on learning and times when it is difficult? Is it the subject matter? Is it the way the subject is taught? Is it a personality clash with the teacher or with other students? Do you bring something with you, mentally or physically, that changes your focus?

Do you learn better by listening to a lecture, by watching something on television or a video, by reading about it, or by hands-on experience? Do you hear well? Is there a physical or mental issue that keeps you from focusing on learning? If so, what could be done to improve the situation? Could you explain to yourself or to someone else, through writing, pictures, or speaking, your best way of learning, the type of subjects you learn best, and the location or situation that is best for your learning focus?

The Parent's Role in Learning

Education begins in the home. The more you as a parent take an active role and offer positive support in your child's learning, the greater the possibility that the child will reach her potential in life.

Parents of gifted and talented children seek out private teachers, private schools, or advanced classes to challenge and inspire their children to higher levels of learning or artistic or athletic achievements. The parents of educationally challenged students or "slow learners" often see more in their children than the education system does. They become advocates for their children, seeking out all available help from the education system and elsewhere.

The more you focus on what is right with your child's learning, the more confidence the child will have to take risks and learn more. When you realize that each one of your children is unique, having been born with something special that may help someone in the world, the process of helping your child learn becomes like providing water and nutrients to a flower. Imagine what it would be like if a flower were never nourished and watered.

ESSENTIALS If you as a parent are willing to take the time to find out how each of your children learns, and if you address some of the questions asked in this chapter or by other types of assessments, you can help your child achieve her highest potential. You may also become the student, and learn more about yourself through your children.

The positive learning experience can start in early childhood, when you are your child's teacher. The more love and encouragement you show the child from the moment of birth, the more confidence the child will have in learning as she grows. A young child can absorb and carry negative feelings throughout her life. If you have not read the chapter on phobias, you may want to refer to hypnotic regressions discussed there for help in ridding your home of negative feelings.

The Teacher's Role in Learning

If you are a teacher, your role in helping the student become confident about learning is extremely important. If you take the time to learn how each student's mind works, you will have a better opportunity to promote a positive learning atmosphere.

When you understand the student's mental makeup and positive learning model, you may be able to develop a learning program that will help him become more confident in his learning potential. Confidence is the necessary foundation for beginning to create a learning trance. Without confidence, a negative, nonlearning trance can just as easily be established. By establishing positive learning anchors for the student, you can help trigger productive learning trances.

When a student arrives at a learning experience, he may already be in a negative trance, induced by himself or by someone else. Many things in the environment can affect him, and what he carries with him can disrupt both himself and the other students. Self-hypnosis can help re-establish the connection between the conscious, unconscious, and universal minds, which promotes positive attitudes and confidence in a productive learning experience. Taking a few moments to get centered at the beginning of a learning experience can help create a positive learning trance. If you are both the student and the teacher, remember to communicate with yourself in the same way as you would encourage others to learn.

As a parent or teacher you should always watch for changes in a student's learning patterns, such as lack of focus, a drop in performance, or a personality change. You may need professional guidance to discover the underlying reason for such a change.

The Student's Role in Learning

When a child is old enough to talk, she may tell her parents things that seem to make no sense. She may have imaginary friends, or she may talk about another period of time as if she had been there. She may see, hear, feel, taste, and smell things that others do not experience at all. Well-intentioned parents may tell her that her experiences are not real and encourage her to forget about them. But when the child stops sharing, she loses a very important facet of her learning ability.

A child can get remarkable images in dreams, which sometimes unfold as nightmares. To the child, all experiences in dreams, whether coming from actual memory or the imagination, are real. When no one else believes her, the child may stop believing in herself. The more you take time to listen to your child's stories, the more you learn about her. The more the child develops confidence in the imaginative ability of her unconscious and universal mind, the more she may be open to the amazing knowledge of the universe.

The sooner a student begins to understand her role in her own learning experience, the sooner she can communicate, to parents, teachers, and herself, what she needs for optimal learning. If she is nonvisual and she knows it, she can avoid a completely visual learning experience, which could be very frustrating to her. When a student understands what her mind can do and what it cannot do, a more positive learning partnership is possible.

ESSENTIALS

Most young children will not be able to focus long enough to have a productive experience in standard hypnosis, so the use of imagery can be an effective way to help them. They usually have excellent imaginations, and suggestions for positive improvements can be created through storytelling.

When you, as a student, are aware of how you use your senses to learn and remember information, you can induce self-hypnotic learning trances to optimize your results. These trances can help you establish a comfortable learning environment by reducing outside stress and creating more focus on learning.

The more you learn to listen to your inner unconscious and universal minds, the more you may in tune to your life's purpose. You may have bowed to pressure from family, friends, or teachers, and thus were subjected to learning experiences that were not optimal for you. If you take the time to quiet your active, conscious mind and listen to the inner voice, you can call upon the wisdom of the ages for guidance. In the words of William Shakespeare, "To thine own self be true."

Self-Hypnotic Learning Trance

Self-hypnosis can be a valuable tool for learning. It can help reduce the stress of tests, help create a better study focus, and aid in memory recall. Self-hypnotic anchors can be created to bring back the benefits of the trance experience instantly. The first step is to establish a time each day to practice self-hypnosis. The more you experience a positive learning trance, the easier it is to focus on learning.

Find a comfortable position, loosen your clothes, take a deep breath, exhale, and let your eyes go out of focus. As you breathe slowly in and out, let the muscles in your body relax. You may notice that some of your muscles are stiff and some of them are relaxed. The more you let stiff muscles relax, the more relaxed you will become and the deeper you will go into self-hypnosis. As you continue to breathe deeply and let your muscles relax, you may be aware of sounds around you, and you will continue to hear them as you go deeper and deeper into self-hypnosis.

In a few moments you may close your eyes and begin to count down slowly from five to zero, suggesting to yourself that you will feel relaxed, positive, and in a comfortable trance when you reach zero. After each count you may suggest that you will relax more and more, and go deeper and deeper into your trance. You may suggest that when you reach zero, your unconscious and universal minds will be open to assisting you in learning, and they will make the right information available to your conscious mind when it is needed. If you are uncomfortable at any time, you may end your trance by opening your eyes or moving your body.

As you count yourself down, you will feel in tune with your senses, and you will be open to the thoughts and positive images that your unconscious and universal minds will send to the conscious surface. You may suggest to yourself that you will experience the feelings of your most comfortable learning environment no matter where you are. If there are loud sounds or talking, you will hear them, but they won't interrupt your learning. You may suggest that you will find yourself able to focus better on your studies and recall more information through sense imagery.

Creating Learning Anchors

When you reach zero, you may feel calm, relaxed, and in a positive mood for learning. You may suggest to yourself that you will feel the same way instantly, wherever you are, when you want to learn and recall information. Suggest to yourself that when you repeat a special word or put your fingers together in a special way you will automatically enter your learning and recall trance. It will be light enough so that no one else will notice, but it will help you feel comfortable about learning and recalling information.

While in self-hypnosis, practice your learning anchors and experience how they work for you. Imagine using them in a situation where you have had difficulty learning in the past. Each time you practice, feel that you are able to focus more and more on your learning and recall abilities. Imagine how, when you are placed in situations or subjects that do not feel comfortable, you could let others know what would help you learn.

Using your sense modalities, imagine how you could make positive changes in your study habits to help you reach the best of your potential, when necessary changing or modifying the places or people with whom you study. Consider that your dislike of a subject may only be temporary resistance toward a greater goal. Imagine that you have been given the wonderful potential to help many people in your life, and the more you learn the more it will help you fulfill that potential.

Posthypnotic Suggestion

Suggest to yourself that every time you practice self-hypnosis, you will become more and more in tune with your learning and recall potentials. Suggest that you will be open to the knowledge that comes from the unconscious and universal minds, and that you will be guided in the right educational direction to be in tune with your life's potential. Suggest that you will remember and use your instant self-hypnotic anchors to help you learn and recall, whenever and wherever you need them.

When you are ready, count yourself back up to five, reinforcing your suggestions as you count. You may suggest that when you reach five, you will feel good about your learning and recall potential. You will also be able to communicate calmly to others about what you need to create a productive learning experience. When you awake, take a deep breath and feel calm, relaxed, and comfortable about having a productive learning experience.

CHAPTER 15

Hypnosis and Work

This chapter considers how self-hypnosis and related concepts of communication can be utilized in the workplace. You will learn how to understand your coworkers' mental imaging models so you can communicate with them in an effective manner. You will examine the concept that you were born with a certain life's work and how to be in tune with it.

Hypnosis at Work for You

If you define hypnosis as communication and imagination, then its concepts fit in to all parts of your life—including your work or profession. Whatever your working role is, whether you are in the lowest entry-level position or are the CEO of a large company, the way you communicate with the people you work for, with, or hire can have a major impact on your success. This is also true when dealing with clients, patients, or customers. The better you are at communicating in a way that each person can understand, the greater your potential to create and promote a successful working environment. In earlier chapters, you have learned how your own mind works.

How Do Others Think and Communicate?

The next step is to learn how to identify the thinking and imagery processes of those you work with: boss, fellow worker, employee, or customer. If you have the opportunity to work one-on-one with another person, and if he is willing, you can use this book as a source to assess how you each communicate. It is also possible to study the other person without him knowing that you are developing a model of the way his mind works. As you build your model, you can experiment with different types of communication, written or oral, to see if he understands the message you are sending him.

When two or more persons communicate, hypnotic techniques are used. Almost every word or sentence can create an image, which is compared to a past memory or a future event. During the brief period of time that the comparison takes place, you are actually entering a light trance. While in the trance, you may absorb a positive or negative mood that stays with you after the trance has ended.

When you try to communicate with a person in a way she can't identify with, the communication may be misunderstood. You have probably had the experience of trying to explain how to do something and getting very frustrated when the person doesn't get it. People often are assigned to jobs that do not take advantage of their strengths and expose their weaknesses instead, which results in poor job performance.

When you understand each person's mental makeup, it may help improve productivity and create better working relationships.

To be sure that you have covered all your communication bases, besides speaking with another person, also put the information into a written memo. Always keep a copy for yourself, and include the time and date of the communication.

The Mental Makeup of Others

When communicating with someone else, especially at work, it is important to be careful that the message you send is received accurately. Unless he is aware of different communication styles, a person will communicate using the style that is best for him. If a visual person tries to describe something to a nonvisual person, he probably will not get his message across. You can learn a great deal about another person by observation.

Observing Visual Ability

Most people are visual to a certain degree, and they will be able to create a picture in their minds. To follow visual directions, a person must be able to see the image in his mind. Ask your coworker a question that requires him to create a visual image, and watch his eye movement.

A visual person's eyes will go upward and move to one side or the other. If he is watching a moving image in his mind, his eyes will probably move as if he were actually watching something float across the room above his head. It is possible that your coworker may close his eyes to get a better view. If you see this happening when you give a visual description, you can ask the person if he sees what you are saying. A very visual person may need to work in an environment that is organized and uncluttered, and he also may be affected positively or negatively by lighting situations.

Sometimes a visual person sees so much around him that he becomes distracted easily. We all keep two different images in our heads: the big picture, where we see both the whole and ourselves as a part of it, and a much smaller view, in which we focus only on our own part. The more that all workers can see the relationship between the large and small images, the more likely it is that the workplace team will be successful.

Observing Hearing Ability

Many people have a hard time staying focused on what someone else is saying. The mere sound of a voice can create a trance, and the listener drifts off into the unconscious world, hearing only her own inner voice. It can be very frustrating to give someone verbal directions, knowing she isn't listening. She will probably miss a portion of your instructions, and the results will be unproductive. There are ways to observe whether someone is hearing what you are saying.

When you speak, watch the eyes of the people you are talking to. Do they focus on your mouth, do they dart about between your ears, or do they just go out of focus? Do they look confused? When a person's eyes go back and forth between her ears, it usually means that she is listening to herself talking in her mind. A good way to tell if your coworker is listening or not is to ask a question that requires her to make a comment that is directly related to what you just said.

ALERT

Always watch for stressful situations that may develop around you in the workplace. Besides focusing on what you are doing, observe the unspoken communication of other people. Observe their body language, their patterns of speech and voice level, and their eye movements. By doing so, you may avoid a conflict.

The flooding hypnosis induction is designed to create confusion in the subject by reminding him of several different things to be aware of at the same time. This results in his being unable to focus, and his unconscious mind is opened up to suggestions. A person with a strong hearing sense will find it hard to stay focused on one conversation.

If you have a problem keeping someone's attention, you may want to choose a different location for your conversation. Once you have determined that a person doesn't listen very well, you can try a different technique, perhaps including visual backup. Give him clear diagrams or written descriptions, or have him watch a video. You can also provide him with a hands-on demonstration.

Observing Kinesthetic Ability

The kinesthetic individual will feel the communication. He may combine visualization with the kinesthetic mode, or he may hear and feel at the same time. A kinesthetic visual response may include an eye movement that proceeds up to the visual image screen and then downward and possibly out of focus. The person may take a deeper breath than normal when he is feeling an image. His body language may reflect how he feels—a stiff and rigid stance shows resistance, and a relaxed stance shows calm and acceptance.

Someone with a strong religious or belief background will often look straight upward, toward the heavens. Learning how to work with someone's beliefs may help you develop a better working relationship. Once you determine someone's belief system, whether or not it is the same as yours, you can build rapport with her by showing respect. It is important to treat each person as a unique human being.

A kinesthetic person is often a hands-on person. She learns and communicates by feeling. Watch for hand movements when you are talking with her. She may need to feel the work with a hands-on experience in a step-by-step progression. She may need to step away from her work occasionally to clear her mind.

The kinesthetic person may be prone to taking on other people's moods or worries. She may bring these worries to work, which could affect her productivity. She also may suffer from a loss of self-esteem. It sometimes takes patience to work with a kinesthetic person.

Observing Smell and Taste Abilities

A person's sense of smell or lack of it can affect the workplace. Someone with a strong sense of smell will often seek fresh air or attempt to keep the air smelling fresh where he works. He may be sensitive to certain smells and find it hard to focus when the air isn't right for him. Someone with a poor sense of smell, however, may come to work unclean or wearing dirty, smelly clothes that offend other workers. It may be a challenge to communicate that he needs to change his habits.

Watching someone breathe or the way he moves his mouth can give you clues about how he processes through taste and smell. You might ask what his favorite smells or favorite foods are, and if he is strong in these senses, he'll respond with movements of the nose and mouth. Many people have favorite memories of a relaxing smell, which you may trigger verbally to help them relax and be more receptive to your communication.

Working with Other People

How you coexist with others in the workplace will, to a great extent, determine how successful you are and how rewarding your job feels to you. By using the same positive and negative model-building technique you would use on yourself, you can develop a model of your coworkers. The more you understand your own and other people's models, the better your chance to implement communication techniques that will be understood by your fellow workers.

FACTS

Violence in the workplace has increased at an alarming rate over the past few years. Many companies have downsized and expect the employees who remain to pick up extra duties. When pressures become too great, people may release them in negative ways, causing property or product damage and the possibility of a violent confrontation.

For each coworker, develop a list of positives. How does she see, hear, feel, taste, or smell? Can she understand both the big picture and the little picture involved at work? Is she self-motivated, does she take on tasks readily, or does she need encouragement and supervision? Is she argumentative or agreeable, reliable or unreliable?

What are her strengths and weaknesses? Is she assigned to the right job, or is she trying to do something she isn't suited for? Does she hear what you say to her, and if not, how can you communicate with her in a different manner and in a nonargumentative way?

Once you have determined a person's positive and negative mind models, think how you could use your knowledge of his imaging strengths to promote a better working relationship. After you have developed a communication plan, try it out and compare the results with the way you and he used to communicate. What worked and what didn't? What could you try next time for a better result?

Practice Communicating Through Self-Hypnosis

Use your own self-hypnotic trance to practice communicating with other people. You may ask your unconscious and universal minds to help you build a positive and effective dialogue. You may ask that the right words come from your lips when they are needed. You'll need to have patience with yourself and patience with the other person. The more you practice communicating during self-hypnosis, the more patient you may become in the actual situation.

Just as in all hypnosis applications, the more consistently you practice, the more you build your positive communication habit. You can develop positive anchors with coworkers to help create avenues for better understanding. The anchors can serve to establish better moods, in which both parties are more receptive to the exchange of information.

Self-Hypnosis and Your Work

You can use a self-hypnosis exercise related to work every day. This exercise can be done in a deep relaxed state, in a light awareness state, or by triggering your instant self-hypnosis anchors. When you first start using self-hypnosis, you may want to use the longer relaxation exercise that you will experience now. If you are ready, find a comfortable, relaxing position, loosen your clothes, take a deep breath, exhale slowly, and let your eyes go out of focus. As you continue to breathe in and out slowly, you may allow your muscles to relax.

ALERT

You will notice that some of your muscles are tight and stiff, while others are relaxed. The more you allow the tight and stiff muscles to relax, the more relaxed you will become.

In a few moments you may allow your eyes to close, as you begin counting slowly down from five to zero. If for any reason you want to end your trance, you may open your eyes or move your body, and you will awaken, calm and relaxed.

As you count slowly downward, you may suggest to yourself that you will go deeper and deeper into self-hypnosis. As you reach zero, you may suggest that you will be in a deep self-hypnotic trance, and you will feel positive and relaxed as you communicate with your unconscious and universal minds.

You may suggest to yourself that no matter what takes place at work, you will do the best you can to produce good results. If you have concerns related to your work, you may ask your universal mind for the best possible resolution. You may suggest that after you have finished your self-hypnosis, you will continue to be open to helpful communications from your unconscious and universal minds.

Autosuggestion and Anchors for Work

As you continue to count yourself down, suggest that with each count you will feel more in tune with your unconscious and universal minds. When you reach zero, suggest that you are open to communication. Any worry or concern that you have may now be turned over to the unconscious and universal minds.

You may ask that when you speak to yourself or others, the right words will come out of your mouth, and that you will take actions that are best for the whole. Feeling a strong connection, ask that you may be in tune with your minds and remain positive and calm no matter what takes place at work. Suggest to yourself that this feeling will stay with you wherever you are, and that the more you need it, the more you will feel it.

If you have a religious belief, you may ask for miracles to take place when needed, and you may ask your angels or guides to watch out for you and give you the right words and actions. You may remember how you feel when you are in contact with your belief, and this feeling will automatically be with you whenever you need it. You may also give yourself a special word or touch anchor that connects you with your belief, angels, or guides, and anytime you want to feel connected, you may trigger it by using these special anchors.

While you are in your trance, experience your anchors and feel how they can be used when you need them for work or anything else. You may experience them several times, and each time you will feel them getting stronger and stronger.

When you are ready, count yourself back up to five. At each count, you may suggest that you will feel your belief, angels, or guides with you, and that you will be open to communication with the unconscious and universal minds. As you count yourself up, you may feel that you have something with you that can help bring about work-related miracles for yourself and others. You may suggest to yourself that you will be in tune with your life's work, and that you will be on the lookout for assignments from the universal mind.

Suggest to yourself that you may trigger your anchors anytime you need to. Also, you may ask that you will be open to the right words to speak or write and the right action to take in relation to your life's work. The more you practice self-hypnosis, the more you may connect automatically with your unconscious and universal minds, in tune with your beliefs and your life's work.

A Career Is Not Just a Job

Some people believe that each of us is born with a life map to follow, which gives us the opportunity to grow and progress in our universal studies throughout our lives. Your life map was placed in your unconscious mind at birth, and each action you take is either in or out of tune with it. Your life's work is part of the map, and how you do your work will affect your soul's growth during your lifetime.

People choose careers for different reasons. You may have picked a career for its high income potential. You may like to take risks and reach for the brass ring of success in business; if so, you are labeled an entrepreneur. You may become a healer, an educator, a politician, a craftsperson, or even a laborer. It takes many people doing different things to provide balance in the world.

You may change jobs or careers several times during your life. Or you may find yourself stuck where you are, without the knowledge or ability to make a change; you may feel trapped, held captive doing something that seems to lead nowhere. If so, you may become bitter, and your frustration can be reflected in your work, in your home life, and even in your health. Your world can become stale and stagnant, as you wait for the day you retire, or you die at your job.

ESSENTIALS

It can be frustrating to work at something that you know is not what you should be doing. You may feel trapped where you are at the moment. Self-hypnosis can help you become patient and help you receive guidance from your unconscious and universal minds about the direction of your life's work. There may be a reason for your resistance.

Have You Chosen Your Life's Work?

How do you feel about your work or career? Is it your life's work, or is it only a means of earning a living until you finish your education or discover your life's work? Whether your current job is your life's work, or whether there's something inside of you that knows you need to be doing something different, self-hypnosis can help you stay in tune with your life's goals. Find a quiet time each day to communicate with your unconscious and universal minds—it can be good for your mind, body, and soul.

Self-Hypnosis and Career Goals

Perhaps the unconscious and universal minds are sending you a communication indicating that what you had thought was the right choice for your career may not actually be the right choice. What you are doing at the moment, however, may be part of a transition into your life's work. Through self-hypnosis, the universal mind can help you stay in tune with your assignments. Your career may be the means for connecting you with your life's assignments. Your life's work covers much more than just your career; it may also include your relationships and creative talents.

Your own free will, your ability to choose your life's direction, may prevent you from reaching the highest potential in your life's work. You may have spent your whole life preparing for your life's work, and then you may not even know that you are doing it. Sometimes you may feel resistance that keeps you from going in your intended career direction: this resistance may actually be working *for* you on behalf of your life's work. The more you pay attention to messages from the unconscious and universal minds, the more likely it is that you'll be in tune with your life's work.

FACTS

When you are young, you may be under a great deal of pressure to choose a career that will satisfy someone else's wishes—to enter a family business or profession, to choose a career that is like your parent's, or to bring honor to the family through your work. You may want to communicate with the universal mind for guidance in choosing a career.

If you have mixed feelings about your career choice, you may want to use a self-hypnotic trance to seek guidance from the unconscious and universal minds. Using the exercise that was presented earlier in this chapter, suggest to yourself that when you reach zero, you will ask for guidance from the unconscious and universal minds and you will be open to the answers. You may ask the universal mind that the right miracles take place to help guide you to be in tune with your life's work. Suggest that when you count yourself back to five, you will be aware of the communications you received from the universal mind.

If you are especially creative, one of your greatest problems may be how to make a living using your natural gifts. You may have a hard time setting a fair price for your work, and you could end up discouraged and out of money. You can use self-hypnosis to ask the universal mind for help in letting your creative work be a life's work that helps others. You may ask that you will be able to earn enough to make it possible for you to continue your work. Ask permission to charge a fair price and to have confidence that your creative work will reach the people who need it.

Using the Imagery of Hypnosis at Work

The image concepts of hypnosis can be used successfully in almost every kind of work. The medical profession promotes a wellness image to patients by the visual appearance of the facilities and staff. The term *placebo effect* describes, among other things, the phenomenon that a patient feels better in a healthy-looking environment. Emergency workers' language use can have a strong impact on the person they are rescuing: the wrong words could literally scare the patient to death.

Some salespeople realize that they have hypnotic power, and they won't sell to someone unless they feel the customer will benefit from the purchase. Others use this ability for financial gain without regard to the customer's well-being. The ability to use hypnotic imagery carries a great deal of responsibility. If you know how to manipulate the critical thinking ability of other people, you have a powerful tool that you can used for good or ill.

Do you, or would you, use your ability to help another person improve her life if she so desires, or would you try to manipulate her for your own personal gain? Can you see the entire concept of your life's work, or do you see only a small portion of the whole? The more you use self-hypnosis to be in tune with your life's work, the greater the probability you'll be on track and reach your potential.

When a salesperson or other professional develops a positive image with her clients or customers, it is called developing rapport. The imagery used by the salesperson produces a hypnotic buying trance in the customer, which tends to make him willing to buy whatever is offered.

CHAPTER 16

Improving Your Personal Relationships

I n this chapter you will look at different types of personal relationships—with your family, friends, pets, love interest, or soul mate. You will explore how your past relationships may influence current ones, and how you can use self-hypnosis to help improve them.

Sailing the Waters of Life

Imagine two sailors starting off together on a great adventure. They gather their supplies and decide on their first port of call. On a bright and sunlit morning they both sail out of the harbor, full of optimism for a safe and exciting journey. Together, the two friends sail side by side, keeping in constant communication with each other, sharing the joys of their adventure.

Suddenly the wind begins to shift, and each skipper turns his attention to his own vessel, working the sails and zigzagging back and forth across the ocean, taking one tack after another. One of the sailors begins to notice that the two boats are starting to move apart, so he turns his vessel and attempts to follow the other's direction. He tries to send a message to the other skipper, but all attempts at communication fail and the distance becomes greater and greater until the two boats are no longer within sight of each other.

ESSENTIALS

The story of the two sailors provides a good analogy for the relationships you may have during your life. Some relationships seem to carry a bond that stands the test of time, while others start out with a fiery passion that slowly fizzles until the last ember dies out.

Now each sailor is alone on the dark ocean, and his thoughts turn to his own survival. The skipper with less experience and poorer equipment may fear that he will face an emergency he cannot handle. His boat may sink, run aground, sail far off course, or by some miracle, it may find the way. This is also true of the other vessel as it sails on ahead, the skipper blinded by his own self-confidence, not heeding the warnings of an angry sea.

The two sailors may never see each other again. They may both continue to sail the ocean; perhaps they'll hook up with other sailors, or they may continue on alone. They may reach their intended destination, or they may visit new ports along the way. They may have a fulfilling journey or one that is filled with fear and despair. The two sailors may find each other again and continue to sail together, or it may be that their interests and destinations have changed and they'll decide not to travel together again.

Family Relationships

Your life is intricately woven around relationships, some lasting for only a few minutes, others lasting a lifetime. Your first relationships are the bonds you form with your parents. Relationships with other family members and close friends come next.

Family relationships can be either building blocks or stumbling blocks to your personal growth. Conscious and unconscious memories from your childhood can have a major impact on the rest of your life. Experiences from the past may have negative or positive impacts, depending on the types of relationships and their lingering effects.

If your family life was filled with love and support, it encouraged you to grow and develop toward your life potentials. The members of a loving family are encouraged to take risks in order to achieve their dreams, but these risks are mitigated by the knowledge that someone will always be there to offer a helping hand. If your family was supportive, you can use this as a model as you grow in life.

You may have no sense of what a family is. Perhaps you were abandoned, either physically or emotionally, at an early age. Your childhood may have been filled with abuse, and now that is the only way you know how to reach out to other people. Abuse often leads to abuse, and the cycle may continue for generations unless something breaks the negative pattern.

ALERT

Traumatic childhood experiences can have a severe impact on the social development of an adult. If you have memories like these buried deep in your unconscious mind, you may find that professional help is the best way to find permanent resolution. Ask your doctor for guidance.

Clean Up the Clutter

Self-hypnosis can be a valuable tool to help resolve negative patterns created by family relationships during childhood. You may have experienced mental or physical abuse. You could have been overprotected, or you may have absorbed phobias from a family member. Negative patterns could have originated in a situation that you witnessed as a child and buried in your unconscious mind.

You may not be able to identify certain emotions that you experience when you seek, begin, or maintain relationships. You may notice a pattern that replays every time you attempt to begin a new relationship. Your relationship failures could be physical or intellectual, they could relate to work or your personal life, they could take place at a distance or close by, they might involve family or friends, or they may be romantic.

To resolve the clutter of negative patterns from the past, first identify, as clearly as you can, what you would like to change. If you can define a negative pattern objectively, gather as much memory information as possible. It is important to look into the past from your present perspective; you will use this information to change your old, negative patterns in the future.

Self-Hypnotic Regression

The affect-bridge self-hypnotic technique can be useful to help resolve the impact of negative situations and relationships from the past. Select a current feeling that can be disruptive or that sabotages situations or relationships in your life. You need experience only a small part of your feeling, just enough to move back through your memories.

If you become uncomfortable at any time while in self-hypnosis, all you need to do is open your eyes or move your body, and you will come out of your trance, feeling calm and relaxed. You may experience your trance through all your senses: seeing, hearing, feeling, tasting, and smelling.

Find a comfortable position, loosen your clothes, take a deep breath, exhale, and let your eyes go out of focus. You may be aware that some of the muscles in your body are stiff and some are relaxed. Whenever you feel a muscle stiffen, you may relax it as you begin to go deeper into your trance. When you are ready, you may close your eyes and begin to count yourself down from five to zero into deep hypnosis. You may suggest to yourself that you will go deeper and deeper into hypnosis with each number.

When you reach zero, you may feel calm, relaxed, and ready to move your feelings back through your memories. As you breathe easily in and out, let yourself experience your most recent memory of the feeling. Experience the feeling with all your senses, just enough to remember the most recent time you felt it.

Take the Feelings Back and Resolve Them

Once you have a clear image of the feeling, go back to another memory, perhaps six months ago. When you have done that, go back a year and do the same thing. Continue regressing backward, from one similar feeling or emotion to the next. It is possible that you will experience other feelings and images, which may be related to the one you started with. You may let each image pop up from your unconscious mind and observe it without trying to analyze it.

Go back to the earliest image that you can remember, and if you can, watch the whole situation, including yourself at that age. Hear what is happening and feel it, but only to a point that gives you a clear image. Did the situation actually take place the way you remembered it?

ALERT

Repressed memories have the potential to bring powerful and possibly disturbing past experiences up to the conscious surface of your mind. If you feel that you might discover such experiences during your self-hypnotic regression, you should seek competent professional guidance before attempting regression on your own.

Compare how you experienced the scene as a child with how you observe it now as an adult. Was the child's perspective correct, or were the feelings absorbed by the child different than what an adult would have felt? Were the child's feelings the fault of the child, or were they someone else's fault? Was the child a part of the situation or a witness to it?

Comfort the Child Within

Now you have an opportunity to speak to yourself as a child. You may tell her that you love her, and that you now understand how and why she feels this way. You may explain to her that she did not cause these feelings and that she does not have to be held captive by them anymore. You may tell her that she may now focus on a future that is filled with love and new adventures.

You may bring your childhood self forward to reunite with your present self. You may suggest to yourself that you will now give the child within a chance to grow and experience a life filled with patience and understanding. You will treat your inner child with the same respect that you would give to another person. When you are ready, you may slowly count yourself back from zero to five, feeling reunited with a part of yourself that you may have lost as a child. When you reach five, you may awaken and feel whole again, with a new perspective on the future.

ESSENTIALS

One effective counseling technique is to reunite as an adult with your inner child. Once your adult self recognizes what is necessary for the inner child to reconcile past negative experiences, you can provide comfort and love to bring the two parts of yourself together again. For the first time as an adult, you may discover the world through the eyes of a child.

Social Relationships

Your family relationships can have a strong impact on your social relationships. If you grew up under stringent control, you may seek too much freedom when you finally leave home.

While in a relaxed state of self-hypnosis, you may ask yourself the following questions. Do you have problems with social relationships? If so, does it follow a cycle, developing into a recurrent pattern that continues until the relationship ends? Do you always expect more or less than your friend does?

Do you avoid social relationships? If so, why? Are you comfortable with other people? Do your family relationships, past or present, affect your social relationships? How do you feel about your social relationships?

Changing Social Relationships Through Hypnosis

Do you want to change the way you experience social relationships? If you do, you may use self-hypnosis to examine how you developed your model of social relationships. Go back over them to find their beginnings just as you did with family relationships. Once you have done so, build a positive model for change, experience it in your mind, check for resistance, and give yourself permission to install this new model in your unconscious mind. You may believe that this change is good, not only for you but also for others, and you may be open to new experiences.

Rejection of Human Relationships

There are people who avoid social and romantic relationships because of unpleasant experiences from the past. If this is the case with you, you may turn instead to a sure source of unconditional love—pets. Regardless of how the rest of life is going, your nonhuman friends can be counted on to respond to your affections. It may seem that your animals have become human.

Or you may turn away from relationships and absorb yourself in nature, your work, your research, or your art. You may spend your life working, reading, and watching television or going to the movies. If you have turned to nonhuman relationships, chances are it is due to the negative effects of an earlier family, social, or romantic relationship.

If you have turned away from relationships, you can use self-hypnosis to help yourself resolve the problem and reintegrate with people. Re-establishing old relationships or developing new ones could benefit both you and others. Someone else might reach out to you, but the desire and willingness to change must come from inside. If you give yourself permission to have patience, you may move forward one step at a time.

The first step in resolving relationships from the past is to establish a new and positive relationship with yourself in the moment. To accomplish this, understand how you can take steps to resolve the past, and use your awareness of how your minds work together to enhance communication in the future. The more you believe in your purpose for change and the more you practice positive imagery, the greater the chance you'll experience relationships in a different and more rewarding way.

Your Soul Mate

Have you ever met someone for the first time and felt as if you had known him all your life? Perhaps there was such a magnetic draw that you couldn't bear the thought of being separated from him ever again. It is possible that this strong attraction, which started out as a social friendship, will blossom into an intimate relationship. Unfortunately, some soul mate encounters turn into fatal attractions.

The soul mate trance begins at the first contact, and one or both of you quickly loses all sense of critical reasoning. It often makes no difference that you are involved in another relationship: you are blind to anything but yourselves. If you have other intimate commitments, they are thrown into turmoil and stand a good chance of ending. When the dust settles and reality sets in, the two of you are alone together and may find you really aren't suited for each other in this lifetime.

To understand a soul mate attraction, you might try self-hypnotic regression to bring the connection between the two of you into perspective. The technique for a past life regression will be covered in detail in Chapter 17. The objective here is to go back over the lives of your soul in search of a previous connection between you and the other person. What might have been an appropriate relationship in a past life may not be appropriate for this lifetime.

Intimate Relationships

Intimate relationships, more than all others, require the effort and skill of two sea captains who are committed to sailing through life together.

It takes a commitment to grow together, share the load, constantly revise the course of life, and above all keep the channels of communication permanently open. Your communication flows back and forth on many levels, spoken and unspoken.

ESSENTIALS   Without communication, your intimate relationships are in danger of failing. The more you work to understand how your partner's mind processes information, the better the chance you'll keep the communication channels open and be receptive to each other's messages.

The concept of hypnotic imagery and communication can be very helpful in maintaining an intimate relationship. It is important for you to have a full understanding of your mental makeup and that of your partner. You can accomplish this through discussion and observation. Know how each of your minds works in the past, the future, and the present. Build mental models of each other's strengths and weaknesses, creative gifts and fears, and likes and dislikes.

Learn to watch each other's physiology, and listen for what each of you is saying without speaking. Learn each other's comfort zones, and develop spoken and touch anchors to convey intimate feelings such as love. Consider creating hypnosis scripts for each other that will help facilitate and heighten intimate moods. Create touch anchors to help trigger those special feelings.

Lasting Relationships

All relationships, from a casual friendship to a fifty-year marriage, take effort and commitment if they are to continue to grow. Communication, respect, and treating each other like unique human beings can help sustain your associations. Unfortunately, it is easier to develop negative anchors than positive ones. It is only natural to see what is wrong with your partner and remind her of it. Often, even when you try to help someone, you may tend to rub her weakness in her face, which often causes resentment.

A relationship begins with mutual interest. With time your interests can change, and the common bond can be lost unless you both keep the communication lines open. Each of you has to take an interest in your partner's growth, as well as in his failures. When you supply constant support and appreciation, you deepen the bond. But also respect your relationship's boundaries and maintain a good balance. Your knowledge of positive hypnotic communication can be applied at all levels of relationship development.

You can use self-hypnosis to work with the unconscious and universal minds, suggesting and requesting that you will always, somehow, know the right, positive words to say to build and sustain your relationships. The more you suggest to yourself that you will be open to positive relationships, the more you will come to use positive anchors that can enhance communication. The more you ask for the proper resolution of relationship conflicts, the more open you will become to the miracles that can take place.

Understanding Relationships

Throughout your life you will enter and end relationships of one type or another. How you are affected and how you affect others shapes the course of future relationships. You may want to consider how you enter a relationship and how you could improve on future partnerships. Good relationships require experience, trust, patience, and a mutual desire to continue on together.

At the beginning of a relationship, you may see only one side: the potential for something good and wonderful. This is particularly true if you feel the need for a relationship. You may be convinced that with a little love and encouragement, your lover will overcome any faults he may have.

Relationship Cycles

Relationships follow basic patterns, having a beginning, middle, and sometimes an end. You begin with some sort of mutual communication, something the two of you have in common. A relationship can start almost anywhere or anytime, with or without warning. Your relationship trance is established in the beginning, and just like in the beginning stages of hypnosis, your critical reasoning ability is gradually eliminated. At this point the relationship can take one of several different directions.

Dangerous Relationships

Relationships of all kinds have the potential to turn destructive and dangerous. Remaining open to communication from the unconscious and universal minds can help you keep in tune with your internal warning system. You may have gut feelings that make you concerned about a relationship. Even though things seem to be going well, you may observe, hear, or feel something that indicates something is amiss.

Your physical, mental, or spiritual well-being can be endangered in a relationship. The other person might control you through abuse, and you could turn to destructive habits to escape: overeating, drugs, or alcohol. You may become confused and lose your connection with your universal belief, feeling that there is no place you can turn for help and guidance.

ALERT

You may need a period of time to escape a negative relationship, especially if you do it without help. You may develop elaborate plans to leave, then wait and watch for a time when you can execute them. Contact a shelter or other women's support organization for help if you are afraid in your current situation.

You may be so involved in a relationship trance that you fail to hear the warnings of friends and family. You may blame yourself for the situation you are in, or you may feel that you are not worthy of anything better. Perhaps you are not giving yourself the opportunity to look for an escape route. Self-hypnosis can help provide a balance and keep the spark of freedom alive. The abusive partner can't know what you are doing within the safety of your own mind.

Self-Hypnosis for a Balanced Relationship

You can induce a self-hypnotic trance to evaluate your relationships in several ways. The ideal situation is to identify a place where you can be alone for a period of time so you may experience deep self-hypnotic relaxation. You can also practice self-hypnosis in bed before going to sleep, while listening to music, especially through headphones, or while you exercise. You can develop anchors that keep you constantly in touch with the unconscious and universal minds. Through self-hypnosis you can escape for long enough to evaluate your current relationship situation through all your senses, in the past, future, and present.

Questions about Your Relationship

Once you have reached a good level of connection and communication with the unconscious and universal minds, you may ask for help and guidance. What is the current status of your relationship? Is it open, honest, and positive? Is it meeting your expectations or your partner's?

Is this relationship healthy for your mind, body, and soul? Is it healthy for your partner or for other people who are affected by it? Are you defensive about it? Do others support you or warn you about the relationship? If so, why?

How does this relationship compare with others you have experienced? Has this relationship changed? If so, are the changes positive or negative, and do they follow patterns from the past? What are you telling yourself about the situation you are in? Are you listening to yourself?

What can you offer to make the relationship grow and be a positive one? What could your partner do for positive growth? Is this possible? Is this relationship worth continuing? If the relationship continues in the same way, how will it affect you mentally, physically, and spiritually?

Self-Hypnosis and Future Relationships

As you move into the future, you may be filled with fear or with confidence. The more you work with the unconscious and universal minds, the greater your opportunity to be in tune with the future. While in your self-hypnotic trance, you may want to ask that you be given the correct guidance by all the positive sources inside yourself. You may ask the universal mind for help in resolving past relationships so you can enhance communication in your current relationships. You may ask for help resolving current relationships that may be failing, and you may ask for help as you seek and become open to future relationships.

ALERT

Your past situations may play a large role in the way your future unfolds. Some of the realities of your life may control, to a certain degree, the options you have in the future.

If you are experiencing conflict in your current relationship, you may ask the universal mind to whisper the right thoughts or words to both of you. If you have concerns for other past, current, or future relationships, or if you feel the lack of a relationship, you may ask the universal mind to help carry the burden of your worries. You may ask for help to prepare yourself physically, mentally, and spiritually for your life's direction, work, and relationships, so that you may be in tune with the flow of the universe as you enter the future.

CHAPTER 17

Understanding Your Past Lives

In this chapter you will examine the concept of past lives and how they may influence your current life through karma that is carried over from one lifetime to another. Furthermore, you will learn several different self-hypnotic past life regression techniques.

Do You Believe in Past Lives?

People in Eastern cultures are more likely to believe in past lives than those in the West, perhaps because the Catholic Church and most of the Protestant denominations do not accept the concept of reincarnation.

FACTS

Reincarnation is the belief that the soul experiences more than one lifetime, or incarnation. In each incarnation the soul continues learning the lessons from previous ones. The soul can learn the lessons at its own speed, as it has free will. In some lifetimes the soul may learn rapidly; in others lessons may need to be repeated.

It is not necessary for you to believe in past lives for this chapter to benefit you. According to one theory, the process of past life regression is a psychological drama of the mind. If this is your belief, your own imagination can help bring about positive resolutions to conflicts within the conscious and unconscious minds.

The Soul's Purpose

Imagine for a moment that in the beginning, the universal mind created souls, which were born from the creator's sacred mist. Each soul had a direct link to the universal mind and all its knowledge. At first it had no physical form and consisted of the purest energy. These souls were unlimited in their ability to travel through space. These early incarnations were as long as several earth lifetimes.

Even though the soul had access to all knowledge, it did not have experiences to go with the knowledge. So each soul was given a map, which was encoded within it, to follow as it made its way through its experiences. Once the soul's experiences have been completed and match its knowledge, it returns to pure energy, where it exists around the earth plane to aid other souls who have not yet learned all their lessons. In addition to the map each soul was given free will. It can choose not to follow the map during an incarnation, but the lessons will have to be continued in another lifetime.

Some believe that the soul began to develop a physical form during its early incarnations. Therefore, it is very possible that people in ancient times knew more about the universal mind than we know today.

ESSENTIALS

The labyrinth, a design that appears in early cave drawings, could have indicated what a soul map looked like. The labyrinth is shaped like a brain, with a right and left hemisphere. When you reach the center of an actual labyrinth, you experience a balance of mind, body, and soul.

The Assignment of Old Souls

Edgar Cayce called the existence of old souls on earth "the invisible empire." This empire lives in a reality that coexists with our world on earth. Its purpose is to watch over souls that still are in their human incarnations. If you become aware of this empire, your dimensions of reality are expanded to include that which is unmanifest. Unmanifest reality is something that is real, but which cannot be experienced through the senses. This reality is manifested at times to help the soul that is still in human form.

Each soul in human form may have at least one old soul assigned to watch over it and help it out if it wants help. The human soul can be its own worst enemy when it uses its free will to try to satisfy the ego mind. This self-desire part of the soul expects everything to be centered on the human, rather than on the universal.

Is it possible that old souls are part of the miracles you experience in your life? Have you ever been at a point where there seemed to be no hope left—when all of a sudden, out of nowhere, you received an answer to your prayers?

Has a stranger ever appeared at a time of need, only to disappear when you try to thank her for her kindness? If so, what do you think is looking out for you: angels, guides, the universal mind, luck, or an old soul? Perhaps an old soul can manifest itself in many different forms, so each human mind receives a form it will accept.

Influences of Past Life Soul Memories

Are you being influenced by past life memories? These are often just below the surface of your conscious mind, and they can affect your life without your even knowing it. You may relive past life memories in your dreams or feel recognition in places you have been before. You may react to people in ways that indicate a previous relationship, even though you never met them before.

Living the Past in the Present

Do you have a passion for a certain time in history? If so, do you like to study or imagine what it would have been like to have lived during that time? Do you cut your hair in a certain way or wear clothing that relates to a certain time period? Do you belong to a group or organization devoted to reenacting historical events? Do you belong to a historical society or subscribe to a period publication?

Do you live in a period home and furnish it or your apartment in a historical theme? Do you prefer older tools or cooking methods and resent modern conveniences, such as television and computers? Do you enjoy playing games or doing crafts that reflect a certain time period? Do you prefer one historical style of music?

ALERT

It is always important to keep yourself well grounded in your spiritual belief when experiencing and investigating past lives. If you do not have a protective belief, you may be thrown off balance by your encounters with the unknown.

Do you enjoy creating art or writing stories about certain periods of history? When you visit certain historical sites, do you feel a connection? Do other people tell you that you should have lived during a certain period in history? If you could live during any time in history, when and where would it be? Can you think of any other connections that may attract you to a certain period in history?

Dreams of Past Lives

You may connect with your past lives through dreams; perhaps you experience an episode that recurs over a certain time span. Maybe you had the dream in childhood, and it disappeared as you grew up. Your dream may reappear at certain times, related to events or situations in your life. The dream may leave you with certain emotional feelings that stay with you long after it is over.

Do you experience recurring dreams from a different period in history? In your current life, do you know any of the people in your dream? Does your dream relate to family members? Have any other members of your family had the same or similar dreams?

Do you dream different dreams from the same time period? Do you have any recurring dreams from different historical periods? Do your dreams relate to fears, phobias, or other traumatic events? Do your dreams have common themes? Can you think of any other dreams that might be related to a past life?

Self-hypnosis can be used to go back through a dream that may be related to a past life. Suggest to yourself that when you reach zero, you will enter the dream from which you want information. You may always step back out of your dream, open your eyes or move your body, and awaken calm and refreshed. Once you have developed a clear dream image, investigate and experience it in a similar manner to other past life regressions. Collect as much information as possible relating to themes or people that may help you work on and resolve karma in your current life.

The Feeling of *Déjà Vu*

Have you ever had the feeling that you have been some place before, although you are visiting it for the first time? Have you ever visited a historical place and spontaneously gone into a trance from a different time: watching the scene, hearing the sounds, feeling the emotions, and even smelling the smells of this other time period. Did you ever experience a trance like this that was so powerful you felt disorientated when you came out of it?

Have you ever found yourself automatically using words or phrases from a different time period, without consciously thinking about it? Do you feel as though there are people, family members, or friends whom you may have known during a different lifetime? Do you have a different relationship with certain members of your family, perhaps a mother who is like a sister? Do you feel related to some of your friends?

Driving down the highway, have you ever imagined that you were traveling in a different time period? Have you seen a person change before your eyes into someone from a different period of time? Especially if you were tired, have you observed scenes that appear to be from a different time, only to find them normal the next time you saw them?

Childhood Memories

A very young child may tell stories that make no sense to his or her parents:

- She might call her parents by different names.
- He might tell his parents stories about "before."
- She might demonstrate artistic ability—drawing, painting, writing, or music—that was never taught to her, at least not in this lifetime.
- He might be able to speak another language.
- She might know a lot about a place although she is visiting it for the first time, or she may know about the people who lived there during a different time.

When your child is very young, he may remember information that relates to your past lives as well as his. Pay close attention, encourage him to talk about "before," and record his stories before he forgets them.

Did you experience any past life memories when you were young? Perhaps you may be able to ask other family members who remember more than you do. Young children may have vivid memories of past lives, which fade as they grow older. Through hypnosis your unconscious memories of early childhood may be brought back to the surface. These memories are a good platform for a past life hypnotic regression.

Cycles of Souls and Karma

Many people believe that a soul travels through its labyrinth journey with other souls, and they work out their lessons of the universe together. With each incarnation the play is a little different, giving each soul an opportunity to perform a different role.

Whenever something is left incomplete or unresolved at the end of a lifetime, it will be addressed in another. This is called *karma*. If two souls have had a difficult relationship, they will have a chance to resolve this karma. Sometimes one person will resolve his part of the karma while the other person does not; the second person will have to do it over again next time.

Past Life Regressions

There are several methods for doing past life regressions. The calendar technique takes you backward through your current life and your birth to what happened before. In the affect-bridge regression you take a feeling back to images from the past. The reading or video library regression helps you experience an image that comes up from your unconscious mind. You can also use automatic writing or hypnosis to examine dreams of different lifetimes.

ESSENTIALS

If you have a good imagination, you can experience a past life through waking hypnosis. All you need to do is focus on an image and experience it in all five senses. You can move about in the image and collect information that relates to themes and people in your current life.

There are several purposes for doing a past life regression. You may simply be curious to experience who and what you may have been before. You may have a deep curiosity about past lives, and you may already have an idea of where and when you lived before. A past life trance might even aid your creativity or psychic abilities, without your knowing it.

In past life therapy you look for answers to mental or physical afflictions by regressing into a past life. The clue could be an unresolved phobia, a fear, or a bad dream. You might want to overcome a bad habit or an addiction, or to understand a behavior pattern, a health problem, or a relationship. The general therapeutic purpose of past life regression is to discover something from the past that can help resolve and positively change something that is negative in the present.

Calendar Regression

To prepare for a past life regression, you will begin with a basic relaxation technique to help induce a deep self-hypnotic trance. Find a comfortable position, take a deep breath, exhale, and let your eyes go out of focus and your muscles relax.

When you are ready, you may close your eyes and slowly count yourself back from five to zero, suggesting to yourself that you will be able to have clear images in all your senses: sight, hearing, feeling, taste, and smell. If at any time you want to end your past life regression, you may open your eyes or move your body, and return to a calm, awake state.

Once you reach zero, you may imagine a calendar on your visual image screen, and turning back one month, remember a positive event in your life. Experience it in as many senses as possible. Next go back another month. Let yourself experience clearer and clearer images as you go back, one month at a time, for half a year. When you have completed this, return to a pleasant memory a full year ago.

Continue your regression, going back in five- or ten-year intervals, until you reach birth. If you are able to image it, you may go back through your birth to the womb. Your mother's experiences while you were in the womb may have had some influence on your life, either negative or positive, and it may help you to understand them. When you have completed this process, continue going back. You may experience a light and a tunnel, complete darkness, or something else.

Continue back until you experience something. The image may be faint at first and hard to understand. You may use your senses to investigate the image. Make note of the temperature, smells, sounds, emotions, and anything else you may experience. If nothing is there, continue going back until you experience something.

Deepening the Past Life Regression

When you have established some type of image, allow yourself to experience as many details as possible. Feel your hair. How long is it? How coarse does it feel? Feel your body and the material of the clothes you are wearing, if any, to determine the texture, the weight, the type of fabric, the length, and the feel.

Look down at your feet, and describe what you see and feel. What do your feet look like, how large are they, and if you are standing, what does the surface feel like? If you can observe yourself, do so at this time and describe what you see. If you cannot dissociate, look for something that you might see your reflection in, and then describe yourself. How old are you and what do you look like?

ALERT

Gather as much information as you can during the image: historical factors, the location, other people who may be present, and your own emotions. You may want to record your words while it is happening or immediately after you have finished, describing your experience in writing or on tape.

What is happening around you, what are you doing, and how do you feel? If something in the image is distressing, turn down the intensity, observe it from a distance, or move yourself to a different image during the same lifetime. You may move either backward or forward.

Review the Lessons

When you have established a clear image, suggest that you will review this lifetime, stopping at specific images that relate to your current life. When you are ready, move to the end of this life, experiencing only enough to give you knowledge of how you felt when you died. Next go back over the theme of the entire lifetime, seeking to understand how it may relate to your present life, and also looking for any people in that life who may be involved with you now.

Compare that lifetime to this one. How does the theme of that life compare with your current one? What can you learn from your past life persona that will be useful as you go forward in this life? Now imagine how the things you have learned could positively change your future.

Did you recognize any of the people in your past life? If so, compare your relationships in the past with the relationships you currently have. What can you learn from this comparison to help you understand your current relationships? Imagine how you could use this knowledge to bring about positive changes in the future.

When you are ready, count yourself back up from zero to five, and awaken from your trance into your current life, calm, relaxed, and ready to use the positive information you have learned from the past to help you move forward on your life's journey.

Affect-Bridge Past Life Regression

After you have counted yourself down to zero, focus on an emotion, a picture, an interest, a fear, a phobia, a pain, or something else that has occurred in your life, and let an image come from the unconscious mind. Remember to tell yourself that you may end your trance for any reason by opening your eyes or moving your body, and you'll return to the surface of your mind feeling calm and relaxed.

SSENTIALS   Affect-bridge past life regression is a good technique to use if you want to locate the roots of a phobia, a fear, or another emotional reaction that you can't explain in regard to your experiences of this lifetime. Once you have a satisfactory explanation, you may go on to resolve the condition.

Once you have focused on your topic, take yourself back through your life, imaging different situations where you have had the same or a related experience. When you have gone back as far as you can, suggest to yourself that you may now be open to any related image coming from the unconscious and universal minds.

While you are in hypnosis, allow yourself to accept whatever you image without questioning it. After your self-hypnosis session has been completed, you will have an opportunity to analyze your image experiences. Once you have established an image, follow the procedure that was given in the calendar regression. Gather as much information as possible, and look for a theme and relationships with other people that may give you insights regarding your current lifetime.

When you have finished reviewing this past life, you may want to look for other lifetimes that relate to it. You may experience more than one lifetime during your affect-bridge regression. After each life, look for relationships with others and themes that may help resolve karma in your current life.

When you have gathered as much information as possible, count yourself up from zero to five, and awaken calm and relaxed into your present life. As soon as possible, write down or record your experiences and impressions of your past life regression.

Library Regression

Another excellent past life regression technique is the library regression. This and the following regressions are good if you are used to reading or watching television or videos. Suggest to yourself that when you reach zero, you will enter a library that has a series of books, or one book with many chapters, containing the history of your past lives. You may choose a volume or open to a chapter that relates to the reason you are pursuing a past life regression. You may always close the book, select a different volume or chapter, or move about in the history of your soul, anytime you want or need to.

The video library technique is similar to the reading library technique. When you have counted down to zero, you may select a disk, videotape, or television channel on which you can view and experience a past life that provides the information you are looking for. Once you have focused on your picture, you may watch, or if you are able, step into the picture and experience the regression through all your senses. You may go back and forth in the image to gather information, and look for people and themes that may relate to resolving karma in your present life.

ALERT

There can be a danger in experiencing a past life reading in which you were rich, famous, or otherwise gifted. It may be tempting to try to relive that past life in your current one. If you become absorbed by the grandeur of your past, you may miss the lessons of this life.

Automatic Writing

Automatic writing is another method you can use to explore past lives. Position yourself in front of your computer, or let your hand rest on a piece of paper ready to write, and count yourself down. When you have reached a comfortable level of self-hypnosis, suggest to yourself that you will relax and let your mind wander. While you are doing this, suggest that the information you are looking for will automatically come up through the unconscious and universal minds, and will be written down for you to read when you wake from your trance. When you have finished, count yourself back up to the surface of your mind and read what you have written.

CHAPTER 18

Increasing Your Psychic Ability

In this chapter you will learn about psychic trances and abilities, and the psychic's role in history. You will examine your own psychic gifts and learn to recognize when you're in a psychic trance. You will experience a white-light self-hypnosis induction, meet your guides and angels, and maybe even try astral projection.

Psychics Through History

Psychic powers and abilities have been part of human culture since history was first recorded. Ancient astrologers got their information from the stars. The Greeks visited the Oracle at Adelphi. Sages, witch doctors, medicine men, and even biblical prophets looked into the unknown for answers. People have invoked psychic powers to manipulate the weather, defeat their enemies, cure the sick, or create prosperity and peace.

These days, almost anytime you turn on the television you find a physic selling her services. You can dial a psychic hot line or reach one on the Internet. A psychic is waiting for you at the mall or tearoom. You'll find best-selling books on the subject, and popular psychic shows are on radio and television. People are always willing to spend money in hopes of seeing into their future.

QUESTIONS?

What does it mean to be psychic?
Psychics are able to obtain information from sources that have no scientific proof. Their information comes in many different ways and forms. There are two different types of psychic information: intuitive and spontaneous.

Intuitive Psychic Information

Intuitive psychic information is developed in your unconscious mind. Through your five senses, you collect and store the material that leads to your intuitive insight. You may consciously remember when you collected some of the information, however you absorbed much of it subliminally, without conscious awareness. All of this material is stored in your unconscious mind.

Self-hypnosis is a great tool to recover repressed memories, memories that your conscious mind is no longer aware of. Have you ever had a long-forgotten memory suddenly pop into your head? It was there all along, stored below the surface of your consciousness.

There may have been a situation or a question that you considered in your conscious mind for a while, and then you went on to other thoughts. Many times, your unconscious mind takes that question or thought as a suggestion and continues to work on it long after you have stopped thinking about it consciously. Your unconscious weighs all the information collected, sometimes comparing different situations separated by long periods of time. When it is ready, your unconscious sends its response up to the surface of your mind, and you become aware of information that seems to come out of the blue.

Spontaneous Psychic Information

Spontaneous psychic information comes through the universal mind. It suddenly appears without warning, usually when you are in a suggestible state of mind. You may already be in a light trance, absorbed in thought, and your eyes may have gone slightly out of focus—at this time you are open to the incoming information.

Spontaneous psychic information may come to the surface of your mind in such a powerful image that it totally consumes you. Your conscious mind is just along for the ride as you slip deeper and deeper into the image. A spontaneous psychic trance is similar to a habit trance: once it starts, it will run its course until it is finished. When the trance ends, you may be left in a state of confusion.

Spontaneous psychic trances do not happen all the time; conditions need to be just right. You may be tired and unable to focus on anything specific, or your life may be in a state of disarray. The information that comes to you may make no sense at all, it may concern an event taking place somewhere else, or it may be the answer to an unsolved mystery. If you do not know how to screen out or shut off the information, it may flood your mind when you are unwittingly open to a spontaneous psychic trance.

Who Is Psychic?

When you hear the word *psychic*, you may think of a woman dressed like a gypsy who holds office hours at the mall, or the man who answers a psychic phone line and tries to keep you dangling on his every word as you pay by the minute.

But the truth is, everyone is psychic to one degree or another. Some of the best psychics never let anyone know about their gifts, perhaps considering these unwanted abilities a curse. These people may spend most of their lives hiding inside their own minds.

Have you ever heard the phone ringing, picked it up, and without thinking greeted the caller by name? Have you ever thought about someone you haven't heard from in a while, only to have contact with him within a short period of time? Has anyone else ever told you that he was thinking about you just before you contacted him?

Did you ever have a hunch about something, which later came true? Have you had the same thought at the same time as someone else? Have you ever exchanged gifts or cards with a friend, only to find you gave each other the same thing? Have you ever dreamed about an event that came true? Have you ever sensed that a family member or friend had a health or other problem?

How Psychic Are You?

If everyone is psychic, how do you recognize your own ability? In general, psychic information is imaged by your sense modalities, just like they process other images. Chances are that you already receive and use psychic information, perhaps without even realizing it; it has been part of your life since birth. In fact, your strongest psychic experiences may have taken place in childhood.

ESSENTIALS

Some people believe that past life experiences contribute to your psychic ability in your current life. If you were a fortune-teller in one life, your unconscious mind may still know how to do it. You may have memories of astral projection, and you may still be able to travel with your mind in this life.

As a child, you may have shut off your psychic abilities as soon as you learned you were doing something different, which might not be accepted by others. Perhaps you thought your premonitions were negative, and when the event actually happened, you blamed yourself. Maybe you lived in fear of what you perceived as an evil power. Psychic abilities, like any other talent, can dry up if you don't use them.

Psychic Ability and the Senses

Psychic abilities are directly tied to your mental makeup. If you are visual, you will experience your psychic trances visually. If you are strong in more than one sense, you will receive information through several senses. If you are experiential, you will experience what happens in your trance, or if you detach, you will view the image from a distance. If you have several imaging strengths, you may receive information from more than one perspective.

Mental Telepathy

Mental telepathy is the direct linking of two or more minds, in which one knows what the other is thinking. This is common in families. One member may have a worry or an illness, and another member instinctively knows to contact them. Mothers are especially linked with their children, and the same may be true for husband and wife, especially if they feel they are soul mates and have been together through several lifetimes.

FACTS

You can try an experiment using telepathic communication. Arrange a time with a friend or family member when you can take a few minutes in a quiet place to send and receive a message. Let one person send the first time, while the other writes down the information, and then reverse the procedure the next time. Compare notes.

Close friends can also experience telepathy. Again, they may have been together before, so their minds are naturally linked. You can also step directly into another person's mind, seeing and experiencing exactly what she is describing. Due to this telepathic link, you may even understand more about the situation than the person who is sending the information does; as a receiver you may be able to add to the sender's understanding.

You may image telepathic information in one or more of your five senses. Do you get visual images from someone else's thoughts? Do you hear what he is thinking? Do you feel his emotions? If he thinks of a smell or taste, can you image what it is?

Clairvoyance, Clairaudience, and Telekinesis

Clairvoyance is the process of gathering information psychically through the senses, without the telepathic link. A clairvoyant may be able to identify one card out of a deck of cards or tell you what you have in your pocket. She may get this information visually, auditorily, or kinesthetically. Some people can use both telepathy and clairvoyance— they can link with someone else's mind and observe things in the other person's location.

ESSENTIALS

You can try a remote-viewing experiment with a friend or family member. Find a quiet place where one of you can imagine what the other is doing at that moment. Focus on the other person, and gradually enlarge your view as you develop a stronger image. Make notes and compare them with your partner.

In clairaudience you image psychic information by hearing it. You might perceive a conversation that is taking place or hear other sounds: mechanical, natural, or musical. Even if you don't know the location, you may be able to identify it by the sounds. Sounds may also be linked to the kinesthetic sense and convey emotions. Clairaudient images may be specifically targeted, or they may be completely spontaneous.

You may be able to hold an object in your hand and receive an image of its history: you may image different places it has been, who owned it, and even the emotions that were experienced by people who were near it. You may hear sounds related to the object, or you may get a psychic image by smelling the object, which in turn produces information through your other senses.

Psychic Trance Tools

Although some psychics can receive information instantly, others use tools to help them go into a trance. Just as a hypnotist may use a strobe light or a spiraling disk to encourage the subject's eyes to go out of focus, a psychic may use objects like a crystal ball, tea leaves, swirling water, smoke, or a burning candle to help induce a hypnotic trance.

As a psychic begins her work, she may go through a ritual, which allows her to relax gradually and deepen her trance. She has given herself the suggestion that she will receive the necessary information from the universal mind, although she may use different terminology.

E ALERT

Use extreme caution with the psychic communication tool called the Ouija board. You might start out intending to have fun with the spirits, only to learn that the spirits aren't playing. The game may trigger negative energy that can disrupt your life.

Other psychics may use sounds, such as running water, nature sounds, music, bells, gongs, or wind chimes, to help induce a trance. Others use smells like burning incense, candles, or perfume, which transport them into a psychic trance. A kinesthetic reader will use the touch of an object or a person to produce the same effect. Massage therapists, who are often very intuitive, receive readings on their clients as they give them a massage. People learning massage or a hands-on healing technique such as Reiki often have spontaneous and unexpected psychic experiences, which may catch the beginning practitioner totally off guard.

Some psychics read tarot or other kinds of cards. There may be a set of guidelines for the use of specific cards, but many psychics get their own impressions, often touching the client and reading his vibrations. A dowser receives his information from the movement of the stick, the pendulum, the rods, or the sensations in his fingers. When the information he is imaging is correct, a psychic may feel a sensation in his head, stomach, feet, or third eye (in the center of the forehead). A psychic may write, sketch, or doodle to help maintain his trance.

Receiving Information

Each psychic has her own source for information. She may go directly to her imagery or she may use spiritual helpers, often called *guides*. A guide usually presents himself when the psychic has gone into a trance; he takes over the psychic's personality and communicates accordingly. This technique is known as channeling, and the information may be spoken or automatically written through the psychic.

The guide may provide information about or messages from a dead relative of the person receiving the reading. The guide may have advice on world events or present a universal philosophy for the good of humankind. He may provide a health or life potential reading for a client. Sometimes the information provided by the guide is published in a book, which generally lists the psychic as the author and gives credit to the source.

QUESTIONS?

Can a psychic really predict the future?
When a psychic gives a reading that involves the future, it is based on current conditions. If these conditions don't change, the prediction may come true. If conditions are changed, then the future outcome may also be changed.

An astrologer reaches to the heavens for information, using ancient formulas to offer self-knowledge and predict the future. Many people center their lives on their daily horoscopes. People play the stock market, make choices about careers or mates, and make other life decisions according to the positions of the stars and planets. Some believe that your future has been mapped out at the very moment of birth.

Past, Present, and Future

Psychic information can pertain to the past, the future, or the present. Information gathered from the past is called retro-cognition, and it can be about a person, place, or object in this lifetime or an earlier one. During a psychic reading you may receive information about the future, based on past events or situations.

A past life reading provides information even if you haven't experienced a past life regression, but it may make you want to try a hypnotic regression to find out more. A past life reading can validate psychic abilities that you may suspect you have, and give you the confidence to use them.

Precognition is the knowledge of something that may happen in the future. This kind of psychic talent often causes young people to shut down their abilities. A premonition that turns out to be true is often unwelcome, especially when the result is negative.

The Psychic Responsibility

The professional psychic has a choice: does she tell the client exactly what she sees, or does she give him the suggestion that he may want to be aware of a potential problem in the future? If a person is told of a traumatic future event, and if he believes the prediction, he may unconsciously do what is necessary to make the prediction become a reality.

Some psychics get information and instantly relay it to their clients: in conscious channeling, the psychic is awake yet she receives and relays information from the universal mind. The flow of information may be just a trickle, or it might be a great flood. The psychic must be willing to let the information come through, since her conscious mind could seek control instead of accepting a universal message.

What to Do with Too Much Information

Before you develop and use your psychic abilities, gain as much understanding as possible about what may happen during a reading. If you don't have the proper understanding and balance, your gift may become a curse. If your ego takes responsibility for your gift, it may be too much of a burden to bear. Remember who really provided your gift and how it should be used.

Proper balance and groundedness is essential in developing your psychic abilities. Grounding yourself connects you with the universal mind, and your belief that you are using your ability for positive good enables you to withstand any self-doubt. Do what is natural for you, and when you are certain that the information you receive is for the good of all, then you can let it flow. If the universe gave it to you, the universe will help you use it correctly.

ALERT

It is very tempting to regard unknown forces as a game you can play anytime you want. However, once you become open to the world of the psychic, these forces can be unnerving, unless you take the proper mental precautions for totally grounding yourself in your belief system.

Without the assistance of universal consciousness, you may open a floodgate of information. Once the psychic flow starts, you may get much more than you want or need. It is hard to block, so it's best to get out of the way, and let it go where it goes. You may pick up on events that have no personal connection to you and that you can't do anything about.

Some psychics ground themselves with a white light that shields them from absorbing their subjects' problems. Some go to their belief systems and ask for healing or the right information. Others ask that they receive only the information they are supposed to receive. Some psychics go through elaborate rituals to protect themselves. With the proper grounding, you may experience the world of the psychic unafraid.

Recognizing Your Psychic Trances

Are you aware of your psychic gifts, and when and how you receive information? A psychic trance is different from an induced trance, as it often happens on its own. You may have been getting psychic signals for a long time, but you didn't pay attention to them or you just shrugged them off as unimportant. Now is the time to start paying attention to what you are telling yourself. Just remember that how you receive information will be different from everyone else.

Once you have identified your psychic trance state, be aware of when it starts and take note of the information you are receiving. It may come as a feeling, a voice, a sound, a picture, a smell, or even a taste in your mouth. You may not understand what is coming in, and that's okay as long as you don't totally disregard it. Ask your belief system to only give you information that can be helpful to yourself or others.

You may receive intuitive information from someone else, who may not even knowing he is providing it, or it may come through a conversation with a friend or a stranger. You may have been thinking about a subject or searching for an answer, and suddenly you see a sign, pick up a book, or find the information on television or the Internet. You can use self-hypnosis to suggest to yourself that the universal mind will provide the answer, and then pay attention to your experiences in the moment.

The White-Light Psychic Trance

To use self-hypnosis to help develop your intuition, find a comfortable position, loosen your clothing, take a deep breath, exhale, and let your eyes go out of focus. As you breath slowly in and out, you may allow your muscles to relax. In a few moments, when you are ready, you may begin to count yourself down from five to zero into a deep and relaxing hypnotic trance.

The white light can be an excellent tool for healing, both for yourself and others. You may mentally send the light to anyone, anywhere in the world, or you can feel it flowing through yourself. The light can also represent universal love and peace, and it can be sent with that intention.

You may suggest to yourself on each count that you will feel a beautiful white light spreading throughout your body, starting at the top of your head and your third eye. You may feel the love and protection of the universal mind as it flows within and around you.

Spreading the Light

If you are ready, you may begin counting downward, and on the first number you may feel your connection with the light as it flows down from the universe. If at any time you want to or need to, you may open your eyes or move your body and end your trance.

With five, you may close your eyes, and then allow yourself to go deeper and deeper with each count, relaxing more and more as the white light flows in through your third eye. At four you may feel the light spread down through your head and face to your shoulders. When you are ready, go to three, and the light will spread down your shoulders to your elbows, lower arms, wrists, and fingertips. At two, the light may flow down through your chest to your stomach, and you will go deeper and deeper into hypnosis. The white light will now flow down to your knees, as you relax more and more. When you reach one, you may feel the light flow down to your ankles, and it makes you feel so calm and relaxed. The white light is now flowing through almost all of your body. You feel your connection with the universal mind.

Now you may count slowly from five all the way to zero, where you will be totally immersed in the white light and experience a complete connection with the universal mind. You may count five, four, three, two, one, and zero. You may allow yourself to feel totally immersed in the white light of the universe and ready to receive the information it is sending. You may be open to identifying and using the psychic gifts that you have been given for the good of many people.

Meeting Your Guides or Angels

At this time you may ask the universal mind to identify your guides or angels. Let your senses be open to receiving the communication. As they remain open, you may relax and enjoy the light. You may see, hear, or feel your messengers from the universal mind.

Your guide may speak to you and give you the specific information that you are searching for, or she may provide more general wisdom to use in your life. It may take several self-hypnosis sessions to establish a link with your guide. The universal mind is in charge and will give you what is needed at the time you need it.

You may not see your angel, but you may feel her presence. If you have a feeling that she is there, you may remember the feeling so you will recognize it again whenever she comes to watch over you. You may receive other images from the universe, such as animal guides.

Spend as long as you want with the universal mind and your guides and angels. When you're ready, count yourself up from zero to five, to the surface of your mind; you will awaken calm and relaxed, and you will continue to feel a special connection to the white light of the universal mind.

Astral Projection

When you are in your white-light trance, you may want to try astral projection. When you astral-project, you leave your body and travel to other places in or out of the earth plane. If you're ready, you may take a deep breath and feel the beam of white light flowing into your body. You will always be able to open your eyes or move your body anytime you want to end your trance, and be fully awake, calm, and relaxed.

You may now feel yourself lifting up and up, above your body. It is a wonderful sensation as you feel yourself traveling up and up into the universe, safe on a brilliant beam of white light. You may experience beautiful colors or music, and feel the energy of the universe. You may be aware of going through a tunnel, moving further and further into the universe.

You may be aware that you are being taken to a special place where you may learn some information from the universal mind that will give you insights into your psychic gifts. You may go to a place that holds information that you may study, or you may be given it by a special being.

When you are ready, you may descend back to earth and to your body, filled with special knowledge from the universal mind. Count yourself back up to the surface of your mind from zero to five, and awaken calm, relaxed, and in tune with the universe.

CHAPTER 19

Writing Your Own Hypnosis Scripts

In this chapter you will learn how to create your own self-hypnosis scripts. You will understand how to include basic relaxation, future pacing, goal identification, model building, goal experience, and posthypnotic suggestions, and you will also learn how to adapt your script to several different applications.

Hypnosis Scripts

If you lived in a perfect world, you would have a wonderful place to meditate and time to spend there, and you'd resolve all your life's problems. Very few people have the luxury of living in a situation such as this. When you focus on the imperfections of the world you may start thinking negative thoughts, which in turn may influence you to take negative actions. You might go about life in a negative self-hypnotic trance, acting out the script (self-talk) you created unknowingly.

You can get help to rewrite your negative scripts. When you use someone else's script, however, you may or may not have success depending on whether your mind identifies with the wording. If you write your own script, you can choose the wording that makes sense to you. You can design descriptive scripts that take you to special places in your mind, or you can create one-word affirmations. You can rewrite your personal script anytime you want.

Before You Begin

A self-hypnosis script should have a certain sequence. It should begin with a basic relaxation exercise. During this phase, you give yourself suggestions for deepening the trance in the future. Once the induction is complete, you introduce and experience the goal of the session. In the final segment, you suggest that the hypnotic experience will continue when you are back in your waking state.

Before you develop a self-hypnosis script, decide how you will carry it out: will you write it down or create it at the time you conduct your session? If you compose it beforehand, will you memorize it, record it and play it back, or have someone read it to you? Will you include sound, music, or smells to help you focus?

Where and when will you practice self-hypnosis? How long would you like each session to last? Will you have access to a comfortable location, or do you anticipate interruptions? How about the lighting or furniture? Is there anything else that needs to be addressed before you begin, relating to location, other people, or your personal schedule?

Self-Hypnosis Session Goals

What is your goal for your self-hypnosis session? Once you have determined what you want to use self-hypnosis for, ask yourself a series of questions to help you compose your script. You may want to write down the answers to your questions to help you remember. The more emphasis you put on the benefits that others may experience through your hypnosis, the more incentive you will have to reach your goal. Ask yourself:

- What is my self-hypnosis goal?
- Why do I want to accomplish this goal?
- Is this goal realistic?
- How will accomplishing this goal help me?
- How will accomplishing this goal help others?

Define your goal simply and clearly. Keep your suggestions to yourself positive. The unconscious mind is very literal and may hear something in a different way than you meant. An example might be, "I won't smoke anymore," which might mean that you will smoke the same amount as you do now. A better choice of wording is "I will be smoke-free."

Keep your goal simple. The more you repeat key words in your script, the more they will be reinforced in your unconscious mind. Those key words will be remembered and brought to the surface when needed.

Make your journey toward your goal sound, feel, and look exciting to yourself. Your universal mind or belief structure may be used as a support to accomplish what you have set out to do. You may want to ask your belief, guides, or angels for help, and incorporate the feeling of that assistance in your posthypnotic suggestions. You may have a large, life-changing goal, or you may simply want help to relax.

Write Your Basic Relaxation Exercise

You may want to go back and review the section of this book that helps you understand how your mind works and how you naturally go into a trance. What you learned about yourself in those exercises can be used in your self-hypnosis script. As you begin to compose your relaxation induction, consider the strengths of your five sensory modalities. If you can image a relaxing smell, for example, suggest that you will experience it when you start your breathing exercise.

Identify a place where you feel calm and relaxed. This will be the destination of your progressive relaxation script. It may be a real place, a place you remember from childhood, an imaginary place, a place from a past life, or a place deep inside where you connect with the universal white light. If you are nonvisual, you don't have to picture the place; you might tell yourself to focus on a sound, smell, or feeling instead.

ESSENTIALS

Whether you record your script or speak aloud to yourself, the sound and speed of your voice is a factor in how effective your self-hypnotic trance will be. Emphasize key words such as *relax*. Let your voice sound relaxed and calm. This technique is called *pacing*.

The first part of your script should include deep, slow breathing, eye relaxation, and muscle relaxation. You may follow earlier examples in this book, or you can try different ideas. Make sure you repeat your suggestions often. When you tell yourself that you are relaxing, feel relaxed. Focus on your suggestions to yourself.

The first section of the script deals with the moment. Everything you suggest to yourself, you experience at that very moment. Plan to work on your breathing, eye focus, and muscle relaxation for five minutes or more. If outside sounds or movements could interrupt your focus, include them in your script. When you give yourself permission to be aware of them, you won't be fighting to block them out.

Future Pacing

The next section of your script should deal with future pacing: you give yourself a suggestion of what is going to happen while you are focused on the moment. An example would be, "In a few moments, when I say the word *deeper*, I will begin to feel myself sinking deeper and deeper into my chair, as I continue to breath in and out. When I am ready, I will sink deeper and deeper as I say the word."

You can use suggestions such as, "My eyelids will become heavier and heavier," or "I will relax more and more with each count downward." Remember to let yourself anticipate the experience before it happens, and feel it at the right time. Your purpose is to make every suggestion as real as possible so you become open to future suggestions that relate to your goal.

You also want to include a countdown to zero. You can begin on any number you like, but you might try starting with five or ten at first. Include suggestions with each number, such as "I will relax more and more and go deeper and deeper." Begin to introduce the suggestion that at zero, you will be at your destination. With each count downward, suggest that you will be closer and closer to your special place.

The countdown portion of your script could last five to ten minutes, depending on what number you start with. At zero, suggest that you are experiencing the reality of your special place. Include clear descriptions in the sense modalities that are strong for you. Experience the images that you are suggesting to yourself. Then compose your count up from zero to the number you started with, suggesting how you will feel when you get back to the surface of your mind and how you will continue to feel after the session is over.

ESSENTIALS

Once you have finished writing your basic relaxation script, record it, memorize it, or have someone read it to you. Try out your script several times to evaluate how it works for you. The more you become comfortable with your script, the easier it should be to enter a successful relaxation trance.

Scripting Your Goal

After you have fine-tuned your basic relaxation script, you can use it to help you develop a positive and a negative model, if needed, for your self-hypnosis goal. These models can be used to develop your change goal.

If you want to experience a past life or develop your psychic gifts, or if you are seeking communication with your guides, angels, or universal mind, it may not be necessary to construct positive and negative mind models.

Scripts for Positive Change

Develop two models of your change goal while in your basic relaxation trance. List all of the positive benefits that you currently get from the behavior you want to change, and then list all the negative things about it. After you have completed this, ask yourself what would be acceptable to the part of you that doesn't want to change.

Use your five senses when you are collecting this information for your script. Next, using your negative and positive models, construct the change model of your goal. Now you are ready to write the change script. Put the negative experience first, and then experience the change model, which incorporates new benefits for the part of you that resists the change. The more you emphasize the negative at first, the easier it will be to install the positive change model.

FACTS

You can use positive and negative model building to create change models for almost anything you want to improve: sports, creativity, habits, work, or relationships. Your script should include a negative model compared with a positive model that you create as part of your change goal.

The last part of the change goal portion of your script is to experience two different models of the future. The negative future model shows what you would be like if you never achieved your goal. The darker you can write it, the better. The positive future model reflects the positive experience you will have when your change is complete.

Posthypnotic Suggestions and Count Up

The last section of your script reinforces your suggestions for positive change, and you count upward to the surface of your mind.

Reinforce the positive benefits of your change, and suggest that you will continue to experience your change after the session is over. This is called a posthypnotic suggestion. Repeat it several times, telling yourself that when you count yourself up, the suggestions will stay in your unconscious mind.

You may wish to use the following self-hypnosis script checklist:

1. Basic relaxation
2. Future pacing
3. Countdown
4. Change goal experience
5. Future goal experience
6. Posthypnotic suggestions
7. Count back up to the mind's surface

When you count back to the surface of your mind, start from zero and finish on the number you started with. Between numbers, reinforce that you will experience the change goal automatically after your session is over. Also include the suggestion that you will feel calm, relaxed, and positive when you awaken from your trance.

ESSENTIALS

Whenever you induce self-hypnosis, include the suggestion that you may, anytime you want, end your session by opening your eyes or moving your body, and awake calm and relaxed. Always allow yourself to be in control of your own hypnosis.

If you included anything in your script about heaviness on the way down, release it on the way back up. If you have a favorite smell, suggest that you will take a full breath of it when you awaken from your trance. Slowly count yourself upward, reinforcing these suggestions between numbers. Remember to experience everything that you suggest to yourself. When you finish writing your script, you are ready to try it out.

Connecting with Guides, Angels, or Universal Mind

The basic relaxation script can contain the universal white-light technique or any other image that you want to include. When you write a script to connect with your guides, angels, or universal mind, you may want to use the white light as described in the last chapter. You may bring this light into your body, or have it surround you, or experience it inside and around you at the same time. With each number, move the light progressively through or around your body; you can begin with the light at your head or at your feet, whichever you are most comfortable with.

In the future-pacing section, suggest that when you get to zero, you will be connected to the light, you will feel its protection, and you will be in contact with your guides, angels, or universal mind. Use your senses to create the imagery that gives you the most powerful experience. You may include an opportunity to communicate directly with your source. Leave time to experience what you are looking for when you use this type of self-hypnosis. The amount of time you remain connected may vary from a few minutes to as much as an hour, depending on the strength of the communication.

You may want to verbalize the information being passed through you and record it for examination after the session is over. You might have a friend ask questions of your guide, and the answers will come through you. Whatever your goals are, make sure you include them in your script. When you count yourself back to the surface, suggest that you will awaken full of positive energy from the white light of the universal mind.

Scripts for Pain Control and Stress Relief

Before writing a pain control script, consult Chapter 10, which addresses the subject. Decide which method will be the most effective for you. Start with a basic relaxation exercise, and suggest that you will experience the positive feeling of your imagery at zero, when you reach your special place. You will want to leave as much time as you need to experience the positive effects of your imagery. Constantly reinforce the goal results, and when you are ready, you may include that you may count yourself back to the surface of your mind or drift off into sleep.

To write a wellness script, image what you want to change as it is now. Then develop the healthy image that you want to replace the old one with. As you compose your script, include the suggestion that when you're deep in your trance, you'll experience the healthy image replacing the negative one. Give yourself the posthypnotic suggestion that you'll continue to feel the wellness benefits after the session.

For stress control, use a basic relaxation exercise to transport yourself to your special place. In this script, include relaxing imagery and positive feelings. You may want to ask your universal mind, guides, or angels for spiritual help to resolve conflicts or worries. In your posthypnotic suggestions, state that you may step out of your stress anytime you want by feeling the positive effects of your special place in your mind.

Scripts for the Universal Mind

Writing a script for yourself is an excellent way to heighten your awareness of how to use your knowledge of your mental makeup. You have the opportunity to experience the magic of your own imagery, and you also have the chance to get in tune with the universal mind and to create and continue a communication with your belief system.

The Benefits of a Belief Structure in Self-Hypnosis

Belief in a positive outcome is the most powerful feeling you can experience in self-hypnosis. The more your script includes strong suggestions that something good is going to happen and will continue to happen, the more your body and mind will respond to that suggestion. Even when the odds for a change through self-hypnosis are not very high, emphasizing a purpose for the change can bring miraculous results.

It can be a powerful incentive to believe that your change will benefit others. When your improvement can be used to help others, it may motivate you to have a stronger belief in the change, whether it is for your own wellness, to improve a habit, to enhance your creative talents, to create a better relationship, or to improve your sports performance. Including the benefits to others in your self-hypnosis script may enhance your success.

The more you ask the universal mind for permission to do the best you can do, and then rely on it to provide what you can't do, the more powerful an image belief you can create. If you are not used to asking for something from the universe, this may be difficult for you. Start slowly with your requests, be honest in your conversations with the universal mind, and ask that its will may be that you do the right thing. It is okay not to know what to put in your script to communicate with the universal mind.

The first few times you use self-hypnosis to communicate with your belief system, you may just relax in a peaceful silence when you reach zero. Even if there are no messages, you may feel how special the universal mind is just by being in its presence. If this is the case, use your script to suggest that this peace or other positive feeling will remain with you after the session has ended. Include the opportunity to breathe in and out, feeling your deep connection with the universal mind.

Scripts for Your Life's Work

Your belief structure is your contact with your life's work. In your script for communicating with your universal mind, you may include a section for addressing your assignments in life. You may ask for guidance as you struggle with decisions, large or small. You may ask to feel your angels or guides with you, always watching out for you wherever you go. You may ask that you be given the right decisions from the universal mind.

FACTS

The more you include positive affirmations in your script, reinforcing that you are not alone in your earthly travels, the more this experience will be reinforced in your unconscious mind. You may repeat a key word or phrase over and over like a mantra, such as "Believe," "May the angels watch over me," or "May it be Your will that things work out for the best of all."

In your posthypnotic suggestions, include the thought that your belief system will always be with you. Suggest that you will continue to receive positive communications from your universal mind, guides, or angels. You may also include that you will be aware of the miracles that take place around you. The more you use words that keep you in contact with your beliefs, the easier it will be to react to life situations in a positive way.

Past Life Scripts

A past life regression script begins with a basic relaxation exercise. Once that is accomplished, there are several different methods to access a past life memory. You may want to record the induction or have a friend read it.

Decide on the method of regression that you want to use: affect-bridge, calendar, movie, television, book, open door, beam of light, or another of your choosing. You can experiment to find the best one.

You may want to suggest that you go to a life that will help you understand a question that you have about this lifetime, and review that life, looking for a theme, for people connected with you now, and for the last thoughts in that life. When the session is over, compare that life to your present one for positive improvement.

Continual Scripts

Continual scripts are the words or thoughts that you are constantly saying to yourself or to the universal mind. If you are not aware of your continual scripting, you may be creating a negative script for yourself. You are always receiving negative influences from your own mind or from other people, and if you reinforce them, you are scripting negatively.

You can give yourself posthypnotic suggestions that you will create a positive script wherever you are. You can suggest that when something is negative, you will trigger an anchor that lets you escape for a brief moment so you may compose a positive response. Continue to use the positive to override the negative.

Communication with your belief system can be a continual script. When you have a constant dialogue with your universal mind, guides, or angels, you can live in a life trance. You may suggest to yourself that every thought you have will be in tune. You may ask yourself whether you were personally responsible for the thought, or whether it was given to you by the universal mind to use for the benefit of others. In your posthypnotic suggestions, you may include that you will be open to the thoughts of the universal mind and to their becoming a manifest reality.

ALERT

Being open to universal thoughts also opens you to psychic insights. You may find that as you hold a continual dialogue with the unconscious and universal minds, you will receive psychic information out of the clear blue sky.

CHAPTER 20

Hypnosis: A Way of Life

Self-hypnosis can be used in almost every part of your life, but you need to understand the dangers that may occur if it is misused. Stay in tune with your life, and self-hypnosis will accompany you as you move into the future of your own making.

Everything Hypnosis

As you have learned from this book, you can apply hypnosis to almost everything you experience. Whether the experience was in your past, is currently taking place, or is expected in your future, the moment you create or recall an image, you are in a self-hypnotic trance. You are in a trance even when you try not to be—your focus places you in an awareness trance.

The way you understand and use trance states can help or hinder you. Entering a trance is a great way to step back and assess the current situation. It can be detrimental, however, if you become caught up in a negative trance.

How can you recognize and use trances for positive results? You should now be able to recognize your own trances. You should be able to step back and examine your thinking patterns, and identify your image strengths and weaknesses. There is always something new to discover about yourself, so you are encouraged to review different sections of this book as you continue to understand and expand your mind strength model.

No one really knows you better than you do yourself—but you may not recognize what you know. This can be especially true in an area where you are naturally gifted. Someone else may have to convince you or guide you to use your abilities. If others constantly comment on something you do well, you may want to listen.

If You Can Never Get Started

It is okay to begin. The moment you think about something, you have already started the process of beginning. You may experience both positive and negative trances as you imagine getting started. You might recall other projects that you have started and didn't finish, creating self-doubt about your ability to ever complete this one. You might remember past failures that still live on in your unconscious mind.

Ask yourself what you can do in your project and what you are uncomfortable doing. Ask yourself what good would result for someone else if you started and completed it. Ask yourself what you need to get started and to finish. Perhaps you need assistance with part of the project.

FACTS

The fear of failure can stop you from beginning. You may compare your results to others that you feel are much better than yours. Sometimes you may imagine the end goal, but it seems too far away and unobtainable. Many images can enter your trance when you think about starting something.

As you move into the future, you now have knowledge and self-hypnosis ability that can help you reach your goals. You can make adjustments to the goals you've already established and create new goals. Always let your three minds be involved with your decision-making and growth. The more you ask the universal mind for help, the more you will be open to receiving and recognizing help when it arrives.

If You Never Finish

You may start projects and never finish them. You may put your whole self into a project for a while, and somewhere near the end you just give up or abandon it. You may have begun an educational course, a college degree, a remodeling project, or something else, but no matter how hard you try to psych yourself up in the beginning, deep inside you know you will never finish.

Review your past projects and look for a pattern in the reasons you abandoned them. Use your imagery to create a clear picture. Ask yourself what you can learn from the past and how that knowledge will help you in the future. Talk to the part of yourself that doesn't want to finish and ask what might be done to change your negative failure image. How could your whole being work together to get the best results?

You may use self-hypnosis to help you learn from past experience so you may make better progress this time. You may give yourself permission to move forward a little bit each day.

Consider your goals, step by step, from the comfort of your trance. You may imagine how you are helping others by working toward the conclusion of a project. You may give yourself permission to do the best you can, as you use your new knowledge of hypnotic imagery.

If You Always Have to Finish

Are you a person who hates to leave anything unfinished? You know that it will stay on your mind until it is done. Did you ever finish a project, only to learn that there was more to it? Perhaps you have an attic or garage full of completed items that didn't fit the purpose after they were completed. They may take up as much space as the uncompleted projects of the person who never finishes.

When you begin a project, do you step back and examine the whole in your mind? Do you feel totally or partially responsible? Can you delegate duties easily? Do you ask for help and guidance from the universal mind?

You can always use self-hypnosis to help you allow your project to take the course of completion that is best for all. You may imagine that the unknown is constant, and that the parts will be assembled in the order that the universe designs. You have the opportunity to be a part of the universal flow. There is a time to begin and a time to finish.

If You Experience Resistance

Do you get flustered when things don't move in the direction you expected? Do you feel that you know exactly what you are supposed to be doing and what direction you are supposed to be headed in? How do you handle things that get in the way of your progress?

ESSENTIALS
When resistance is happening to you, it's usually not much fun; it means that something is not going the way you want it to. If you are patient and work with the resistance instead of fighting it, you may find it was really for your benefit.

Do you force your way through, eyes straight ahead, chasing your dream or goal? Do you listen to the advice of others or the whispers from within? Do you carry resentment toward people or situations that get in the way or hold you back?

When life's resistance keeps you from moving forward, you may use self-hypnosis to examine the course of events. You may listen to your inner self and communicate with the unconscious and universal minds. You may ask for help to know the direction you should be going. You may remind yourself of your life's assignment and the role you are playing at the moment. When the resistance lifts, you may be aware of why it was there in the first place.

If You Collect Things

Do you spend your life collecting things? Perhaps you cannot resist bringing home a bargain. You go to the dump and find treasures in someone else's junk. You stockpile for a rainy day. More and more stuff accumulates as time goes by.

You may collect books, planning to read them someday soon. Your bookcase spills over with a vast library of knowledge waiting to be read. You know that you have all the parts and pieces to assemble almost anything you need. You are prepared.

As the years go by, the items you have accumulated lie in disrepair, as the elements take their toll. The information in your library becomes outdated and is no longer useful. The books are covered with dust. You may not see the change, however, as you continue to collect more for Someday.

ALERT

When you consider stockpiling items for the future, be aware of the trance you are in at that moment. Ask yourself where you are going to put the new addition and whether you already have other items that are related to it. If you are unsure, you may want to consider not adding it to your collection.

If you let what is in your mind gather dust and remain unused, it, too, may go the way of material goods. A vast library of knowledge in the universal mind is also waiting for you to open it. Through self-hypnosis, you may step back and examine what to save and what to pass on to another collector. You now have the opportunity to start assembling vast amounts of material from your soul's stockpile of experience, if you so choose.

If You Can't Let Go of the Past

You may cling only to the past, holding on to things that used to be. You surround yourself with familiar items, not wanting to face the uncertainty of something new. You resist change with all your might.

Time and time again you fall back on what you know, no matter whether or not it is right at the moment. As time slips by, you get further out of date. In your mind, however, nothing has changed. It is the same as it always has been.

QUESTIONS?

What might happen if I remain in the past?
Your comfort zone will shrink as you find that you do not now enjoy some of the things you used to enjoy. Old friends may drift away, but new ones are hard to come by. You will be left alone with your mementos and possessions.

With your knowledge of self-hypnosis, you may now view the old and new from a comfortable trance state. You can imagine trying and experiencing something new before you actually do it. You may ask for help from the unconscious and universal minds to represent the integrity of the past as you journey into the future. Even as you read these words, the past has extended itself into what used to be the future. Through self-hypnosis, you may represent both the old and the new.

The River of Life Self-Hypnosis Meditation

Here is a self-hypnosis meditation that can give you the opportunity to put your life in perspective. You may want to tape it and experience it from time to time when the need arises. Find a comfortable place, loosen your clothing, take a deep breath, exhale, and let your eyes go out of focus. When you're ready, close your eyes and begin.

Imagine a Drop of Water

For a moment, imagine a drop of water that forms high up in the clouds. Part of its contents comes from previous drops that have been drawn upward from the earth by the rays of the sun. The other part comes from the elements of the atmosphere. Many drops of water have gathered in this cloud and await their journey to the earth far below.

It is time for your drop of water to descend, and as it leaves its misty environment, it is frozen by the cold air and floats gently down in a snowstorm, landing high up on a mountain in the middle of winter. Here it lies dormant with countless others, waiting for spring thaw. Eventually, the sun's warm rays melt the snowflakes, and together they begin to trickle down the mountainside. More and more join in, and the trickle becomes a stream. It cascades along in a great hurry to get to the valley far below.

Some of the droplets splash out onto rocks beside the stream and are drawn up to the heavens again on a golden ray of sunshine. Others provide nourishment to the plants and wildlife along the way. Many of the drops thunder over the waterfall in a vast show of strength and majesty. As the stream reaches the valley, it joins other streams and a river is formed.

The River Flows

Your small drop seems almost insignificant as the torrent of water pushes onward. Sometimes the river drifts lazily and meanders through fields where crops and cattle are raised. Sometimes it shows rage and attacks anything that stands in its way. Sometimes obstructions, such as natural or manmade dams, block its way. Still, your drop continues its journey toward the giant ocean.

Many people come to the banks of the river. Some come to appreciate its beauty. Some drink of its water. Some come to swim, fish, or skim over its surface. Some come to throw their garbage into it.

The river flows through cities that try to harness its power. Pollution threatens to poison it and destroy its character. Development tries to change its course. Gallons upon gallons of water are siphoned off for various purposes. Somehow your drop has survived and continues its trip to the great ocean beyond.

The View from Above

For a moment, imagine that you could view the journey from high above. You watch as your drop flows along toward the ocean. You can see the distance it has traveled to get where it is now. You see the drops that it has traveled with: some are still there, while others have chosen a different course. Faintly in the distance, you can see the great ocean.

As you look ahead, you see that the river comes to a fork, and the drops have to decide which direction to travel. One route is direct but passes through polluted cities and comes up against the dams. There is great pressure to follow this direction, and many of the droplets quickly join the flow.

The other route seems to have no direction. It meanders through fields and woodlands. It has many visitors on its banks, where the other route has few. Time does not seem as important, and the pace is slow and comfortable. It is not the way for drops that are in a hurry.

The Choice of Routes

As you look down at your drop, you realize you can choose the direction it will take. Which direction will you choose? Will you join the majority of other drops and take the fast route? Will you choose the route that meanders through beautiful countryside?

ESSENTIALS

You now have a choice about the route your life will take. You have the opportunity to view your life's travel from above. You may go back over your route and learn from the past. You may consider and plan your direction.

As your drop drifts toward the fork, it says good-bye to old friends that don't know which direction they are heading. Alone and unsure at first, your drop begins the next leg of its journey. A gentle breeze carries the sweet smell of lush meadows and fragrant forests. Many adventures await the drop on its meandering journey to the great ocean beyond.

You Are Now a Self-Hypnotist

You are a hypnotist. You always have been. You always will be. The difference is that you now know what you are. Now that you have learned self-hypnosis, you have a great responsibility and an opportunity.

You have a responsibility to use your skills in a manner that does not take advantage of people who do not understand. Hypnotists sometime become consumed with their abilities. They want others to think that they possess a special magic power, and they begin to believe that they do. They develop a great desire for control.

It is tempting to use the knowledge of hypnosis to influence others for self-gain. You have learned how to observe others and study the way their minds work. You can build models of people's mental strengths and weaknesses. You have the ability to induce trances in yourself and others. You do not have to count a person down into deep hypnosis, as your words alone can create powerful images.

Should You Hypnotize Others?

So why not hypnotize your friends and family? You may have taped your own self-hypnosis induction, and then listened to it while experiencing a trance. That same tape might also induce a hypnotic trance in others. You may have written an induction script that could also work on others, if you were to read it to them. Some people go into trance easily.

Yes, it is possible to hypnotize others using what you have learned in the book. What you haven't learned is how to handle situations that may crop up during a routine hypnosis session. The stage show hypnotist skillfully creates phobias and other hallucinations in his subjects. To his subjects the suggestions are real, and they will react accordingly. The slightest miscue can produce unexpected results.

Dangers of Hypnosis

A well-meaning lay hypnotist who is trying to help someone may make the situation worse. If the subject has some sort of mental imbalance, this could be amplified during the session. A trained hypnotist watches the subject's every expression, word, or body movement, and is ready to end the trance at a moment's notice. As you may be aware, the scripts in this book always include the opportunity to end a trance anytime you want.

FACTS

People who are prone to seizures should not be hypnotized. The trained hypnotist watches the subject for head movements that might indicate some kind of distress. At any abnormal sign, she quickly brings the subject out of his trance in a calm and relaxed manner.

Past life regressions can also be dangerous. If a subject encounters something stressful in a past life trance, she will experience the entire trauma as if it were happening at that very moment. An untrained hypnotist may panic in this kind of situation and be unable to make the right suggestions to remove the trauma.

Hypnosis Is a Lifelong Study

There are many ways to continue your study of hypnosis. The first and most important is to practice daily self-hypnosis. The more you experience it, the more you will learn from it.

You can find many books on the subject of hypnosis, each one with a slightly different view. There is a great deal of information on the Internet, though much of it has a sales pitch attached. There are tapes, CDs, and videos on the subject. If you have never seen one, you may want to attend a hypnosis stage show. You might even want to volunteer as a subject.

How to study hypnosis:

1. Take a self-hypnosis course at a local college or hospital.
2. Study at a hypnosis center.
3. Enroll in a hypnosis certification course.
4. Take a college hypnosis course.
5. Enroll in a college clinical hypnotherapy degree program.

Have you ever been to a certified hypnotherapist? It is an excellent way to observe and experience how a professional conducts a session. Perhaps there is a self-hypnosis course being offered at a hypnosis center, hospital, or community college near you. An itinerant hypnotist may come to your area and offer a habit change seminar. He will usually saturate the local media a few days before he arrives.

Many excellent hypnosis training programs offer certification courses, if you wish to practice professionally. It is a good idea to compare the courses of study from several different programs and get references from individuals who have taken the trainings previously.

ALERT

Be aware of hypnosis certification courses that promise a wide range of practice skills after only a short period of study. Weekend training sessions do not meet the certification requirements of most states.

Some distance study programs offer college degrees. If you are interested in pursuing more study, consult the Web addresses listed in the back of this book. Each state has different requirements for certification to practice hypnosis, so you will want to make sure you are taking courses that fulfill your local requirements.

Just Imagine

Have you ever stood on a dock by the ocean and watched the boats come and go? You probably saw some small dinghies and some expensive ocean-going yachts. Some craft may have been working boats, while others were for pleasure. Did you wonder where the boats were going and what great adventures would be in store for them? Have you ever wondered what it would be like to sail on one of them?

Have you ever been at an airport and watched a small plane take off into the sky, and wondered what it would be like to fly to distant places? Have you imagined going on safari to a wild jungle or visiting a remote island beach in the tropics? Have you wondered what it would be like to dive to the depths of the ocean or soar in orbit above the earth? Have you ever imagined what it would be like to explore the Antarctic?

Have you ever thought what it might have been like to live when the great mysteries of the world were being constructed, and perhaps have access to ancient knowledge that people forgot long ago? Have you ever wondered about what the mind really has locked inside it? Have you ever wondered what being human is all about?

Setting Sail

The choice is yours. You may go to the water's edge and imagine what it would be like to sail off on an adventure. You may seek passage on one of the vessels or purchase your own boat. You can take a day trip to see how your sea legs hold up under the conditions of the ocean. There are many ways to experience the lore of the ancient mariners.

ESSENTIALS

You have just completed your first sailing course on the waters of self-hypnosis. You now have the basic skills to navigate the course of life. You have the knowledge and the guidance of the universe available to the beckoning of your mind. You have the ability to set the course, stay on track, and weather the storms and unknowns. The adventure is yours if you are willing.

Just as the ancients followed the labyrinth map of their souls, you may find your way in the same manner. Your map is there just below the surface of your mind. Just imagine.

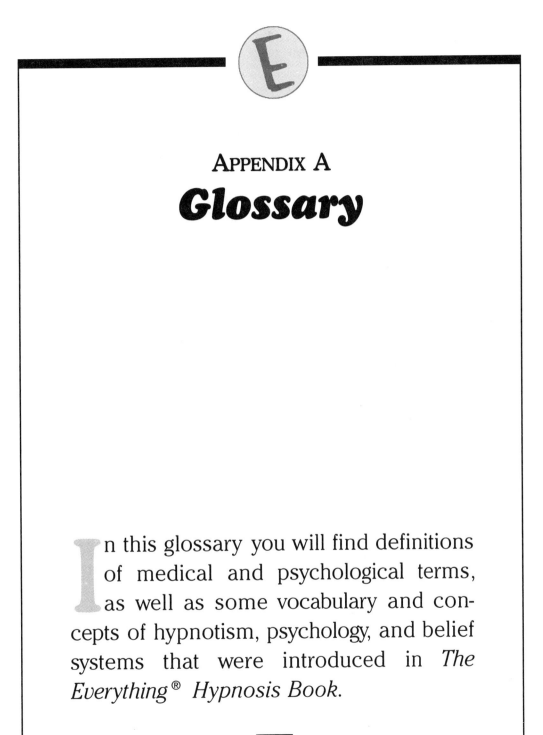

APPENDIX A

Glossary

I n this glossary you will find definitions of medical and psychological terms, as well as some vocabulary and concepts of hypnotism, psychology, and belief systems that were introduced in *The Everything*® *Hypnosis Book.*

ADD/ADHD: Attention deficit disorder/attention deficit disorder with hyperactivity.

AFFECT-BRIDGE TECHNIQUE: A method of hypnotic regression that takes a feeling back to images from the past to look for the root of a stressful emotion.

ANCHOR: A physical or nonphysical reminder that recreates a previous emotional state.

ASTRAL PROJECTION: The process of leaving the physical body and traveling to other places in or out of the earth plane.

ATLANTIS: A mythical island first written about by Plato; the subject of many psychic readings by Edgar Cayce.

AURA: The energy field around a person or object.

AUTOMATIC WRITING: Writing that comes from your unconscious mind while in a light trance.

AUTOSUGGESTION: The mind's continuation of a posthypnotic suggestion that operates to produce mental or physical effects.

CALENDAR TECHNIQUE: A method of hypnotic regression that takes you back through life in reverse chronological order.

CLAIRAUDIENCE: The ability to image psychic information through the sense of hearing.

CLAIRVOYANCE: The ability to gather psychic information through the senses, especially the sense of sight.

COGNITIVE BEHAVIOR THERAPY: A method used to desensitize a person through slight exposure that is gradually increased.

COMFORT ZONE: A place or state of mind where you feel safe and have little or no anxiety.

CONSCIOUS MIND: The surface of your mind; the communication center where you process thoughts and ideas.

CONVERGENT-THINKING MODEL: A thought process that eliminates options until none remain.

CRITICAL THINKING: The ability to examine problems objectively in order to make rational decisions.

CYCLE OF SOULS: The belief that souls travel with other souls through multiple incarnations to work on universal lessons.

DEPTH TESTING: Techniques to determine the trance level that you can reach.

DIMMER SWITCH TECHNIQUE: An induction that uses the image of turning down a knob or slide control to turn down the intensity of pain or other sensations.

DIVERGENT-THINKING MODEL: A thought process that searches for options in problem solving.

DOWSER: A person who uses a device to locate underground water, mineral deposits, or other unseen things.

FLOODING TECHNIQUE: The use of several sensory stimulants at once to confuse the conscious mind and allow a suggestion to be given to the unconscious mind.

GUIDED IMAGERY: Verbal communication that creates a trance experience related to a specific destination.

HOLMES-RAHE SOCIAL READJUSTMENT SCALE: A scoring system that totals significant events that might impact a person's health over a specified period of time (usually one year).

HOLOGRAM: A three-dimensional image.

HYPNO-ANESTHESIA: The use of hypnosis to block pain during surgery.

HYPNO-BIRTHING: A hypnotic technique to relieve stress, anxiety, and pain, and to help muscles relax during the birthing process.

HYPNOSIS: An altered state of consciousness where the unconscious mind accepts suggestions.

HYPNOSIS INDUCTION: The process of going into a hypnotic trance.

HYPNOSIS STAGE SHOW: A demonstration of hypnosis for the purpose of entertainment.

HYPNOSIS WHEEL: A revolving disk that, when gazed at steadily, helps the eyes go out of focus.

HYPNOTHERAPY: A profession that uses hypnosis to aid self-improvement.

HYPOTHALAMUS: A gland located in your brain; it produces hormones that signal other glands to go on high alert or to calm down.

INCARNATION: One lifetime in a soul's series of lives.

INSTANT SELF-HYPNOSIS: A hypnotic trance created at the moment an anchor is triggered. *See also* **ANCHOR.**

KARMA: Unresolved experiences from past lives that carry over into the next life.

KINESTHETIC: Related to the sense of touch or feeling.

LABYRINTH: An ancient sacred form; a path intended to bring balance, spiritual connectedness, and joy to those who take it.

LIBRARY TECHNIQUE: A method of hypnotic regression where you select an imaginary book relevant to a past life you are seeking information about.

LIFE MAP: The potential conditions for soul development with which each person is born; how we use our free will determines whether we will achieve our potential.

MANIFEST REALITY: Everything that can be touched, seen, heard, smelled, or tasted.

MEDITATION: A state in which you quiet the mind, finding peace as thoughts drift away into space.

MENTAL TELEPATHY: Nonverbal communication through the mind.

METRONOME: A device that keeps time by making rhythmic clicking sounds. Though generally used by musicians, it may also be used in hypnosis.

MIND CONTROL: The ability to influence someone else's thoughts or actions.

NEURO-LINGUISTIC PROGRAMMING (NLP): A communication technique developed by Grinder and Bandler to develop and change thinking processes.

PAIN AMNESIA: A state in which your pain remains in the unconscious mind because you are focusing on something else.

PACING: The process of leading a person to a desired action or state of mind.

PAIN DISSOCIATION TECHNIQUE: A method of self-hypnosis used to escape pain by distancing yourself from it.

PAIN TRANSFERENCE TECHNIQUE: A method of self-hypnosis used to move a pain from one part of the body to another part.

PARTS THERAPY: A form of therapy that creates a dialogue between the different parts of a person.

PHOBIA: An anxiety disorder; usually a fear of certain situations or objects.

POSTHYPNOTIC SUGGESTION: A suggestion given during a hypnotic trance that remains operational after the trance has ended.

PRAYER: The act of sending thoughts to a specific source (for instance, God); usually with the expectation of a positive response.

PRECOGNITION: The knowledge of something that may happen in the future.

PSYCHIC: One who has the ability to obtain information from sources that have no scientifically proven basis, such as intuition or supernatural contact.

PUSH METHOD: A hypnotic technique that uses visualization to force a positive image through a negative one.

REFRAME: The installation of a new habit into the unconscious mind.

REINCARNATION: The belief that the soul experiences more than one lifetime.

RETRO-COGNITION: Psychic information gathered from the past.

SELF-HYPNOSIS: The process of inducing a trance state in yourself.

SOMNAMBULISM: The state of performing motor acts (such as walking) while asleep; the deepest level of trance experience.

SOUL MATE: Someone you feel that you may have known in another lifetime.

SUBCONSCIOUS: *See* **UNCONSCIOUS MIND.**

SUGGESTIBILITY: The capacity to be influenced by suggestion.

SUGGESTIBILITY TEST: A means of measuring a person's potential to enter a hypnotic trance.

TELEKINESIS: The ability to get a psychic image from an object by touching it.

THIRD EYE: A spot in the center of the forehead that may feel tight and swollen by strong emotions, and through which the universal mind may be contacted.

THINKING MODEL: A model of the way you compile information through your senses.

TRANCE: An altered state of consciousness in which the unconscious mind is open to suggestion and loses its ability to make critical decisions.

TRANCE READINGS: Information acquired psychically while in an altered state.

TRANSFERENCE: The redirection of an emotional feeling onto something or someone else.

UNCONSCIOUS MIND: The storage area of the mind that contains all your past experiences; also referred to as the subconscious.

UNIVERSAL CONSCIOUSNESS: An awareness that is reached through the unconscious mind; the source of information and answers that have no scientific explanation; your belief system.

UNIVERSAL MIND: The part of your soul where you enlist the unknown to give strength and produce miracles. *See also* **UNIVERSAL CONSCIOUSNESS.**

UNMANIFEST REALITY: Something real that cannot be seen, touched, or explained readily.

WHITE CLOUD INDUCTION: A hypnotic technique that takes you to a safe place where you can detach yourself from an undesirable situation or condition and examine it (or not) without negative feelings.

ZONE: A state of hyper-focus, usually experienced by an athlete at the peak of performance.

Additional Resources

The two sections of this appendix contain, first, a suggested reading list of books that cover topics discussed here in greater detail, and second, a list of organizations you can contact for more information or assistance.

Suggested Reading

Ackerman, Diane. *A Natural History of the Senses*. (NY: Random House, 1990)

Andrews, Ted. *How to See & Read the Aura*. (St. Paul, MN: Llewellyn Publications, 1993)

Bandler, Richard and John Grinder. *Reframing: Neuro-Linguistic Programming and the Transformation of Meaning*. (Moab, UT: Real People Press, 1982)

Bernstein, Morey. *The Search for Bridey Murphy*. (NY: Doubleday & Co., 1956)

Bolduc, Henry Leo. *Self-Hypnosis: Creating Your Own Destiny*. (Virginia Beach, VA: A.R.E. Press, 1985)

——. *The Journey Within: Past-Life Regression and Channeling*. (Virginia Beach, VA: Inner Vision Publishing Co., 1988)

——. *Your Creative Voice: Reaching and Teaching from Your Experience*. (Independence, VA: Adventures Into Time Publishers, 1996)

Caprio, Frank S. and Joseph R. Berger. *Healing Yourself with Self-Hypnosis. A Modern Guide to Self-Improvement and Successful Living*. (Englewood Cliffs, NJ: Prentice-Hall, 1963)

DeBecker, Gavin. *The Gift of Fear: Survival Signals That Protect Us from Violence*. (NY: Little, Brown & Company, 1997)

Ford, Arthur. *Unknown but Known*. (NY: Harper & Row, 1968)

Grinder, John and Richard Bandler. *Trance-Formations: Neuro-Linguistic Programming and the Structure of Hypnosis*. (Moab, UT: Real People Press, 1981)

Haven, R. A. *The Wisdom of Milton Erickson*. (NY: Irvington, 1985)

Hilgard, Ernest R. and Josephine R. Hilgard. *Hypnosis in the Relief of Pain*. (Los Altos, CA: William Kaufmann, Inc., 1983)

Kirkpatrick, Sidney D. *Edgar Cayce: An American Prophet*. (NY: Riverhead Books, 2000)

LeCron, Leslie M. *The Complete Guide to Hypnosis*. (NY: Harper & Row, 1971)

Lethbridge, T. C. *The Power of the Pendulum*. (Penguin Books, London, 1976)

McClain, Florence Wagner. *A Practical Guide to Past Life Regression*. (St. Paul, MN: Llewellyn Publications, 1992)

McGill, Ormond. *The Encyclopedia of Genuine Stage Hypnotism*. (Colon, MI: Abbott's Magic Novelty Co., 1947)

Montgomery, Ruth. *A World Beyond*. (NY: Coward, McCann & Geoghegan, 1971)

Naparstek, Belleruth. *Your Sixth Sense: Activating Your Psychic Potential*. (San Francisco: Harper Collins, 1997)

Rhodes, Raphael H. *Hypnosis: Theory, Practice and Application*. (Secaucus, NJ: Citadel Press, 1978)

Roberts, Jane. *The Seth Material*. (Englewood Cliffs, NJ: Prentice-Hall, 1970)

Rosen, Sidney. *My Voice Will Go With You: The Teaching Tales of Milton H. Erickson, M.D.* (NY: W. W. Norton & Co., 1982)

Schlotterbeck, Karl. *Living Your Past Lives: The Psychology of Past-Life Regression*. (NY: Ballantine Books, 1987)

Simonton, O. Carl, Stephanie Matthews-Simonton, James Creighton. *Getting Well Again: A Step-by-Step, Self-Help Guide to*

Overcoming Cancer for Patients and Their Families. (Los Angeles: J. P. Tarcher, 1978)

Stearn, Jess. *The Search for a Soul: Taylor Caldwell's Psychic Lives.* (NY: Berkley Books,1994)

Stephens, Elaine. *Whispers of the Mind: A Complete Program for Unlocking the Secrets of Your Past Lives.* (NY: Harper & Row, 1989)

Sugrue, Thomas. *There Is a River.* (NY: Henry Holt, 1942. Reprinted by Holt, Dell, A.R.E. Press, 1997)

Other Resources

American Lung Association
✐ *www.lungusa.org*

American Medical Women's Association
✐ *www.amwa-doc.org*

American Pacific University (hypnosis training)
✐ *www.ampac.edu*

American Psychological Association
✐ *www.apa.org*

American Society of Dowsers
✐ *www.dowsers.org*

Anxiety Disorders Association of America
✐ *www.adaa.org*

Association for Research and Enlightenment
✐ *www.edgarcayce.org*

Association of Waldorf Schools in North America
✐ *www.awsna.org*

Association for Psychological Type
  (Myers-Briggs Indicator)
✐ *www.aptcentral.org*

Attention Deficit Disorder Association
✐ *www.add.org*

Calorie Control Council
✐ *www.caloriecontrol.org*

Children and Adults with Attention-Deficit/
  Hyperactivity Disorder
✐ *www.chadd.org*

Edgar Cayce Foundation
✐ *www.edgarcayce.org*

Federal Consumer Information Center
✐ *www.pueblo.gsa.gov*

Focus on the Family
✐ *www.family.org*

HypnoBirthing
✐ *www.hypnobirthing.com*

International Board for Regression Therapy
✐ *www.ibrt.org*

National Guild of Hypnotists
✐ *www.ngh.net*

National Home Education Network
✐ *www.nhen.org*

National Institute of Mental Health
✐ *www.nimh.nih.gov*

National Women's Health Information Center
✐ *www.4woman.gov*

Search for God (discussion groups)
✐ *www.edgarcayce.org*

White Mountain Hypnosis Center, Madison, NH
Dr. Michael R. Hathaway, D.C.H.
(hypnotherapist and hypnosis training)
603-367-8851

Index

THE EVERYTHING STRESS MANAGEMENT BOOK

By Eve Adamson

Trade paperback,
$14.95 ($22.95 CAN)
1-58062-578-9, 304 pages

T*he Everything® Stress Management Book* provides the most effective methods of stress reduction and helpful hints on how to prevent stress from building up before it leads to chronic health problems. It explains the latest, most potent techniques for quelling anxiety, including simple exercises, stress-fighting foods, aromatherapy, yoga, and massage. Full of charts, tables, important warnings, and useful tips, *The Everything® Stress Management Book* is a complete guide on how to achieve your life's goals—without wearing down your body.

OTHER *EVERYTHING®* BOOKS BY ADAMS MEDIA CORPORATION

BUSINESS

Everything® **Business Planning Book**
Everything® **Coaching and Mentoring Book**
Everything® **Fundraising Book**
Everything® **Home-Based Business Book**
Everything® **Leadership Book**
Everything® **Managing People Book**
Everything® **Network Marketing Book**
Everything® **Online Business Book**
Everything® **Project Management Book**
Everything® **Selling Book**
Everything® **Start Your Own Business Book**
Everything® **Time Management Book**

COMPUTERS

Everything® **Build Your Own Home Page Book**

Everything® **Computer Book**
Everything® **Internet Book**
Everything® **Microsoft® Word 2000 Book**

COOKBOOKS

Everything® **Barbecue Cookbook**
Everything® **Bartender's Book, $9.95**
Everything® **Chinese Cookbook**
Everything® **Chocolate Cookbook**
Everything® **Cookbook**
Everything® **Dessert Cookbook**
Everything® **Diabetes Cookbook**
Everything® **Low-Carb Cookbook**
Everything® **Low-Fat High-Flavor Cookbook**
Everything® **Mediterranean Cookbook**
Everything® **Mexican Cookbook**
Everything® **One-Pot Cookbook**
Everything® **Pasta Book**

Everything® **Quick Meals Cookbook**
Everything® **Slow Cooker Cookbook**
Everything® **Soup Cookbook**
Everything® **Thai Cookbook**
Everything® **Vegetarian Cookbook**
Everything® **Wine Book**

HEALTH

Everything® **Anti-Aging Book**
Everything® **Diabetes Book**
Everything® **Dieting Book**
Everything® **Herbal Remedies Book**
Everything® **Hypnosis Book**
Everything® **Menopause Book**
Everything® **Nutrition Book**
Everything® **Reflexology Book**
Everything® **Stress Management Book**
Everything®**Vitamins, Minerals, and Nutritional Supplements Book**

All Everything® books are priced at $12.95 or $14.95, unless otherwise stated. Prices subject to change without notice.
Canadian prices range from $11.95–$31.95, and are subject to change without notice.

HISTORY

Everything® **American History Book**
Everything® **Civil War Book**
Everything® **Irish History & Heritage Book**
Everything® **Mafia Book**
Everything® **World War II Book**

HOBBIES & GAMES

Everything® **Bridge Book**
Everything® **Candlemaking Book**
Everything® **Casino Gambling Book**
Everything® **Chess Basics Book**
Everything® **Collectibles Book**
Everything® **Crossword and Puzzle Book**
Everything® **Digital Photography Book**
Everything® **Family Tree Book**
Everything® **Games Book**
Everything® **Knitting Book**
Everything® **Magic Book**
Everything® **Motorcycle Book**
Everything® **Online Genealogy Book**
Everything® **Photography Book**
Everything® **Pool & Billiards Book**
Everything® **Quilting Book**
Everything® **Scrapbooking Book**
Everything® **Soapmaking Book**

HOME IMPROVEMENT

Everything® **Feng Shui Book**
Everything® **Gardening Book**
Everything® **Home Decorating Book**
Everything® **Landscaping Book**
Everything® **Lawn Care Book**
Everything® **Organize Your Home Book**

KIDS' STORY BOOKS

Everything® **Bedtime Story Book**
Everything® **Bible Stories Book**
Everything® **Fairy Tales Book**
Everything® **Mother Goose Book**

EVERYTHING® *KIDS'* BOOKS

All titles are $6.95
Everything® **Kids' Baseball Book, 2nd Ed.** ($10.95 CAN)
Everything® **Kids' Bugs Book** ($10.95 CAN)
Everything® **Kids' Christmas Puzzle & Activity Book** ($10.95 CAN)
Everything® **Kids' Cookbook** ($10.95 CAN)
Everything® **Kids' Halloween Puzzle & Activity Book** ($10.95 CAN)
Everything® **Kids' Joke Book** ($10.95 CAN)
Everything® **Kids' Math Puzzles Book** ($10.95 CAN)
Everything® **Kids' Mazes Book** ($10.95 CAN)
Everything® **Kids' Money Book** ($11.95 CAN)
Everything® **Kids' Monsters Book** ($10.95 CAN)
Everything® **Kids' Nature Book** ($11.95 CAN)
Everything® **Kids' Puzzle Book** ($10.95 CAN)
Everything® **Kids' Science Experiments Book** ($10.95 CAN)
Everything® **Kids' Soccer Book** ($10.95 CAN)
Everything® **Kids' Travel Activity Book** ($10.95 CAN)

LANGUAGE

Everything® **Learning French Book**
Everything® **Learning German Book**
Everything® **Learning Italian Book**
Everything® **Learning Latin Book**
Everything® **Learning Spanish Book**
Everything® **Sign Language Book**

MUSIC

Everything® **Drums Book (with CD), $19.95 ($31.95 CAN)**
Everything® **Guitar Book**
Everything® **Playing Piano and Keyboards Book**

Everything® **Rock & Blues Guitar Book (with CD), $19.95 ($31.95 CAN)**
Everything® **Songwriting Book**

NEW AGE

Everything® **Astrology Book**
Everything® **Divining the Future Book**
Everything® **Dreams Book**
Everything® **Ghost Book**
Everything® **Meditation Book**
Everything® **Numerology Book**
Everything® **Palmistry Book**
Everything® **Psychic Book**
Everything® **Spells & Charms Book**
Everything® **Tarot Book**
Everything® **Wicca and Witchcraft Book**

PARENTING

Everything® **Baby Names Book**
Everything® **Baby Shower Book**
Everything® **Baby's First Food Book**
Everything® **Baby's First Year Book**
Everything® **Breastfeeding Book**
Everything® **Father-to-Be Book**
Everything® **Get Ready for Baby Book**
Everything® **Homeschooling Book**
Everything® **Parent's Guide to Positive Discipline**
Everything® **Potty Training Book, $9.95 ($15.95 CAN)**
Everything® **Pregnancy Book, 2nd Ed.**
Everything® **Pregnancy Fitness Book**
Everything® **Pregnancy Organizer, $15.00 ($22.95 CAN)**
Everything® **Toddler Book**
Everything® **Tween Book**

PERSONAL FINANCE

Everything® **Budgeting Book**
Everything® **Get Out of Debt Book**
Everything® **Get Rich Book**
Everything® **Homebuying Book, 2nd Ed.**
Everything® **Homeselling Book**

All Everything® books are priced at $12.95 or $14.95, unless otherwise stated. Prices subject to change without notice.
Canadian prices range from $11.95–$31.95, and are subject to change without notice.

Everything® **Investing Book**
Everything® **Money Book**
Everything® **Mutual Funds Book**
Everything® **Online Investing Book**
Everything® **Personal Finance Book**
Everything® **Personal Finance in Your 20s & 30s Book**
Everything® **Wills & Estate Planning Book**

PETS

Everything® **Cat Book**
Everything® **Dog Book**
Everything® **Dog Training and Tricks Book**
Everything® **Horse Book**
Everything® **Puppy Book**
Everything® **Tropical Fish Book**

REFERENCE

Everything® **Astronomy Book**
Everything® **Car Care Book**
Everything® **Christmas Book, $15.00** ($21.95 CAN)
Everything® **Classical Mythology Book**
Everything® **Einstein Book**
Everything® **Etiquette Book**
Everything® **Great Thinkers Book**
Everything® **Philosophy Book**
Everything® **Shakespeare Book**
Everything® **Tall Tales, Legends, & Other Outrageous Lies Book**
Everything® **Toasts Book**
Everything® **Trivia Book**
Everything® **Weather Book**

RELIGION

Everything® **Angels Book**
Everything® **Buddhism Book**
Everything® **Catholicism Book**
Everything® **Jewish History & Heritage Book**
Everything® **Judaism Book**

Everything® **Prayer Book**
Everything® **Saints Book**
Everything® **Understanding Islam Book**
Everything® **World's Religions Book**
Everything® **Zen Book**

SCHOOL & CAREERS

Everything® **After College Book**
Everything® **College Survival Book**
Everything® **Cover Letter Book**
Everything® **Get-a-Job Book**
Everything® **Hot Careers Book**
Everything® **Job Interview Book**
Everything® **Online Job Search Book**
Everything® **Resume Book, 2nd Ed.**
Everything® **Study Book**

SELF-HELP

Everything® **Dating Book**
Everything® **Divorce Book**
Everything® **Great Marriage Book**
Everything® **Great Sex Book**
Everything® **Romance Book**
Everything® **Self-Esteem Book**
Everything® **Success Book**

SPORTS & FITNESS

Everything® **Bicycle Book**
Everything® **Body Shaping Book**
Everything® **Fishing Book**
Everything® **Fly-Fishing Book**
Everything® **Golf Book**
Everything® **Golf Instruction Book**
Everything® **Pilates Book**
Everything® **Running Book**
Everything® **Sailing Book, 2nd Ed.**
Everything® **T'ai Chi and QiGong Book**
Everything® **Total Fitness Book**
Everything® **Weight Training Book**
Everything® **Yoga Book**

TRAVEL

Everything® **Guide to Las Vegas**

Everything® **Guide to New England**
Everything® **Guide to New York City**
Everything® **Guide to Washington D.C.**
Everything® **Travel Guide to The Disneyland Resort®, California Adventure®, Universal Studios®, and the Anaheim Area**
Everything® **Travel Guide to the Walt Disney World Resort®, Universal Studios®, and Greater Orlando, 3rd Ed.**

WEDDINGS

Everything® **Bachelorette Party Book**
Everything® **Bridesmaid Book**
Everything® **Creative Wedding Ideas Book**
Everything® **Jewish Wedding Book**
Everything® **Wedding Book, 2nd Ed.**
Everything® **Wedding Checklist, $7.95 ($11.95 CAN)**
Everything® **Wedding Etiquette Book, $7.95 ($11.95 CAN)**
Everything® **Wedding Organizer, $15.00 ($22.95 CAN)**
Everything® **Wedding Shower Book, $7.95 ($12.95 CAN)**
Everything® **Wedding Vows Book, $7.95 ($11.95 CAN)**
Everything® **Weddings on a Budget Book, $9.95 ($15.95 CAN)**

WRITING

Everything® **Creative Writing Book**
Everything® **Get Published Book**
Everything® **Grammar and Style Book**
Everything® **Grant Writing Book**
Everything® **Guide to Writing Children's Books**
Everything® **Screenwriting Book**
Everything® **Writing Well Book**

Available wherever books are sold!
To order, call 800-872-5627, or visit us at everything.com